the paralegal profession
A Career Guide

by

NEIL T. SHAYNE

1977
OCEANA PUBLICATIONS, INC.
CONDYNE/TRANS-MEDIA DISTRIBUTING CORP.
Dobbs Ferry, New York

Library of Congress Cataloging in Publication Data

Shayne, Neil T.   1932-
   The paralegal profession.

   1. Legal assistants — United States. I. Title.
KF320.L4S5   340'.023   77-4914
ISBN 0-379-00684-7

THE PARALEGAL PROFESSION
A Career Guide

NEIL T. SHAYNE
1501 Franklin Ave.
Mineola, N.Y. 11501

Bar Admission	1954 New York
Present Position	Senior Partner Law Firm - Shayne, Dachs, Weiss, Kolbrener, Stanisci and Harwood
Teaching and Consulting Positions	Faculty and Program Chairman, Practicing Law Institute (1969-Present)
	Faculty and Program Chairman, American Management Association
	Lecturer - American Bar Association American Trial Lawyers Association
	Director Paralegal Program, Long Island University, Brooklyn, New York 11201
Professional Listings	Who's Who in America
Present Paralegal Positions	Member of the certifying board of the Nassau Association of Legal Assistants
Publications	Books: Author, *Making a Personal Injury Practice Profitable,* Practicing Law Institute, (1972);
	Author, *Pre-Paid Legal Services,* American Management Association, (1974);
	Editor, Course Handbook, *Casualty Insurance Executives Workshop,* (1971) Practicing Law Institute;
Law Tapes	"Prepaid Legal Services," distributed by Condyne Law Tapes, Dobbs Ferry, New York
	"Survival for the Young Attorney", distributed by Condyne Law Tapes, Dobbs Ferry, New York
Featured Columns	"Economics and Law", Bi-Weekly Column, *New York Law Journal,* (1973-Present).

TABLE OF CONTENTS

CHAPTER V - A SURVEY OF THE AMERICAN LEGAL SYSTEM

CHAPTER VI — THE EDUCATIONAL TRAINING OF THE PARALEGAL

CHAPTER VII — OBTAINING EMPLOYMENT AS A PARALEGAL

CHAPTER VIII — MOST OFTEN ASKED QUESTIONS ....

APPENDIX I — NEW YORK STATE BAR ASSOCIATION COMMITTEE ON PROFESSIONAL ETHICS, GUIDELINES FOR THE UTILIZATION BY LAWYERS OF THE SERVICE OF LEGAL ASSISTANTS

INTRODUCTION

The paralegal or legal assistant is a child born of the necessity for lawyers and other professionals, for that matter, to operate their businesses on an economic basis.

In the not too distant past, a young lawyer would be willing to "clerk" in a law office for $15 to $25 a week. A legal secretary would have been delighted with a job that paid $35 a week and did not require her to work more than a half day on Saturday. The American Telegraph and Telephone Company was willing to place an office telephone call for 10 cents. Letters emanating from a law office would reach a destination with a 3 cent stamp. Large, airy law offices in prestigious buildings were available for less than $4 per foot. The cost of running an office was not a major factor and attorneys were able to practice law without an undue concern to expenses like "overhead," "bottom line," and "debt service."

Studies of the legal system indicated that a vast majority of the public was not being represented by legal counsel as a result of its inability to pay for the increasing cost of legal services. We will learn that prepaid legal services and the economic factors dictate the delivery of legal services at a reduced rate.

The paralegal emerged from a combination of these factors.

The purpose of this book is multi-faceted. It should serve as a textbook for a general paralegal program. The thrust of the book is to acquaint the paralegal with the legal profession. The practical applications of the work performed by a paralegal are detailed throughout the manuscript.

The Watergate scandal and feelings of dissatisfaction with our government have mandated the necessity for understanding the ethics of all professions and certainly the legal profession. "Ethical Considerations Relating to Paralegals" are reprinted in their entirety.

The book describes the job placement market for paralegals and includes suggestions for obtaining employment as a paralegal. No longer will a degree from a university guarantee employment. Thus, it is my concept that the programs and the materials for the paralegal must include job orientation and job placement.

Neil T. Shayne

CHAPTER I

An Overview of the Paralegal
As a Professional

Emergence of Paralegalism

The urbanization of our society, which tends to complicate relationships, the high degree of government involvement in our lives, and other factors expose us all to law and regulation which inevitably lead us to need legal services, whether we be the largest business corporation or the most humble citizen or the much neglected average wage earner.

A great failure of the legal system in our society is that it has been unable to deliver legal services to many in need of them at a reasonable price. The problem is two-fold, as it is with medical care. Delivery of services must be made more economical, and the money to pay for services must be made available to those who are unable to afford them at any price. It is the delivery of legal services in a more economic fashion which relates to the subject of this volume, paralegals. While in fact there are many technological innovations which do make the modern law office more efficient than its predecessors, it is clear that the major cost component of legal services is professional labor. Lower the labor cost and you lower the price of services.

Paralegals: A New Concept

What, now, is a paralegal?

Paralegals are nonlawyers who perform functions traditionally performed by lawyers. The fundamental theories on which the use of paralegals is based are as follows:

(1) A legal matter can be broken into small tasks. Each task need not be done by the same person.

(2) Not all of the individual tasks involved in handling a client's problem require a lawyer to do them. Actually, most of what a lawyer does every day was not learned in law school. Instead, it was learned on the job. Certainly there are others in society who possess the aptitude to do some parts of the work.

The basic concepts involved are not new. Industry adopted these concepts when it turned from the piecework method of production to the production line. The advent of nursing and the other medical subsidiary professions marked a similar change in the practice of medicine. The truth is that there has been use of paralegals for many years. There were always many legal secretaries who did work in one office that was done by lawyers in another.

What is new about all this is the concept of formally trained paralegals who can, within a particular type of practice, do a wide variety of tasks that involve a real understanding of the substance of a transaction or lawsuit.

Perhaps the most useful summary statement of the role and the function of the paralegal is that offered by the American Bar Association's Special Committee on Legal Assistants. (While "legal assistant" and "paralegal" are much inter-used, this Guide throughout will use the increasingly prevailing term, *paralegal*):

> "Under the supervision and direction of the lawyer, the (paralegal) should be able to apply knowledge of law and legal procedures in rendering direct assistance to lawyers engaged in legal research; design, develop or plan modifications of new procedures, techniques, services, processes or applications; prepare or interpret legal documents and write detailed procedures for practicing in certain fields of law; select, compile and use technical information from such references as digests, encyclopedias or practice manuals; and analyze and follow procedural problems that involve independent decisions."

Again, many legal secretaries do perform in some paralegal capacity. In fact, however, such secretaries have been trained to do substantially more than a beginning secretary. A detailed discussion of the differences between a legal secretary and the paralegal appears in a later chapter in this Guide in connection with the educational training background of the paralegal. It is enough to note at this point that the job or the responsibility of the legal secretary is light years away from that of the trained paralegal.

Role and Functions of the Paralegal: A Summary of the Private Sector

Although in a subsequent chapter the reader will be presented with a highly detailed example of what the paralegal is actually expected to do in a given legal area situation, it might nevertheless be useful to have a general description here at the outset of this Guide.

In the area of *Estate Planning and Administration,* the paralegal graduate should be able to assist in the preparation of legal documents associated with the planning of estates. In the administrative phase he or she should be able to participate in the collection of assets, valuation of assets, maintenance of records, notification of beneficiaries, preparation of wills and trusts for review; complete federal and state tax returns; apply income principal rules to estates; apply accounting rules to estates; draft court forms from account records; prepare periodic statements for estates, trusts and individuals; transfer securities into names of people entitled to them; draw checks for signatures of executors; follow through on collection and delivery; monitor to charitable clients; file tax waivers; and prepare closing documents.

In the area of *Corporate Law*, the paralegal should be prepared to undertake, under the supervision and control of a lawyer (as actually in all of these tasks he or she works under such supervision and control) the following tasks: prepare initial and amended articles of incorporation, satisfy state filing requirements, prepare drafts of stock certificates and securities, maintain stock ledgers and books, draft resolutions authorizing cash and stock dividends and stock splits, draft employment agreements, draft qualified stock option plans and agreements, draft buy-sell agreements, prepare Blue Sky materials, draft underwriting agreements and resolutions authorizing the role of securities, prepare registration materials for regulatory agencies, draft acquisition and merger transactions and draft closing papers and closing binders.

In the *Real Estate* area, the paralegal should be prepared to perform all the routine matters and prepare the appropriate documents involved in the more common types of real estate transactions, and conveyances and actions, including deeds, contracts, leases, deeds of trust, mortgages, actions to quiet title and foreclosure actions.

In *Domestic Relations,* the paralegal should be prepared to undertake tasks associated with domestic relations matters, including preparation of initial documents such as the complaint, answer and summons; pleadings associated with the action; and findings of fact, conclusions of law, and order for judgment.

In *Civil Litigation,* the paralegal should be familiar with and able to prepare all documents associated with the trial of a civil action. In addition, he or she should be prepared to digest transcripts of depositions and trial testimony, index documents and/or exhibits for trial, and act as librarian for all trial documents.

Beyond all this, the paralegal will be expected to have *communications skills* that include the ability to record, analyze, interpret, and transmit facts and ideas orally, graphically or in writing with complete objectivity, and to locate continuously and master new information pertinent to the assignment.

Closely related to this functional requirement of communication skills is that very basic tool and skill of any legal professional, legal research and legal writing. Since this is not essentially a "how-to" book, we will not attempt here to offer material about how one goes about doing legal research. But for the purpose of acquainting the reader with what it is a paralegal is expected to know and to do, it will be enough to point out that the principles of legal research address themselves to the following kinds of questions which will give some notion of what is involved in this area of paralegal activity:

1. How many kinds of law books exist?
2. What are citations?
3. What are the components of a law book?
4. How does the researcher "find" ambiguity?
5. What is constitutional law and how is it read?
6. What is a statute and how is it read?
7. What is a regulation and how is it read?
8. What is a court opinion and how is it briefed?
9. What is legal authority?
10. What is the principle of analogy and how is it applied?
11. How is the table of contents and an index used?
12. What is an annotation?
13. How does the researcher start his research?
14. How is applicable constitutional law found?
15. How is applicable statutory law found?
16. How is applicable regulatory law found?
17. How is applicable case law found?

There are several kinds of legal writing apart from research within a law office:

1. Letters
2. Instruments (contract, deed, will, bond, lease, etc.)
3. Pleadings (complaint, answer)
4. Memoranda
5. Briefs

Instrument writing requires great precision as does court pleadings. The paralegal must have a thorough knowledge of substantive and procedural law in order to perform this function. While there are standard forms available for many instruments and pleadings which require a minimal amount of data fill-in, the paralegal must always be prepared for the not unknown or unusual situation where the standard form simply will not fit the facts of a particular client. In such a case, adjustments in the standard form must be made.

But it is the in-house memorandum (intended primarily for personnel in the law office) which is an analysis of a legal problem or of some aspect of a legal problem which is the most frequent writing requirement in the law office. Since the memorandum is most often prepared preliminary to the final draft of instruments, pleadings and briefs, and the paralegal may be asked to write memoranda on legal problems that must be resolved before the instrument, pleading or brief is sent out of the office, it is a vital skill he or she must have the facility to develop in his training.

Role and Functions of the Paralegal: Public Sector

We turn now to the public sector as a source for employment of trained paralegals.

With the ever-growing activities of government on all levels, federal, state, and local, it is inevitable that various government entities should be increasingly employing paralegals. The Civil Service Commission estimated that in 1975 the federal government employed 30,000 paralegals and predicted an even larger role for them in the coming years. The Commission itself has developed a new Paralegal Assistant Series that includes the following functions: (a) analyzing legal material and preparing digests of points of law for internal governmental agency use; (b) maintaining legal reference files and furnishing attorneys with citations to pertinent decisions; (c) selecting, assembling, summarizing, and compiling substantive information on statutes, treaties, and specific legal subjects; (d) collecting, analyzing, and evaluating evidence as to activities under specific federal laws before an agency hearing or decision; (e) analyzing facts and legal questions presented by personnel administering specific federal laws; answering questions by collecting interpretations of applicable legal provisions, regulations, precedent, and agency policy; and, occasionally, preparing informational and instructional material for general use; and (f) performing other paralegal duties "requiring discretion and independent judgment" in applying specialized knowledge of particular laws, regulations, precedent, or agency practices based thereon.

Paralegals are employed by the National Labor Relations Board, the Federal Trade Commission, Equal Employment Opportunity Commission, Department of Justice, and Department of Health, Education, and Welfare.

A recent publication, entitled *Paralegal Personnel for Attorney General's Offices,* published by the National Association of Attorneys General, is an example of the opportunities for paralegals in the state level in the public sector. When one considers how many state and local governmental agencies there are which are likely to need trained paralegals to help carry out their functions it can readily be seen that the potential job opportunities are tremendous. The Manual referred to here discusses the potential use of paralegals in just one section of the legal profession: the Attorneys General offices, and it recommends the use of such paraprofessionals. Benefits are noted which are equally applicable to private sector law firms:

An economic benefit, whenever a paralegal replaces a lawyer and thus frees him for other work.

An increased level of office productivity, permitting the district attorney to expand his "discretionary" caseload in such areas as consumer fraud.

An improvement in the quality of office work, deriving from a better match up between work needing to be done and the workers' aptitude to do it.

The Manual further noted that, "Similar success was shown in a survey of over one hundred private practitioners who used paralegals; all respondents said that their own output had been increased. The fact that many private law firms now employ as many as twenty-five paralegals bears out this finding."

While the National Federation of Paralegal Associations is essentially the organ for private sector paralegal organizations, the National Paralegal Institute, established in 1972 by the Office of Economic Opportunity, is primarily concerned with promoting the training and utilization of paralegals in the public law sector. This includes legal services to the poor, group legal services, government agency work, and the criminal justice system. It is in this public sector where readers here who are most interested in those "most interesting and exciting facets of the law" such as environmental law will find what they are looking for!

The thrust of this book, however, is essentially private sector paralegalism but always considering those issues which are shared in common by both sectors.

The Economics of Paralegals for Lawyers and Their Clients

Turning to the all-important matter of the economic implications of paralegals in terms of basic economics for the lawyer and client, it must first be noted that paralegals have a much lower hourly billing rate than even the youngest lawyer in a law firm. It has been found, for example, that on the average, the paralegal's time is billed at a rate of $20 per hour. The combination of salary and overhead applicable to the paralegal in a large city firm is about $15,000 per year. If the paralegal is able to bill 1,500 hours at $20 an hour, that would yield a gross billing of $30,000 a year. After subtracting the paralegal's overhead the firm derives a reasonable profit from use of the paralegal.

If it takes the paralegal twice as long to perform a task as it would have taken a lawyer whose time is billed at $40 an hour, then there is no money to be saved by the client. On the other hand, many of the tasks performed by paralegals can be performed for a total hourly charge, i.e., billing rate times hours, that is less than a lawyer's. This is even true when comparing the costs of a paralegal to a young lawyer, because lawyers are not trained in law school to do the every day work of legal practice, while paralegals are trained to do just that type of work.

Question: Will use of paralegals save the public money? Indications are that many matters which are presently billed on an hourly rate are being billed for less as they are shifted to paralegals. Unfortunately, there are other situations where these savings are not passed on to the public. But ultimately there is hope and reason to believe that the use of paralegals will tend to make the cost of legal services more reasonable and increase the profitability of lawyers. In other words the dividend that may be realized will probably be split between the clients.

Prepaid Legal Service Programs

Closely connected with this subject of the economics of the use of paralegals in the legal profession is the emerging development of prepaid legal service plans which provide legal services economically for that part of the public which does not qualify for legal aid and to whom the payment of legal expenses imposes a heavy burden. The onset of prepaid legal service plans will require a form of legal services that can be performed by the paralegal under the auspices of a qualified lawyer.

Prepaid legal service plans are plans whereby a group arranges for payment for legal services in behalf of its individual members pursuant to a pre-arranged agreement with the legal profession. They are similar to group medical plans. Unions, lodges, trade associations, industrial corporations and similar groups are all potential prospects for prepaid legal services. Funding for these plans is generally accomplished by minimal assessments payable from wages of group members. Philip J. Murray, staff director of the American Bar Association's Special Committee on Prepaid Legal Services, predicted that this new approach to the delivery of legal services will be used by 25% of the public within the next five years.

The past several years have seen the introduction of prepaid legal services and the firms involved in this type of practice tend to develop highly specialized structures because the work they handle falls into a routinized pattern. Unlike the large law firm, they depend economically on the profitable processing of a high volume of low fee matters. The use of paralegals can make the difference between processing low fee work at a profit rather than a loss. These firms, therefore, offer a potential market for the employment of large numbers of paralegals.

Paralegal Professional Organizations

But to return to the development of the paralegal movement, it should be noted that a number of national organizations have taken an interest in how this emerging occupation develops. As the paralegal movement has gained momentum and recognition, paralegals began forming associations which is in the American tradition. By May 1974 representatives of eight such associations met and established the

National Federation of Paralegal Associations. During its first year, the Federation served as a communications network to alert and inform members of issues and events that affected paralegals. In 1975 the Federation assumed a new structure and became a professional association for paralegals. At that second meeting it was further resolved that Federation members would take an active role in developing and regulating the "profession." There are about twenty new organizations in the process of forming and joining the Federation.

The Legal Assistant Section of the National Association of Legal Secretaries has formed a separate organization, the National Association of Legal Assistants (NALA). Unlike the Federation, which consists of organizations, membership in NALA is on an individual basis.

American Bar Association Views the Paralegal Movement

In 1968 the American Bar Association's (ABA) Special Committee on the Availability of Legal Services reported to the House of Delegates that "legal services would be more fully available to the public" if the legal profession were to recognize that "freeing a lawyer from tedious and routine detail" would conserve the lawyer's time and energy for "truly legal problems." Accordingly, three recommendations were made:

1. The legal profession should recognize that there are many tasks in serving a client's needs which can be performed by a trained non-lawyer assistant working under the direction and supervision of a lawyer;

2. The legal profession should encourage the training and employment of such assistants; and

3. A special committee of the ABA should be created to consider the subject of lay assistants for lawyers.

These recommendations were adopted by the House of Delegates and the Special Committee on Lay Assistants (now the Standing Committee on Legal Assistants) was established. In 1969 the Special Committee sponsored limited surveys of law firms around the country and found that there was "a significant" use of nonlawyers.

In 1974, this same Committee issued a Report which surveyed the "Characteristics Important for (Paralegals) as Viewed by Employing Firms" which we offer here as a useful piece of information for readers of this Guide who are considering a paralegal career:

Characteristics	Very Important	Important	Not Important
a. training as a (paralegal)	10	6	4
b. ability to understand legal terminology	17	2	2
c. interviewing skills	5	6	9
d. analytical mind	13	8	1
e. at least 4 years college	6	8	6
f. get along well with people	11	10	1
g. willingness to assume responsibility	19	2	0
h. knowledge of bookkeeping	2	7	11
i. willingness to follow orders	11	9	1
j. maturity	17	4	0
k. at least some college or vocational school	7	8	2
l. intend to make a career as a (paralegal)	5	11	5
m. above average intelligence	14	6	0
n. facility in speaking	7	11	3
o. legal secretary experience	0	4	18
p. interest in people	4	12	5
q. writing skills	10	10	0
r. some law school courses	2	2	17
s. ambitious	6	15	0
t. ability to function at a high level under stress conditions	9	10	2
u. understanding the legal process	7	9	5
v. secretarial skills	0	5	0
w. understanding the meaning of "confidentiality"	16	5	0
x. empathy	3	12	3
y. desire to eventually become an attorney	0	0	22

Another survey appearing in this Report of "Tasks Performed in Law Office as Reported by Employing Firms" is also worth reprinting here for the purpose of giving you a further idea of what the functions of a paralegal are in actual practice.

Task	Frequency of Response	
	Usually Perform	Should Perform
(1) Type	0	0
(2) Maintain law library	4	6
(3) Notify client of actions taken	0	5
(4) Do office filing	1	2
(5) Prepare briefs and pleadings	0	4
(6) Docket	3	5
(7) Train nonattorney staff	0	0
(8) Prepare office memoranda	0	3
(9) Operate office machines	2	1
(10) Appear for client in court	0	0
(11) Search and check public records	4	17
(12) Contact client for information	2	10
(13) Prepare fee and disbursement statement	1	4
(14) Draft wills, deeds and trusts	2	5
(15) Plan installation and operation of office machinery	0	0
(16) Notify clients of approaching deadlines	3	10
(17) Serve papers	4	7
(18) File motions	5	7
(19) Shepardize	5	14
(20) Hire and supervise nonattorney staff	2	1
(21) Tax work	14	8
(22) Compile and select citations	4	12
(23) Index documents and prepare digests	10	17
(24) Conduct initial interview with client	0	2
(25) Take dictation	1	1
(26) Investigations	7	16
(27) Develop and implement office procedures	1	2
(28) Prepare probate inventories and inheritance and Federal estate tax returns	12	17
(29) File papers	3	4
(30) Receptionist	1	1
(31) Make arrangements for depositions and hearings	1	6

Firms of 15 lawyers and more will vastly increase their use of paralegals, especially as they learn to better utilize them. Smaller firms, on the other hand, have a limited ability to absorb paralegals. Often, the lawyers have a very general practice, which means that the training received by the paralegal ordinarily cannot fit their practice as well as it would for a specialist. Therefore, more time-consuming and costly on-the-job training is required. This is difficult because of the manpower shortage under which these firms often operate. There are, nevertheless, "strategies" the paralegal job applicant can use in seeking out a position with a small firm and these strategies are discussed in a later chapter in this Guide.

Paralegals and the Practice of Law

The ethical problems which have emerged since the widespread use of paralegals has taken place are an important topic in any presentation like this dealing with paralegalism as a profession. Guidelines issued by the New York State Bar Association are a pioneering effort in that New York is the first state to have such guidelines for paralegals. Ethical conduct of paralegals is also dealt with in the ethics codes promulgated by the two major professional paralegal associations referred to earlier. These three sets of codes are reprinted in Appendix I of this Guide.

Use of paralegals has had a tremendous impact on the way law is practiced in the United States. This impact can be expected to increase in the coming years. Increased use of paralegals, will benefit the public and the lawyers and will create an ever-growing job market for the kind of knowledge and skills paralegals have acquired in their professional training.

CHAPTER II

The Paralegal and the Law Office

Law Office Management As a Specialization

Throughout this guide we will be discussing the kinds of activities a paralegal will most likely be engaged in. These activities are essentially quasi-legal. That is to say, it is *almost* legal or it is *like* legal work as it is carried on by an attorney. It remains to be considered a very difficult face of the paralegal's office responsibility, the role of office manager, administrator or administrative assistant. In the largest law firms this role will usually not be a paralegal's function because in such a setting running the office is a full-time activity leaving practically no time, if any, for really legal pursuits.

According to the American Bar Association's Committee on Legal Assistants (*viz.,* paralegals), some of the tasks of the paralegal as office manager (or legal administrator) are as follows:

1. Design, develop or plan modification of new procedures, techniques, services, processes or applications.

2. Plan, supervise and assist in the installation and maintenance of relatively complex office equipment.

3. Plan productions, operations, or services as a member of the management unit responsible for efficient use of manpower materials, money and equipment.

A more detailed job description in some law offices could be as follows:

The office manager shall administer the affairs of the firm, reporting directly to the managing partner, meeting with him regularly (or with the administrative committee, or an executive committee) to report on business affairs, determine or suggest policies, implement policy, develop necessary procedures, and provide special financial and management information upon request. He shall assist the managing partner in the preparation of budgets. He shall prepare and interpret management reports, expand allocated budgets for non-lawyer personnel, equipment and supplies. He shall plan the utilization of space and acquisition of space as necessary. He shall maintain the firm's insurance. He shall be responsible for investing in acceptable short-term transactions any cash excess of working capital requirements and shall advise the managing partner when sufficient cash is available for long-term investments.

The office manager shall supervise all accounting, secretarial and other nonlawyer personnel functions and systems, and shall have final responsibility and authority in non-lawyer personnel matters, including work assignments, allocation of equipment, authorization of time off or overtime, quality and quantity of work product, hiring, training, salary advancement, discipline and discharge.

The office manager shall also be responsible for the housekeeping function of the firm, including the maintenance, servicing or replacement of office furniture, equipment, carpet, drapes and other decor items. He reviews, modifies, and maintains the filing system, creates and maintains an information storage and retrieval system, including the gathering of all existing office forms in order to provide the office with the material necessary to create coordinated and standard forms. He organizes and maintains the library, keeps the court calendar and works out a mutually acceptable office meeting schedule. The office manager will be involved in developing procedure manuals for use by non-lawyers in order that more work can be delegated to the non-lawyer staff. He may, if requested, become involved in providing assistance to an attorney in a specific area of practice.

In some large law offices, paralegal personnel are directly responsible to the office manager, while in other offices paralegals are directly responsible to the partner in charge of a specific department in the same manner as the partner will supervise associate lawyers. When the office manager is in charge, he may determine the assignment of paralegals to lawyers, help to decide priorities, i.e., defining when "rush" is "very rush," being sure that everyone is following the common practices and procedures of the firm and generally overseeing work flow and allocation of work. The office manager often has the responsibility to help define what functions can be performed by a paralegal who will be supporting an attorney. For example, development of a master information list (a questionnaire used by a paralegal to gather information from a client) will probably be initially developed by the office manager for review by an attorney. Such master information lists will then be used as a check-off list by the paralegal obtaining information for the lawyer.

Law Office Management Responsibilities

It is obvious that what has been described thus far is a paralegal who has specialized in his training to take charge of a large law office. Now many if not most paralegals will be working in small law offices where they will be expected to carry out the quasi-legal activities to help the lawyer in his practice of law and yet administrate the management dimension of the office. On the face of it, this may appear to be an impossible undertaking but in fact it is quite possible to fulfill the role! What follows is an outline of paralegal functions in terms of law office administration. In the smaller law office not all of these responsibilities need to be assumed and almost rarely are they assumed at one and the same time so that you will feel defeated. There will be the time and opportunity to do many of these things when you are not involved with a specific quasi-legal task.

1. **Calendar Monitoring**
   (a) Maintain "tickler" system (e.g., court appearance dates, agency filings, process serving, etc.).
   (b) Maintain individual attorney's calendar.
2. **Bookkeeping/Accounting**
   (a) Client billing
   (b) Staff time sheets
   (c) Quarterly and final tax returns of the office
   (d) Budget analysis.
3. **Librarianship**
   (a) Monitor law library collection.
   (b) Keep library up to date through loose-leaf services.
   (c) Inform attorneys of developments in the law as picked up through loose-leaf services.
   (d) Collect data, literature, citations from the library on a specific topic under instructions from an attorney.
   (e) Shepardize cases.
   (f) Index specified subjects (coordinating data from library, office files, etc.).
3. **Office Equipment**
   Oversee the purchase, use and maintenance of MTST, Xerox, Dictaphones, etc.
3. **Training**
   Train office staff on the "business" components of the office, e.g. using office equipment, billings, time sheets, etc.
4. **Office Management**
   Assist in the design and implementation of office procedures via forms, checklists, systems, manpower allocation, etc.
5. **Reports**
   (a) Draft statistical reports, e.g., code data from intake and closeout sheets on every client.
   (b) Budget reports.
6. **Filing**
   Maintain, monitor, index, digest client files.

Office Layout

Decreasing the overhead of and thereby increasing the profit of the lawyer's office is one of the most compelling ways the paralegal proves his/her value and assures tenure at the position. And one of the most effective procedures for accomplishing this goal of reducing overhead is properly laying out the office.

Proper use of file cabinets and file folders is an integral part of overhead reduction. The old type of pull-out file cabinets should be discarded. These cabinets are approximately three, four or five drawers high and take up three feet in length. In order to make them operational, it is necessary to have a secretary sit at least two feet away from the cabinets. Space must be included for the pulling out of the drawers. These cabinets should be replaced by the new horizontal cabinets. The new cabinets go from floor to ceiling and are ten inches in length. The files are put in horizontally and each drawer has twice the capacity of a pull out drawer. These cabinets are not only substantially more economical but also are an aesthetic improvement. They come in all of the standard colors and can be blended in with the decor. The drawers do not pull out. The covers for the cabinet slide into the top thereby creating a minimum of wasted space. Years ago, the price of office space was not a factor and it was not necessary to consider space saving techniques. Today it is a crucial factor in office economics.

It is essential to determine where the secretary or secretaries are going to be physically located and make sure that the files are in close proximity. Many law offices have a file room or a place to maintain the files which can be twenty-five to fifty feet away from the secretaries' area. The expenditure of additional time walking back and forth can be avoided if the files are in the same general area as the secretary.

Folders and Filing Correspondence

Paralegals must know how to make use of time-saving folders as an element of management control. Most law firms still use the large red envelopes as a place for dropping papers during the course of the matter. These red folders have an elastic band which ties around a little knob and serves to hold the papers in one place. Some offices then use these plain oak tags and separate the oak tags under different headings and take the oak tags and put them into the red folder. It has been my experience to observe an attorney spending ten or fifteen minutes looking for the home telephone number of a client. I have noticed secretaries wasting ten or fifteen minutes looking up the opposing counsel's address or perhaps the opposing counsel's file number.

I have heard attorneys state to a client on the phone, "Let me review your file and call you back." This response is given to a very simple question by the client. This problem can easily be alleviated by a simple folder. The folder that I have designed is broken into four parts. The folder itself is very similar to the normal oak tag except it is made out of a hard cardboard finish. It has one additional cardboard insert. This changes the interior of the folder and increases the capacity to affix papers from two interior boards to four.

It has been our experience that the correspondence is never referred to during the handling of the case. Lawyers keep letters that are sent to clients even though many of them serve no function. We lawyers never like to throw things out. It is often necessary to send four or five letters to the same person in order to get information. Almost everything sent out in a law office is sent with a covering letter and these covering letters are kept together with the correspondence on the first side of the folder. It is also our experience that most of the discussions during the course of the law suit do not require a reading or reference to legal motions, affidavits, or pleadings. Attorneys also make numerous copies of the same legal pleadings. We keep all of the pleadings in the second section of the folder. In the third and fourth portion of the folder we keep the information which we feel is most important and should be readily available. In a personal injury action on the third side, we keep all of the medical information. It is easy to discuss the medical aspects of a client's case by merely leafing through three or four or five medical reports. In the other fourth portion we keep all of the information relating to the liability of the case. This would include witness statements, diagram of the accident, police report, accident report, etc. We have found that this makes all information available to any lawyer who happens to be handling the file.

One of the major time saving factors of this folder is that all of the information is written on the outside of the folder. In place of a plain red envelope with a few telephone numbers scratched on it, there is a logical sequence for information to be easily recorded and observed. The outside of the folder has the following information:

1. Name, address, business phone, telephone number of plaintiff.
2. Name and address of defendant.
3. Name, address, telephone number of attorney that forwarded the case, if there is such an attorney.
4. The court in which the case is pending.
5. The county where the court is located.
6. The Index Number, the Calendar Number, and any other court information which is relevant.
7. The attorney for the opposing side or the insurance company for the opposing side, including the address, telephone number, file number, and name of the person who is in charge of the case for your opponent.

We still have additional information on the front cover and that includes every court proceeding. The following information is listed:

1. The date.
2. The trial or motion part.

17

3. The purpose of the hearing.
4. Representative of the plaintiff.
5. Representative of the defendant.
6. If there is a money figure involved, the demand and offer, and then a short space for comments.
7. Under that we have disposition of the case including settlement or verdict, the date, the place, the name of the judge, the defendant's representative, the plaintiff's representative, and the amount.

On the reverse side of the folder, still on the outside, we have a list of all expenses. This serves as a check list for any other system that may be used for recording expenses. This includes the date, the name of the person to whom the money was paid, and the amount. We also keep a simple diary system on the outside of the folder. Many small law firms do not maintain a diary system. The method of deciding what is to be done in a law suit is a review on some sort of a periodic basis. This is poor practice and an economic disaster. There are numerous systems which can be used to make certain that a case comes up for review on some logical basis. The simplest of all is a system which many dentists use to guarantee that a patient will be reminded of a six-month check-up. As soon as a case comes into the office, the title of the action should be placed on a 3 x 5 card and put into one of the little card boxes. If there has to be some work performed on this case in the near future, the card should then be put into the day designated by the month. The card catalog box should be broken into days and months. When the day of the month comes up, all of those cards are pulled out, attached to the files, and brought to the attorney or attorneys who are handling this case. This is a simple "tickler" system which was perfected by the dentists many years ago. It is a simple and efficient way of using a diary system.

Form Letters

The proper use of forms and form letters is a necessary time-saving device. The attorney keeps only that portion of his earned dollars which is not spent to pay his taxes or to maintain his office. A major cost of that office is nonlawyer services. If nonlawyer output can be increased 25% to 50%, there is a proportionate saving. This goal can be successfully accomplished by the use of prepared letters and forms.

Copies of the forms following should be adapted to the particular needs of each office. Forms can, of course, be developed to good purpose for other areas of the attorney's practice.

Letter Correspondence

An attractive letter can be produced by photo-offset. It is possible to prepare original letters, using office stationery, leaving blank spaces where necessary. Electric typewriters with bold black letters can fill in the blanks. Only close inspection will reveal the inserted words, since the typing characters and color match the printed matter.

Apart from the savings in cost of stationery, the firm does not have to use the lawyer's time dictating repetitive letters and legal documents, and the secretary can turn out more work.

Letters can be produced by photo-offset for fairly reasonable sums of money even during inflationary times. However, actual rates vary with both economic times as well as with specific business enterprises and the areas in which they are located, so that it would make little sense to offer specific sums here.

We now offer a sample of model form letters which the reader may find useful both in coming to understand this particular aspect of law office management in prospect as well as actual use in practice.

Dear

Enclosed please find   . Please read the enclosed carefully, and sign at the place indicated by your initials. Have this signed and stamped by a Notary Public, and then return to us in the enclosed, self-addressed, stamped envelope.

If there are any corrections to be made, kindly do so on a separate sheet of paper.

Thank you for your cooperation.

———————————

Dear

Please be advised that we have been retained with respect to your above named patient's claim for personal injuries.

Would you be so kind as to furnish us with your medical report relating to the injuries sustained and medical treatment rendered by you. We would also appreciate it if you would furnish us with a copy of your bill for medical services rendered.

Thank you for your courtesy and cooperation in this matter.

———————————

Gentlemen:

We have been retained as attorneys for the above named with reference to a claim for personal injuries sustained on the above date. We have been advised that our client received treatment at your hospital following said accident.

Enclosed please find duly executed authorization permitting us to obtain a copy of our client's hospital record. Would you kindly furnish us with a photostatic copy of the entire hospital record together with a copy of the bill for services rendered to the patient at your earliest possible convenience.

If there is any fee for this service, kindly advise and it will promptly be forwarded.

Dear Dr.

Would you kindly reply to our previous letter to you, and furnish us with your medical report and bill pertaining to the injuries sustained and treatment rendered by you.

Your prompt reply will enable us to proceed properly with the handling of your patient's case and will be greatly appreciated.

Thank you for your courtesy and cooperation.

Dear

We have been retained with respect to your above named employee's claim for personal injuries sustained in an accident which occurred on the above date.

Would you kindly furnish us with a written statement as to the amount of time your employee was absent from employment following said accident, together with a statement of your employee's average weekly earnings for a period of ten weeks prior to the accident.

If your employee was not paid during this absence or if payments were made and charged against sick leave, pension, vacation or other similar plans, please advise.

If your employee was paid during his absence and such payments were not charged against sick leave, pension, vacation or other similar plans, your reply should be limited solely to the amount of time he was absent from employment and his average weekly earnings.

Thank you for your courtesy and cooperation.

Dear

Enclosed please find duly executed general release together with stipulations of discontinuance in the above entitled action.

The amended rules of the Appellate Division require that our closing statement state the date the stipulation of discontinuance was filed with the Calendar Clerk. It is, therefore, necessary that the original stipulation be returned to us for filing.

Kindly forward your check, together with the signed original stipulation of discontinuance, to the undersigned at your earliest convenience.

Thank you for your courtesy and cooperation.

Dear

Enclosed please find insurance company check in settlement of the above-entitled action. Kindly endorse this check, and return same to us in the enclosed, stamped, self-addressed envelope.

Upon receipt of this check, properly endorsed, we will forward our check to you for your share of the recovery.

Thank you for your cooperation in this matter.

Dear

Enclosed herewith please find copy of a Closing Statement which has been filed with the Judicial Conference of the State of New York and which sets forth the manner in which the proceeds of your action have been distributed. We are also enclosing our check for your share of the recovery in accordance with Item 9 of the Closing Statement.

We were pleased to have been of service to you in this matter and we trust that you will feel free to call upon us whenever the occasion to do so may arise.

Dear Sir:

Enclosed please find original and one copy of the transcript of the examination before trial of your client in the above matter.

Please have your client sign the original before a notary public and return same to us at your earliest possible convenience. The copy is for your files.

Handling Potential Clients

It has already been noted that the purpose of the paralegal is to help reduce law office expenses, permitting the attorney more time to devote to strictly legal matters.

A major problem law offices frequently face is which cases to accept in terms of their profitability for the office, and which to turn down. One important function, then, the paralegal can perform is that of interviewing potential clients. Here, with skillful initial questioning, the paralegal can determine if the law suit warrants retaining an attorney or whether it should be processed by the client instead. Limited questioning, such as that which follows, can quickly suggest which route the client should pursue:

Client: I am here to sue a customer who refused to pay me for wiring and electrical work that was performed in their house and . . .

Paralegal: Excuse me. Would you be good enough to tell me the cost of the work that you performed?

Client: I submitted a bill in the amount of $195.

Paralegal: I will speak to one of the attorneys. However, I must point out to you that I believe the cost of handling this case in this office would be probably more than you can expect to receive. Are you aware of the small claims court?

Client: I think I have heard something about it, but I don't know how it is used.

Paralegal: In our state we permit people to bring a law suit in the court without hiring an attorney. The purpose is to avoid expenses in all matters in which a person is making a claim of less than $500. The procedure is very simple. Merely proceed to the Small Claims Part of the District Court and they will be happy to mail a summons out for you for a cost of $2. The person you are suing will be able to respond without hiring an attorney. The case will be heard by a judge or an arbitrator who is a member of the local bar association.

Client: Well, I didn't realize I could use that service and I thank you very much for your time.

Paralegal: You are most welcome, and if you have any further problems, I am sure that the law firm will be delighted to assist you in any way.

In this situation, the paralegal did not need to take a long, detailed history before ultimately advising the client that the matter could best be handled outside the office in the Small Claims Part of the District

Court. Almost any other approach by the paralegal might probably have resulted in a wasteful expenditure of time reaching the same conclusion! The paralegal should always be mindful that there are many cases which would be best handled through the client's own resources. Questioning at the outset should aim at that result in the best interests of both the office and the client.

Needless to say, no matter would be finally determined before the paralegal has consulted with an attorney in the firm concerning the case at hand. In this way the firm's option of accepting or rejecting a case remains open until it has been reviewed at the appropriate level.

There are some attorneys who believe that it is a good practice to accept any case even though it is not financially sound. The theory is that sooner or later a client giving you unprofitable business will call you on a profitable matter. It has been my experience that quite the converse is true. The client appreciates an honest answer and is made to realize that no law firm will be able to do a competent job on a matter that is totally and completely unprofitable. A more significant factor is the human nature of most people. Many clients are under the impression that if a law firm handles an insignificant matter they are not qualified or competent to handle a more serious matter. My firm processes a great deal of personal injury work and the following story is not uncommon.

Paralegal: Mr. Shayne asked me to talk to you and obtain a history and the facts relating to your case.

Client: That's fine. However, I will be able to speak to Mr. Shayne before I leave, will I not?

Paralegal: Yes, of course. You told me that you sustained a severe sprain to your neck, and it was necessary for you to be hospitalized for a period of four weeks following this accident.

Client: Yes, that's correct.

Paralegal: It is important that we determine if there was any pre-existing injury or condition to your neck. As I will outline later, the insurance company will be able to obtain this information, and therefore it is necessary that we are forearmed.

Client: I had a minor sprain to my neck last year and the case has not been settled yet.

Paralegal: Did you retain a lawyer?

Client: Yes, I did.

Paralegal: Can you tell me the name of the lawyer?

Client: Mr. Smith.

Paralegal: May I ask you why you did not bring this case to the attorney that is handling your previous accident?

Client: I gave a very simple case to this lawyer and he was unable to settle it.

Paralegal: What were the facts?

Client: I was proceeding along Main Street when another car, speeding, decided to pass a red light and struck my car right in the middle of the intersection of Main Street and Park Avenue. I was proceeding within the speed limit and had the green light in my favor. I was out of work for a week and went to a doctor five times for a sprain of the neck. Mr. Smith, the lawyer, brought me down to his office for depositions, sent all sorts of legal papers to me to be signed and it was necessary for me to see a doctor from the insurance company. Over a year has passed and he couldn't even settle that case. I know that case was not a particularly big one and perhaps a large case like this one should be handled by a different law firm. I assume that Mr. Smith does not handle very big cases.

Here is a situation which is most unfortunate for the previous lawyer. It is quite apparent that a case like this should not have been taken in the first place and was accepted solely as a favor to the client. We have a case where each driver claims the other passed a red light. This sets up a sharp question of fact which is not readily amenable to settlement. Even if the company is willing to assume some responsibility for the accident, we are still left with a case with very little damage. The client suffered a one-week loss of pay and was treated by a doctor only a few times for a sprain of the neck. This is a law suit which the original attorney probably should have declined in the first instance. It is the type of case which the plaintiff should not have pursued. The time and effort and possibility of success are not commensurate with the time and effort of the client or a law office. I think if the original attorney had stated his position in this matter, the second substantial case would have been retained by his law firm.

Mr. Client, I know that you have a complaint and you sustained some injury. I must point out to you that most probably the other driver will claim that you have passed a red light and he was driving with a green light in his favor. You saw a doctor on only three occasions and you are not claiming any severe injury to your neck at the present time. My office handles cases with a great deal of care and requires more time than you might imagine. We have determined that even before walking into court we must expend twenty hours on each case in order to handle it properly. This is the type of law suit which we feel it is probably not in

24

your best interest to take on because we cannot give it the time that we devote to our other cases. I am certain that there are other lawyers in town that will handle this case, and I would suggest that if you insist on pursuing this claim you speak to them. I must point out to you that every case in this office requires a complete personal and medical study and we must be selective with the cases we take. The insurance companies and insurance company lawyers that deal with us know that we do this type of investigation and know that we are fully prepared. If the occasion does arise where you need any legal advice in the future, do not hesitate to contact our office. If you would like me to recommend one or two young lawyers that might handle this case I will be delighted to do so.

It has been our experience that this type of a discussion with a client will bring him back to us if and when he has a more substantial case. It is true there is a possibility the client will be satisfied with the other lawyer and retain the other attorney for any future business. This course of action nevertheless results in an upgrading of the legal practice. "Upgrading" means that each year a law firm should try to increase the quality of the business that it accepts.

We have been discussing the hourly rate law firm. The larger law firms that charge per hour do not have this problem. Any case that is being accepted by the office mandates that the client will pay the lawyer's hourly rate. Most attorneys still have a set fee for a matter or operate on a percentage basis and therefore the paralegal must look into the facts very carefully to determine whether the case is profitable to handle. The final decision on whether the case will be accepted will be made by one of the attorneys. However, the attorney must be given all of the facts before making this decision.

The paralegal can perform a service for the attorney by suggesting that the attorney keep a *key client index*. It has been the experience of most law firms that there are a few friends or clients who are excellent sources of prospective business. It is unethical to pay a client for any referral. However, it is not unethical to thank them and perhaps occasionally take the referring client out to dinner or to a show to show your appreciation. It is interesting that there are some close friends of the attorney who are never in a position to refer any business and other people who are constant sources of business. Many attorneys feel the law of averages reveals that twenty clients of the firm will average about ten referrals per year.

A key client index would most probably reveal that out of the twenty clients perhaps one or two refer five or six cases. This fact depends on the position of the client. An owner of a business that employs working people may very well be in a position to recommend clients to a law firm. The average worker who has not had much contact with lawyers and is in need of an attorney might ask an employer for a recommendation. The worker also knows that the employer is in constant communication with attorneys and probably could recommend one. There are people who continually make such statements as "My doctor is the finest doctor in the world," "My lawyer is the smartest lawyer in the world," etc. These are the clients who generally refer a great deal of business. It is a useful function to maintain a file indicating who are major sources of business. A simple "thank you" and communication with them is usually enough to assure the flow of business.

The paralegal is not in a position to set a fee on a case; however, it is not unreasonable for the paralegal to discuss how fee structures are set. The following are guidelines recommended by the American Bar Association:

1. Time involved.
2. Nature, difficulty, and novelty of the problem.
3. Amount of money or other interest involved.
4. Attorney's professional standing.
5. Benefits sought for the client.
6. Attitude of the profession toward the type of litigation.
7. Responsibility assumed by the attorney in the case.
8. Probability of success for the client.
9. Necessity of the lawyer's service.
10. Client's ability to pay.

Following are some of the other routine functions a paralegal might perform for the litigation department of a law firm:

Keep up with the answer date and all deadlines, informing the attorneys well in advance.

Prepare lists of witnesses to be deposed and keep up with the whereabouts, addresses, telephone numbers, etc., of all witnesses during the pendency of the case.

Prepare general information interrogatories in each case; that is, questions asking witnesses known to the opposite parties, enumeration of correspondence, etc.

Arrange for court reporters, deposition dates, send out notices of depositions, subpoenas, mileage and per diem payments, make all arrangements for depositions.

Draft routine motions.

Arrange for the lawyer's appointments to interview witnesses.

Paralegals may interview some witnesses and take statements much as claim adjustors and investigators presently do.

Draft removal petitions.

Obtain additional time for answers to interrogatories or filing defensive pleadings.

Draft answers to interrogatories, checking the file and information supplied by the client to insure the accuracy of the answers.

Outline depositions and collate deposition and interrogatory information into categories.

Review depositions of opposite parties and adverse witnesses for inconsistencies and contradictions.

Collect originals of all documentary evidence and make sure the attorneys have originals properly filed and indexed.

Compile pretrial notebooks with all exhibits indexed and essential major points to be covered with each witness, with page numbers of any contradictions and inconsistencies in depositions likely to be used to impeach the witness at trial.

Most of the information required by pretrial orders may be completed by paralegals.

Paralegals can notify all witnesses of the trial date and make sure that all subpoenas for the trial have been issued; that all witnesses are in attendance at the trial, providing transportation where necessary; and make all other arrangements to relieve the trial attorney of worry about the whereabouts of his witnesses.

Paralegals would arrange for the use of a jury service or obtain the jury list for analysis.

Paralegals would notify all witnesses in the case of postponement or continuance.

Paralegals would prepare after-trial letters, thanking all witnesses for their time, etc.

Paralegals would keep current lists of expert witnesses used by the firm and other firms.

Paralegals would draft all routine post-trial papers.

Paralegals would keep checklists of post-trial procedures to insure that appellate procedure is precisely followed.

Paralegals would locate page numbers in the record for the attorney writing the briefs.

Paralegals would keep up with all of the trial lawyer's files, making sure that they were properly organized and indexed and quickly available to him.

Paralegals would collect the client information in personal injury cases such as past and present medical history; history of other accidents and injuries; facts pertaining to the accident forming the cause of action for the present lawsuit; obtain the client's employment history; obtain medical authorizations and list all special damages and obtain medical records.

Paralegals would do all the lawyer's proofreading.

Paralegals also could keep the lawyer current on all cases decided and reported under particular key numbers. For instance, paralegals could review all of the advance sheets from the Supreme Court, all of the Federal Circuit Courts, the District Courts and the State Courts, summarizing particular cases under particular key numbers. Paralegals could, of course, do all of the "Shepardizing" and checking of citations.

Other administrative functions which paralegals could be trained to perform are preparing drafts of bills and transmittal letters, preparing drafts of responsive letters, accepting telephone calls and acting generally as an administrative assistant to the lawyer.

CHAPTER III

Interviewing the Client
and Trial Preparation

Putting the Client at Ease

Many new clients have a fear of the legal process and are afraid of prosecuting or defending law suits. Most clients are uneasy right at the outset. It is therefore important for the paralegal to put the client at ease and to relax him. Asking the client if he would like a cup of coffee or making certain that he is in a comfortable chair can be important first steps. A few innocuous questions are an effective way to start off the conversation easily. For example, "Did you have any difficulty finding our office?" "This kind of weather is probably better suited for tennis or golf than it is for talking about a law suit!" "What did you think of the President's talk last night?"

Once the client gets talking about anything in general there will be a natural flow leading into the problem at hand. Let the client know that you have plenty of time and that you intend to devote as much of it as necessary to make certain you get all the needed information.

Explaining Your Role in the Interview

It is important to explain to the client that you are not a lawyer. You are permitted to discuss your role with the client. You can tell him that you are trained as a paralegal and that you have graduated from an accredited program if that is the case. It is a good idea to discuss the necessity of getting a complete and thorough history. Clients who have dealt with lawyers on previous occasions are fully aware that lawyers are busy people and often cannot give them sufficient time. It should be apparent to the client that as a paralegal you are committed to devote a substantial amount of time to the client's problem and that you are collecting data and information which will be presented to one of the attorneys for discussion. Generally speaking, the client is pleased to learn that an intelligent and responsible person is going to give him this kind of attention. The preliminary discussion indicated here will set the stage for the more complete and perhaps

29

personal information you will want to get from the client.

Encouraging the Client to Talk Before the Questioning

Often clients need someone to talk to who will listen to his full story. A good rapport is usually established with a client by giving him the time and opportunity to give you what he believes to be the whole story with all of its details. The information may not be quite what you want or need, nor is it likely to be in the proper order. But the client's free flow of narrative will nevertheless give you a picture of the information that is required as well as give you some insight that the client himself has about the problem. The client may give an audible sigh of relief after he has let it all hang out, as it were. There appears to be therapeutic value for many people to get things "off their chest."

Keeping Form or Checklist Handy

It is essential that every law office maintain a checklist or form which is to be used in the interview of each new client. This instrument should itemize questions which are most commonly asked. Most law firms do not have such a fact sheet and the paralegal should set one up himself. We are going to use a checklist for a personal injury action in the litigation field as our example or model in this section. We will discuss the reasons for the information that will be elicited, and much of this information could be carried over to any other field of law.

The paralegal should ascertain the name, address, and telephone number of the client, spouse, children, and the person who referred the matter to the office. Both the home and office number of these people are essential to have. It is an irritant to an attorney when he is attempting to telephone a client and the only telephone number recorded is an office number. If the client is no longer working or is on vacation or on sick leave, it becomes necessary to consult a telephone directory to get the home address. The telephone number may not be listed or the party may have moved. In short, both of these telephone numbers should be quickly available and in a handy spot such as outside the folder. Elsewhere in this book we discuss proper folders for use in a law office.

The name and address of the person forwarding the matter is essential because this person might be the only one who has contact with the plaintiff for any extended period of time. It should be noted that a personal injury action occasionally takes three to four years before it is settled or tried. During this time people move, lose their jobs, get transferred, or simply disappear for any number of other reasons. Not surprisingly, then, years may pass when the client has no contact with the law office. Legal pleadings are prepared and forwarded directly to the attorneys for the defendant so that contact with the client is limited.

The paralegal should keep in touch with the client, although this is not done in too many law offices. If the client is not available and information is required immediately it is helpful to turn to the person who referred the case in the first place because he is likely to know the habits of the client and thereby can most likely put you in touch with him.

It is important that you record the occupation of the plaintiff as well as the length of time he has been employed. In a personal injury case, as in most other adversary proceedings, the credibility of the plaintiff is always at issue. Evidence that your client has been employed in a position for a long period of time indicates a sound and stable individual. Whatever else a psychiatrist might say about it, the attorney will have a higher regard for a person's veracity when he has been solidly employed in a responsible position for a reasonable length of time.

One of the most essential elements in conducting an interview with a plaintiff in a personal injury, products liability, or malpractice action is to take a complete medical history from the plaintiff and obtain information relating to each and every injury that the plaintiff has sustained going back as far as the plaintiff can remember. Many an attorney has lost a case because either he or his paralegal who conducted the client interview failed to get all the information he needed for a successful cross examination at the trial.

In a personal injury action all the physical facts must be obtained. Again turning to our model, a physical injury case, the following information should be recorded:

Date and time of the accident.

Place of the accident.

Width of the intersection.

Whether the intersection was controlled by signals, whether there was heavy traffic, how far the plaintiff's motor vehicle or the defendant's motor vehicle may have been from the intersection.

Time traffic light was red or green.

Whether there were any obstructions which would prevent either driver from seeing the other.

The composition of the roadway.

How many lanes could travel in each direction.

Whether there were any parked cars.

Whether the police were at the scene.

The name of the patrolman, the shield number of the patrolman, the police precinct of the patrolman.

Whether the plaintiff was taken to the hospital by ambulance, the name of the hospital, how long a period of time the

31

plaintiff was at the hospital, general injuries sustained by the plaintiff at the hospital.

The name and address of the owner of the plaintiff's car.

The name and address of the operator of the defendant's car.

The name and address of the owner of the defendant's car.

The registration number, year, make, and state of defendant's car.

The insurance broker of the plaintiff and defendant, if available.

The insurance company of the plaintiff and defendant, if available.

Whether there is any medical payments coverage on the plaintiff's car.

Whether there is any collision coverage.

Obtaining Negative Aspects of the Case

One of the most difficult aspects of conducting an interview in any case is to get negative aspects of the case from the plaintiff or client. The client is under the impression that he must impress you that he has been grievously wronged. Under the circumstances, the client will relate all of the positive or strong points in his problem but unlikely to mention anything which diminishes his case.

But once you have in fact elicited all the strong points of the client's history and you have established a rapport with him, you must bring to light any negative factors in the case. You should advise the client that information and investigations are available and will be conducted by the opponent's attorney so that even the most difficult information to uncover will get to the opponent eventually. For example, matrimonial lawyers experience situations where the husband is convinced that he has covered up his tracks in an adultery situation by conducting his affair out of town and fails to relate this to his attorney in a subsequent matrimonial action. But he pays for a dinner with a Diner's Club or an American Express card and an astute investigator for the suing wife uncovers these slips at Diner's Club or American Express. When the attorney for the wife has a series of dinner checks for two it is not difficult to conclude that this husband was not at a bowling party or at an executive meeting which he might have told his own attorney! In short, if any portion of the client's story does not ring true, make certain that you pursue your questioning to a greater depth. Point out to him the old cliche that being forewarned is being forearmed.

Have Client Produce All Written Papers, Documents, Pictures, and Records Connected with the Case

Keep a diary and make certain you acquire all papers and documents relating to your case and forward it to the office.

Very often a client will tell you that he suffered pain and discomfort during the hospital stay. However, when a case comes up for trial, a year or two later, he has no memory of what has taken place. The following are excerpts of a diary which was kept by a patient:

I can't have anything by mouth for another two weeks. I dream of water often.

Intravenous feeding is not painful except when the liquid nourishment infiltrates the vein. This appears to happen when the fluid is going too slowly into the vein. (Actually it is caused by the needle slipping out of the vein). When this happened, my arm became swollen.

My first three nights at the hospital were nights of complete pain. The first night was extremely painful on the heels of my feet. I tried to shift my weight from heel to heel, but the heels burned with pain and the right heel felt as if it were on fire. Apparently the pain was caused because my feet were on a board that had been placed between me and the mattress. This caused my heels to be directly in contact with the board and also caused pressure on the heels by elevating them several inches higher than the rest of the legs. I shall have to lie on my back in this position for more than 3½ weeks. At times it is unbearable.

When the doctors made rounds the next morning, the aides were advised that the foot board was to be placed under the mattress and under my heels. Thank God I was relieved of that torture device.

The last two nights have been nights of horror. I have not slept a wink and am firmly convinced that patients are deliberately tortured by the 11 p.m. to 7 a.m. shift.

I went to therapy and I was able to stand two times at the "walkette" for about ten seconds each time. The therapist told me to extend my legs in bed 100 times a day. This is for thigh muscle strength and I did this exercise 500 times.

Betty gave me a haircut. This is the first time my hair was cut since before the accident. I went for therapy and walked for the first time. I was able to walk fifteen feet on the "walkette" by placing weight only on my right foot and supporting myself with my arms.

It is now 6:30 a.m. I slept rather restlessly last night. I am depressed. I fight it off by thinking of my recovery. Lying on my back since the accident is painful and tedious. Just can't wait until I can get on my side.

At 10:30 a.m. on April 13, 1971, I experienced a sharp pain in my right chest. My first thought was that I had a muscle spasm, but in reality it was a blood clot.

A conference was held between my surgeon, Dr. M., and the internist, Dr. S. A decision was made to operate. The blood clot inflamed the lung causing a temperature and my temperature soared to 104.8 degrees.

The nurse covered my body with cold compresses in an urgent effort to break the fever. The fever and ice baths fought each other to a stand-still.

The first day after the operation I was desperately weak. I lost all contact with the world. The only thing that had meaning to me was my wife's hand — Betty's fingers, the only thing that kept me from slipping into nothingness.

I remember my wife saying, "Joey, open your eyes." I looked at her pleadingly, but I was too weak to keep my eyes open, and I drifted off keeping in contact with the world only by grasping Betty's fingertips.

I was coming back to life. I still had a fever and was disturbed about the condition of the veins in my arms. I looked like a drug addict. My left arm was swollen from the shoulder to the fingers and mottled with the telltale marks of many needles.

If you had waited until three years or two years after this accident and had asked this patient how he felt while he was in the hospital, it is inconceivable that he would have remembered all of these details and feelings that he was able to record in a diary.

Very often, a client will summarize the import of a letter or a written document. When you have the opportunity to puruse the same document, you will be shocked to find that it may be in total conflict with the story that you have received. Ascertain and assemble all of the written documentary evidence that is available. Many of us practicing law believe that the most important hour devoted to a case is the hour devoted to obtaining the facts. There are times when information can be obtained in less time and there are occasions when substantially more time is required. Do not let the press of other duties prevent you from conducting a total and complete interview.

Just at about this point when you are completing your interview you should assure the client that it will be kept in the strictest of confidence. And it goes without saying that you should express no opinion about whether the case will be accepted or what its value may be. After you have now completed the interview it is appropriate to call in one of the partners and introduce the client. A brief synopsis of the case should be related to the partner. If the client has any questions about the legal elements in the case or about the fees, he can raise them at this time.

Before leaving this discussion on interviewing, it would be useful to report the following "classic" history showing how a little extra time

34

resulted in a substantial settlement. The facts in this paralegal-client episode are that a youngster of nine years of age received an injury which resulted in the loss of his right eye. Liability had been established and the job of the law firm was to realize as large a settlement as possible in order to adequately compensate such a tragedy.

Paralegal: How are you feeling Johnnie?

Johnnie: Pretty good I guess.

Paralegal: Well, we haven't spoken to you in some time, and I just wanted to see how you were getting along so I can keep your case up to date.

Johnnie: O.K.

Paralegal: How are you doing in school?

Johnnie: I'm doing very well.

Paralegal: How are your marks?

Johnnie: My marks are better than ever, and I have no trouble reading.

Paralegal: Are you playing much ball?

Johnnie: Yes, I play basketball everyday.

Paralegal: How are you doing in the basket shooting department?

Johnnie: I am the best foul shooter on the team, and I can shoot better than anyone else on the team.

(The paralegal's job was to try and obtain information which would result in a larger settlement. So far, the interview is not going well from a financial standpoint.)

Paralegal: Are you able to jump under the boards and get rebounds?

Johnnie: Well, to tell you the truth, Mr.   , my daddy told me that I can't jump under the boards, because if I get hit in my other eye I will be blind, so I really don't play too close to the boards.

Paralegal: Well, are you playing any baseball?

Johnnie: Yes, I play, and I play very well.

Paralegal: Can you hit the ball all right?

Johnnie: I am the best hitter on the team.

Paralegal: How is your fielding?

Johnnie: I field very well, but my mommy won't let me slide into bases. She says that if dust got into my eye or I got hit in the eye, I would be blind. In fact, I really don't play baseball too much.

Paralegal: Well, how are you feeling otherwise? Do you have any other problems or things which you are worried about?

Johnnie: Well, I guess when I go into New York City and one time I got dust in my eye and I couldn't see and I was very frightened. I thought I would never be able to see again and I started to cry until the dust went out of my eye and I was able to see again."

This case was settled for a substantial amount of money when this dialogue was sent to the insurance company. It is rare that a lawyer would have the time and patience to devote to a series of questions and answers of a nine-year-old child. The diligence of the paralegal in this case resulted in a very substantial settlement for the child as well as an impressive fee for the law firm.

Initial Conference Key Time to Probe Data

The same sort of probing is essential in every field of law to best handle the client's matter, and it is on the initial conference that the paralegal should most concentrate and intensify his or her effort, not only to establish the basis for a good client relationship but also to acquire the information necessary to determine how to best serve the client's needs.

The following article by Sanford J. Schlesinger, Esq. offers valuable insight into the type of interviewing that should be conducted with a client seeking help on his estate matters.

Clients will often go to a lawyer and say, "I want a will"; they are never heard to say, "I want my estate planned." Generally, clients mistakenly believe that estate planning is merely the act of having an attorney draft and supervise the execution of a will. Unfortunately, attorneys often accede to the client's direction without advising him of the intricacies of estate planning and the potential adverse consequences if the planning is inadequate.

Goals of Estate Planning

An estate plan: should have two basic goals; transferring the client's property to the person(s) he or she wishes to receive it, and achieving such with the most favorable tax consequences. To adequately achieve these goals, a substantial amount of information must be obtained from the client. Among the many considerations in establishing a plan to dispose of a client's wealth are the client's (and often related person's) financial condition, the nature of his property, the extent to which he wants various persons to share in his estate, the needs of each intended beneficiary and their capacity to handle the client's largesse, the estate, inheritance and income tax consequences of the transfers, and the continuing need for flexibility.[1] The attorney's task is to evaluate all factors and to ascertain what would be best for

(1) Merians v. Commissioner, 60 TC 187, 189, Dec. 31, 966 (1973); Casner, Estate Planning, Ch. 1 (3rd ed. 1961); Holzman, Estate Planning, Ch. 1 (1967); Trachtman, Estate Planning, Ch. 1 (Rev. ed. 1968).

the client within the framework of the client's wishes and the requirements of the estate tax laws of the Federal government and the inheritance tax laws of possibly several States (and maybe even the City of New York).

Everyone is aware that estate and income tax savings are major considerations in estate planning. However, the attorney must be cognizant of the primary objective of estate planning, the carrying out of the dispositive wishes of the client at the same time as achieving maximum tax savings. If tax savings can be achieved within this framework, they are desirable. If tax savings will distort these desires, they may have to be subordinated to the client's overall planning for disposition of his estate.

Initial Conference

Generally, it is advisable to divide the initial conference with the client into three basic areas of inquiry: personal information and family tree; financial data concerning the client's assets and liabilities at the time of the interview and projected into the reasonably foreseeable future; a review of the client's dispositive wishes.

Attorneys are aware that clients are often reluctant to furnish personal or financial information in the detail which is required to do a complete analysis. A brief but substantial explanation advising the client as to the various elements of an estate plan, the potential tax savings, and the protection it will afford his next of kin, will generally convince the most reluctant client.

The attorney should not rely on what a client thinks are his assets or his net worth. People often are unaware of the full extent or nature of their holdings until guided by competent counsel asking the right questions.

The client should be advised that, based on the analysis of his holding, the result of the conference may be more than a will, that it may be an estate plan, which can include, among other things, inter-vivos trusts, both revocable and irrevocable, transfers of various assets between and among family members including change of ownership of life insurance policies, preparation of gift tax returns, and various other transactions which may either better accomplish the testator's disposition of his assets and/or achieve greater tax savings.

The first conference affords a good opportunity to explain to the client the different dispositive and tax consequences of various forms of ownership, (i.e. joint ownership, tenancy by the entirety, tenancy in common, Totten trusts), and the effect of beneficiary designations on insurance policies and various benefit plans. It also is advisable to explain to the client which assets are testamentary (pass under the will), and which assets are nontestamentary (pass outside of the will). For example, it has been our experience that, because life insurance generally passes outside the will to the designated beneficiary, many clients believe that life insurance is not estate taxable. It should be explained to the client that life insurance is generally estate taxable,[2] except under certain specific limited ex-

---

(2) Section 2042 IRC.

ceptions, for example, if the decedent does not possess any incidents of ownership in relation to the insurance at the time of his death and the proceeds of the policy may be excludable from his taxable estate.

Questions to be Asked

This article will touch upon only certain basic areas. Accompanying this article [at the end] is an outline of questions concerning the areas of information that must be explored. It is important that the attorney obtain the information in an orderly, usable manner.

The attorney should make longhand notes during the conference in sufficient detail so that a comprehensive record of the meeting is established. Such notes can serve to refresh recollection after the death of the client, and if necessary, upon proper identification of the handwriting, can be introduced in evidence to show that the will was the expression of the testator's intention.

The client should be interviewed alone; the information should be obtained directly from the client, and not from a third party. This procedure is desirable in order to avoid any possible charges of undue influence. If information cannot be obtained directly from the client, it should be read back to the client, and he should acknowledge that he is cognizant of the information that is being read to him.

Personal Information

The client's correct name and any other names he is or was ever known by should be noted. Also, whether or not there are any assets or holdings of the client in any other name or names should be ascertained.

The client should be advised that residence and domicile are not the same thing. The location of the client's current domicile should be established at the first interview. If there is a possibility of conflicting or double domiciles, the problem should be explored with the client and a plan to eliminate the problem proposed as part of the ultimate estate plan.

The client's place and date of birth, citizenship, Social Security number, and data concerning military service and any veteran's benefits should be noted. Whether or not benefits can be expected from any governmental unit other than the United States, i.e. a foreign government, or a state or local government should be ascertained.

Client's Advisers

The attorney should obtain the names and addresses of the client's accountants, insurance agents, and other advisers. Copies of the client's income tax returns for at least three years prior to the meeting and gift tax returns, if any, should be reviewed and analyzed.

Data on the client's employment should be obtained, not only as to any corporate benefit plans, but as to the future prospects of his career and the life style of the client as it relates to his current and projected income.

Family Tree

After this basic personal information has been obtained, the client's family tree should be explored. A major purpose for obtaining the family tree is to ascertain who would be the client's distributees under Section 4-1.1 of the Estates Powers and Trusts Law if the client should die intestate. The family tree will also make it possible for the attorney to demonstrate to the client the different consequences having a will or not having a will will have on the disposition of his estate. This sometimes can be of striking effect to the client and a great encouragement for pursuing estate planning.

For example, under Section 4-1.1 of the EPTL if a client with a wife and two children should die intestate the decedent's wife is entitled to $2,000 plus one-third of the estate and the decedent's children share the remaining two-thirds of the estate (all outright, not in trust). This is almost invariably contrary to the client's wishes.

Marriages

A listing of dates and places of all marriages of the client should be made. If there has been more than one marriage, information concerning termination of the prior marriage(s) should be obtained. If the termination resulted in a divorce or separation, copies of the divorce decrees or separation agreements must be examined. If a spouse predeceases the client, information should be obtained regarding any inheritance from such spouse, including any trust arrangements.

As divorce, separation and differing marital arrangements become more common, marital status should be developed very carefully. This can be significant in determining whether or not a spouse will qualify as such for right of election purposes under Section 5-1.1 of the EPTL as well as for purposes of the marital deduction under Section 2056 of the Internal Revenue Code. (Section 5-1.2 of the EPTL details the bases on which a "spouse" may be disqualified from electing against a decedent's estate.)

Adopted Children

In establishing the family tree you should ascertain whether there are any adopted children, children born out of wedlock or stepchildren, and whether the client wishes such children to inherit, and if so, to what extent.

The analysis of the family tree should include the names, addresses and ages of relatives to a degree of consanguinity which satisfies the practitioner that he has covered all contingencies that could reasonably occur. Therefore, if a client has a wife and children, it is advisable for the attorney (in addition to the wife and children) to obtain information concerning the client's parents, his brothers and sisters, and possibly issue of brothers and sisters.

Obtaining a complete family tree can be useful if any questions of pedigree arise and can avoid laborious investigation after the client dies. In many counties, if the distributees are more distant that the third degree of consanguinity, the family tree must be included in the petition for administration or probate.

In obtaining information as to a client's assets and liabilities, the three basic points of information are ownership, valuation and documentation.

39

The nature of the ownership should be obtained. Are any assets held jointly with another person? If so, with whom, and who made the contributions to the joint account? Who owns the family residence, is it held by tenancy by the entirety, and who supplied the consideration? Are there any "in trust for" (Totten trust) accounts? If so, who is the beneficiary? Who are the designated beneficiaries on, and owners, of, any life insurance policies or annuity contracts?

A preliminary valuation of the assets should be obtained in order to estimate estate tax consequences and to compute what may be available for distribution. This need not be a one hundred percent accurate evaluation, but it should at least be a "ball park" figure. The attorney should not rely on the client's understanding, but should obtain copies of documents wherever possible. The nature of ownership of businesses should be checked, the business could be a partnership, corporation, or sole proprietorship. All shareholders agreements, profit sharing, pension, or employee stock ownership plans should be reviewed to ascertain the true provisions thereof. In doing this the attorney not only better familiarizes himself with the client's affairs, but places himself in a position to give the client some useful advice on matters outside the estate plan.

Deeds and mortgages and other documentation on real estate holdings should be reviewed and the stock and lease of a cooperative apartment should be examined. The attorney must make sure that what the client characterizes as a cooperative apartment is not a condominium or homeowners association. The client's personal insurance policies and income tax returns should be checked to determine overlooked assets or discrepancies in ownership.

The more detailed the data obtained from the client, the better. It is possible that after the estate plan has been completed, the next time this information will be considered, the client will be deceased and, therefore, the best source of the information will no longer be available and the attorney's file may be the only cohesive and hopefully coherent analysis of the client's relationship and holdings.

Often the client's greatest fear concerning estate planning (possibly even greater than the concepts of death and of estate taxes, which we know are inevitable) is the legal fee going to be charged for such.

It is advisable that a statement for services for estate planning should itemize the various results achieved by the attorney and reflect the potential tax savings achieved for the client as a result of the estate plan so that the client is aware of the savings to him in the context of the attorney's fee.

The practitioner should note that under certain circumstances at least a portion of the fee can be tax deductible by the client for federal income tax purposes. Under Section 212 of the Internal Revenue Code, certain expenses incurred by a taxpayer for the production or collection of income, management of income producing property, or in connection with the determination, collection or refund of any tax are deductible by the taxpayer.

In the Tax Court case, *Merians v. Commissioner,* (60 TC 187, Dec. 31, 1966) taxpayers retained the services of a law firm to plan their estates. The legal services included conferences, preparation of a work sheet, preparation of wills, establishment of an irrevocable trust, creation of an insurance trust and preparation of gift tax returns. The taxpayers deducted the entire fee on their income tax returns. Their attorney testified that he spent a great deal of time on tax matters and that most of the time spent on their problems concerned tax advice, but no other evidence was presented on which to base an allocation. The Court allowed a tax deduction for the 20% of the fee.

One of the lessons to be learned from the case is that it is advisable to keep clear records showing what time is expended for tax matters and what time is expended for other matters in estate planning. This case should be reviewed carefully by attorneys prior to preparation of bills on estate planning matters.

Outline of Information to Obtain

Personal Data

Name
Address
Social Security Number
Place and Date of Birth
Citizenship
Military Service—branch and serial number
Date and Place of Marriage(s)
    A. If divorced—date and place of divorce and copy of decree
    B. If separated—copy of decree and separation agreement
    C. Ante-nuptial agreement, if any
Employer's Name and Address
Accountant's Name and Address
Income Tax Returns—obtain three years' copies
Gift Tax Returns—obtain copies
Burial Instructions—cemetery and plot, person to contact
Family Tree—list of relatives—relationship, addresses and ages

Assets

A. Bank Accounts:
    Checking Account—bank, account number, signatories
    Savings Account(s)—bank(s), account number(s), current balance(s), nature of ownership—i.e. sole name, joint (who contributed the funds, date account created), in trust for (Totten trust)
    Safe Deposit Box—bank and location, box number, location of key, persons with authority to enter
B. Real Estate:
    Address, ownership, mortgage (amount, term, interest rate), insurance, estimated value (possible appraisal), location of deed and other pertinent papers
C. Cooperative Apartment:
    Address, number of shares, term of lease, ownership, any loan outstanding, valuation (possible appraisal), location of stock and lease
D. Securities:
    Brokerage accounts—broker, latest statements
    Listing of security holdings and valuation, location of securities
    Custodial Account—name of bank, person to contact
    Name of Company, description and location of securities on which there are any restrictions such as an investment letter
E. Insurance:
    Life Insurance—company and policy numbers, amount, location of policies, insured, beneficiary, ownership

F. Annuity Contracts:

Company, contract numbers, type—joint or survivor, sum certain, etc., valuation of death benefit (if any), location of contracts

G. Automobiles:

Year, make, ownership, valuation, insurance

H. Personal property of particular value:

Jewelry, furs, stamps or coins or other collections, art works (location, valuation)

I. Tax Shelters:

1. Oil and Gas—description, documentation, valuation
2. Real estate participations—description, documentation, valuation
3. Others

J. Business Interests:

Nature of business—i.e. corporation, partnership, sole proprietorship, type of business, financial statements, valuation, names and addresses of person(s) to contract, copies of shareholder or other agreements

K. Other Assets:

1. Commodities—broker, valuation
2. Mortgages or notes owed—valuation, maturity, interest rate, name and address of debtor

L. Company Benefits:

1. Pension—name of trustee, name of beneficiary, valuation, death benefit, location of documents, taxability
2. Profit sharing—name of trustee, name of beneficiary, valuation, location of documents, taxability
3. Stock Options—company, number of shares unexercised, expiration date

M. Interests in Trusts:

1. Trust(s) created by client or for client's benefit—terms of trust, assets in trust, valuation, documentation
2. Trusts of which client is Trustee—title of trust, location of assets, location of records, name and address of attorney for trust

N. Powers of Appointment:

General or limited, valuation, documentation

O. Insurance other than life insurance:

1. Hospitalization and Health Insurance—Blue Cross or other hospitalization, policy number; Blue Shield or other medical payment, policy number, name of company providing Major Medical coverage, disability insurance coverage
2. Personal Property Insurance—Company and policy number, location of policies, broker or agent

Debts

Loans (bank, mortgage, insurance, brokerage account margin) amount, lender, due date

Unpaid charitable pledges

Other liabilities, e.g. guarantees outstanding, obligations under marital agreements

Guidelines on Drafting Interrogation

Before leaving the subject of interviewing the client for the next topic or step, trial preparation, review the following guidelines for drafting your interrogatory of the client.

1. Start out with requests for basic data (*e.g.,* name, address, age, occupation, *etc.*).
2. Avoid questions that call for simple yes-no answers.
3. Avoid questions that call for an opinion from the client unless the opinion might be relevant or provide leads to other facts.
4. Phrase the questions to elicit facts.
5. Know what facts will be important to establish your client's case, and ask specific questions focusing on those facts.
6. As to each fact, ask questions calculated to elicit the client's ability to comment on the fact (*e.g.,* how far away was he, does he wear glasses, *etc.*).
7. Phrase the questions so that the client will have to clearly indicate whether he is talking from first hand knowledge or hearsay.
8. Ask questions on topics that you know or reasonably suspect will bring out potentially damaging answers so that the attorney can be forearmed at the trial.

Preparation For Trial

Preparing a witness for trial is one of the most important ingredients for a successful outcome in a lawsuit, yet it is an activity in which most lawyers are least proficient. The press of time makes it difficult for the attorney to prepare his for litigation. Thus it is that this is an area where the office paralegal can make one of his most important contributions.

The discussion which follows here not only lays out what your *client* should know about how a trial is conducted and what goes on beginning with jury selection and ending with the verdict, but it will review for you the same information which in turn will give you a clear picture of how the legal system actually operates on the trial level as distinguished from the appeals level which we will deal with in a later chapter on the American Legal System.

The paralegal must impress upon the client the necessity for telling the truth. It is important to stress to the client that there are questions which will come up in cross examination in an area where the client has not been prepared. The response of the client must be the truth. The following example reveals a client running into difficulty over a matter of little consequence. Assume the plaintiff has finished testifying and encounters this example of cross examination:

Question: Mr. Jones, is it not a fact that in the last few days prior to your taking the witness stand today your lawyer spoke to you about this case?

Answer: No, it is not true.

Question: Is it your testimony that he did not tell you what to say in this case?

Answer: I did not speak to him about my testimony.

Question: Mr. Jones, didn't I see you speaking to your attorney and the legal assistant less than an hour ago?

Answer: Yes you did.

Question: Weren't you discussing your case then?

Answer: No.

The attorney in summation will point out to the jury that it is inconceivable that any attorney will permit a client to take the stand and testify in a litigation case without reviewing the case with him. A truthful answer from a well prepared client would develop in this order:

Question: Is it not a fact that you spoke to your attorney about this case just within the past few days?

Answer: Yes.

Question: Isn't it a fact that he told you what to say in your testimony today?

Answer: He told me to tell the truth!

Following a brief introductory meeting with the client an indication of how a trial progresses and the usual order of the proceedings is mandated. When a client is made aware of what is happening in a court room, he will have a more relaxed view and the apprehension and anxiety will be alleviated.

The first step in a jury trial is the selection of a jury. The selection of a jury is conducted in two different ways depending on the jurisdiction. Many jurisdictions permit the attorneys to question the potential jurors. In other jurisdictions the judge that is going to try the case will do the questioning. The purpose is obtaining a fair and impartial jury. Jurors will be questioned on their background, on their occupation and whether they have any preconceived ideas relating to the case.

The examination of the jury hopefully will guarantee that the jury is composed of persons that will be able to arrive at a decision jointly.

A concern of the attorney is to be certain that one specific juror does not have any background or experience which would lead that juror to take over the function of the other jurors. If a dispute in a law suit arises from a real estate contract the attorneys for both sides will be certain that a member of the jury is not a real estate broker. A jury composed of 5 or 11 people and one broker would be a jury that most probably would be swayed by the juror with the real estate background and expertise.

The client should be apprised of the fact that the jury does not decide the law of the case. This is the province of the court. The jury decides the facts. In a personal injury lawsuit, involving two automobiles at an intersection controlled by signal lights, the question of which automobile passed the red light would be a question of fact. The question of whether it is unlawful to pass a red or yellow light would be a question of law.

The client should be told that prior to the taking of testimony it is customary for the attorneys to make an opening statement. Generally the plaintiff has the right to open and close. This means that the plaintiff's attorney has the privilege of addressing the jury first. The response is then delivered by the defendant's attorney. Following the taking of testimony the defendants attorney conducts his summation and the plaintiff's attorney has the privilege of closing or responding. Explain to the client that this does give the plaintiff a decided advantage. However the plaintiff has the burden of proof. The burden of proof merely requires the plaintiff to prove his or her case by a proponderence of the evidence. This "proponderance" has been defined as the amount required to tip the scales in favor of the plaintiff. The purpose of the opening statement by the attorneys is to outline the proof to the jury and serves as a guide to what the attorney hopes to prove. The statements by the attorneys during the opening are not evidence and the client should not be disturbed at what the opposing counsel states during the opening statement.

There is no set procedure for the trial of the action. The normal process is for the plaintiff to testify first. The witness plaintiff or defendant should be instructed to answer questions truthfully and briefly. The tendency of a witness to volunteer more information than is requested usually leads to trouble. The following is an example taken from a personal injury action. This question was asked by the defendant's attorney in the cross examination of the plaintiff:

Question: Mr. Jones did you ever see a doctor with relation to any injury to your head prior to this accident?

Answer: No, in fact I never go to doctors.

Question: I notice a scar on the top part of your hand. Did this scar come from this accident?

Answer: No, it did not.

Question: It looks to me that there may have been stitches in that hand?

Answer: Yes, there were.

Question: Did you see a doctor or did you stitch your hand yourself?

Answer: I saw a doctor.

Question: Do you as part of your routine health care ever get a medical check up?

Answer: Yes, I get a medical check-up every year.

Question: This check-up is conducted by a physician?

Answer: Yes, it is.

Question: So that when you told us you never see a doctor you were not telling us the truth. Is that correct?

This particular line of questioning is not of great significance; however, it reveals the difficulty that a witness encounters by giving fortuitous information that is not requested. Describe to the witness that there will be certain objections made by the attorneys during the duration of the witnesses testimony. A witness is disturbed when not permitted to answer a question as a result of rulings made by a judge. Remind the witness that there are certain rules of evidence that must be followed. The fact that a judge may agree or disagree with an objection made by the witnesses attorney is not a significant part of the lawsuit and the witness should not have any concern over the rulings of the judge. Questions must be answered with information that is personally known to the witness and not information given to the witness by third parties. This type of testimony is called hearsay testimony. The purpose of excluding most hearsay evidence is that the attorney for the other party does not have the opportunity to cross-examine the source of the information. The following is an example of hearsay testimony. Examination of the plaintiff by the plaintiff's attorney:

Question: Do you recall being involved in an automobile accident on January 5, 1976?

Answer: Yes I do.

Question: Can you tell us where the accident occurred?

Answer: It occurred on the Long Island Expressway, near exit 36.

Question: Can you tell us what happened?

Answer: I stopped in a line of traffic and was struck in the rear by another vehicle.

Question: Did a time come where you came out of your car?

Answer: Yes.

Question: Can you tell us how you felt at that time?

Answer: I was in pain.

Question: Were there any witnesses to this accident?

Answer: Yes, the driver of the car in front of me told me that the defendant's car was speeding.

Defendant's Counsel: Objection, your honor.

The Court: Sustained.

Explanation: The testimony of the plaintiff repeating what a witness told him at the scene would be hearsay. The proper way of introducing this evidence is by calling the witness into court personally or serving a subpoena upon the witness compelling him or her to appear in the proceeding. There are certain exceptions to the hearsay rule and it is incumbent upon a good paralegal to become familiar with the rules of evidence.

Instruct the client not to be baited by the opposing counsel and under no circumstances get involved in a shouting match with counsel. An argumentative lawyer is not looked upon with great favor by a jury and a witness that keeps his composure and answers in a truthful soft key response will be doing the most to further his cause.

It is important to review all of the facts of the case with your witness prior to his appearance in court. If the case involves an accident the witness should be taken to the scene of the accident and familiarize himself with the area. If the witness is a plaintiff that sustained personal injuries, the witness should be asked to review the difficulty he encountered in either the business or social aspects of his life as a result of the injuries sustained in the accident. Juries are merely human beings that can relate to difficulties in their everyday existence. A sprain of the hand may not appear to be a significant injury with any potential for a substantial recovery. A good searching interview of the plaintiff could produce the following testimony. Direct examination by plaintiff's attorney of the plaintiff:

Question: Mr. Jones, you told us that you injured your hand while falling, is that correct?

Answer: That is correct.

Question: Can you tell us which hand you injured?

Answer: My right hand.

Question: Are you right handed?

Answer: Yes I am.

Question: Mr. Jones, are you employed?

Answer: Yes.

Question: Could you tell us the nature of your employment?

Answer: I am employed as a manager of the Palace Theater.

Question: Does the injury to your right hand prevent you from conducting your business or hamper you in any way?

Answer: No it does not.

Question: Do you participate in any sports?

Answer: Yes, I bowl.

Question: Were you bowling prior to this accident?

Answer: Yes for many years.

Question: At the time of the accident could you tell us what your bowling average was?

Answer: I had a league average of 172.

Question: Are you still bowling?

Answer: I am trying; however, the injury to my hand prevents me from gripping the ball properly.

Question: Are you bowling in a league now?

Answer: No I am not.

The fact that someone has a slight injury does not necessarily mean that a picture may not be presented to a jury which will describe the hardship suffered by the plaintiff. I am certain that at least some of the jury members will have a sport that gives them pleasure and a careful investigation of the plaintiff's social activities can result in producing a more equitable verdict for your client. The following excerpt of a summation was used by my partner, Moe Levine, in a personal injury case with testimony similar to the bowling testimony described:

"Ladies and Gentlemen of the jury, you have heard this plaintiff testify that the injury to his hand did not hamper his business. He testified that he was employed in the same job for 18 years. Perhaps he did not advance in his occupation and perhaps he never will. It is apparent that he has not had an easy life; however, he looked forward with great anticipation to his Thursday night bowling league. When this defendant injured Larry Jones he succeeded in changing his life style. His life was based upon mere survival except for his Thursday night bowling game. It was not merely a bowl-game but a whole evening. It was dinner with his team mates and friends before and a couple of beers discussing the game afterward."

Explain to the client that the attorney will not be able to ask him leading questions and therefore, it is essential that the client review all of the facts leading up to his case and listen carefully when the question is being asked. A leading question is a question which prepares the witness by giving the answer in the question itself.

Question:	When the sales agent signed his contract was your brother also present?
Counsel:	Objection! Leading.
Court:	Sustained.
Question:	The proper question is, "was this contract signed?"
Answer:	Yes.
Question:	By whom?
Answer:	Mr. Jones.
Question:	Was anyone present during this signing?
Answer:	Yes, my brother.

The witness should also be cautioned not to anticipate questions and answer them before the question is asked. The following example indicates anticipating counsel's questions.

Question:	Did a time come when you observed the traffic light?
Answer:	Yes, I saw it was green when I was . . .
Counsel:	Objection! Not responsive.
Question:	Mr. Jones, a time came when you looked at the light?
Answer:	Yes, it was green during . . .
Counsel:	Objection! Not responsive.
The Court:	Mr. Jones, will you please give us the courtesy of answering the questions without anticipating any other questions.

This type of colloquy is annoying to the judge and the jury and can be avoided if the client is made aware of what is expected of him. If there are any weaknesses in the plaintiffs case it is important to bring them out during the direct examination and not wait for the defendant's attorney to pounce upon the plaintiff in cross examination.

Following the direct examination by the witnesses' attorney, there is cross examination conducted by the adversary's attorney. The witness should not be concerned if the defense attorney is making telling points during cross examination. The witness should be instructed that his attorney will have the right to a reexamination called a redirect after the cross examination of the defendant's attorney. The witness should not try and explain inconsistencies during the defendant's cross examination and should restrict himself to yes and no answers. If there is any ambiguity, his attorneys will clear it up by questioning him on redirect examination. Point out to the client that attorneys are also actors and when his attorney appears disturbed at a ruling by the judge, it sometimes is a role played in a jury trial and the sad hapless expression does not mean that "all is lost."

After the witness has testified, make sure that his or her demeanor is proper and under no circumstances should the witness sneer or laugh when other witnesses are testifying.

Many witnesses have a tendency to grimace when another witness is testifying. This type of behavior generally is offensive to a jury and can lead to the following exchange:

> *Counsel:* Your honor I have tried to remain silent, however, I must ask the court to instruct Mr. Jones to refrain from sneering when my witness answers questions.

> *The Court:* Mr. Jones I have noticed your facial expressions within the past few minutes and I find them most disturbing. If you continue to act in this fashion I have no alternative but to ask you to remove yourself from the courtroom.

The type of dress suitable for a courtroom is formal. If the weather is warm and the witness would prefer wearing an open collared sports shirt, discourage him. The witness will never be criticized for dressing in a shirt and tie. Dressing in an informal casual manner can possibly offend the judge or some members of the jury. It is better to be safe than sorry when it comes to proper attire.

Direct the witness to answer forcefully and in a voice that can be heard by the juror furthest from the witness. The witness should look at the jury when testifying. The witness should refrain from looking at the judge or the attorney. His testimony is to be directed at the jury. If the witness has some information that he feels must be imparted to the lawyer, ask him to jot it down on a piece of paper and try and get a note to the attorney. The witness should not come up to the witness table or try to distract the attorney when the case is in progress. After the plaintiff has testified, generally the plaintiff's witnesses are called. The witnesses for the plaintiff should be prepared with the same thoroughness that the plaintiff has been prepared. There are usually some documents including hospital records, photographs and police reports which are introduced into evidence during the plaintiff's case. There are rules of evidence and statutes indicating which records may be introduced. A paralegal should be familiar with these rules and explain to the witness what is actually happening when the lawyers are discussing the admission of documents with the court.

Following the plaintiff's testimony and the testimony of the witnesses, the attorney for the defendant has the right to cross examine the witnesses and after this procedure has been completed the plaintiff will usually rest. The defendant usually will make a motion to dismiss the plaintiff's cause of action because of failure to establish a prima facie case. This motion is almost perfunctory and the plaintiff should not get too distrubed during the discussion of this motion. Motions made during trial can be granted, denied or reserved. If there is a reserved decision on a motion it means that the judge will make the decision after all of the evidence is in or at some other portion of the case. After the plaintiff's case it is the defendant's turn to put on witnesses who will testify on behalf of the defendant. The usual procedure again is for the defendant to testify and witnesses for the defendant to appear. The defendant is under no obligation to produce any witnesses and in some cases the defendant will rest without producing a witness or any evidence. The defendant in these cases is gambling on the fact that the plaintiff has not proved a prima facia case. A prima facia case is necessary in order for the case to be sent to the jury. Following the defendant's case, the defendant will rest and the judge will ask the defendant to sum up to the jury. Summation or final argument is not evidence and is a statement or a discussion made to the jury reviewing the evidence with the hope of swaying the jury to that attorney's point of view. The client should not be too disturbed at the discussion of either attorney during the summation. The plaintiff sums up last and following the plaintiff's summation the judge will issue the court's charge. The charge of the court are instructions that the judge will give the jury relating to the law in the case. The judge will also charge the jury as to what weight they must give the witnesses' testimony and how the law must be applied in this specific case. Following the judge's charge, the jury will deliberate. After the deliberation the jury returns and delivers its verdict. The decision of the jury is called a verdict.

Make sure that there is some easily accessible place on the file for the home and business telephone numbers of all witnesses and persons that are going to be called during the trial of this action.

CHAPTER IV

THE PARALEGAL AND LEGAL FORMS*

As a legal assistant, you will regularly deal with, prepare and review, numerous legal forms. In this chapter, we will briefly discuss these forms in an attempt to create an overview of the role that they play in your daily routine and re-emphasize their purpose, type, and value. Additionally, we will outline the physical systems that are available to aid you in their retention and retrieval. This section is designed to put the new legal assistant in the proper frame of mind to gain the most from the legal form; and to refresh the experienced assistant as to the convenience of the legal form as an efficient tool in the processing of legal documents, in the organization of time, and in the organization of the legal arena.

In the past, before the advent of production printing and copying facilities, legal forms were created totally by hand. Scribes, in order to produce a document, spent unending hours copying documents by hand on scrolls or parchment. On pages 54 & 55 is a photographic reproduction of such a document, an 1883 indenture.

In comparison to this nineteenth century form, the twentieth century legal form has taken huge strides to conserve the attorney's time. In the United States, the first standardized mass-produced legal forms were published in the mid 1800's. This was a significant occurence. It gave attorneys a tool that would enable them to delegate responsibility. These forms gave the attorneys the means to be more orderly, efficient, and organized in their work. It relieved their office(s) of the necessity of drafting each legal document in its entirety.

It would be helpful to view forms in several categories which, by no means, are mutually exclusive.

---

*Adapted from materials prepared by Robert H. Blumberg & Carol Ann Lyons, associated with the leading publisher of legal forms, Julius Blumberg, Inc.

This Indenture

William Foulsham of the second part and the said Arthur James Bunting Edward Curl and Henley Curl of the
and to the use of the said Arthur James Bunting Edward Curl and Henley Curl their heirs and assigns as joint
Bunting and Henley Curl it was provided (inter alia) that the said Edward Curl should from the date of the said Agree
partnership business the hereditaments comprised in the Indenture hereinbefore firstly and secondly described form
and convey the said ... Copartnership for the term and upon the condition in the said Agreement mentioned
Bunting of the one part and the said Henley Curl of the other part the parties hereto agreed to be partners in
day of January One thousand eight hundred and eighty upon the terms and subject to the covenants and provisions
Curl of the one part and the said Arthur James Bunting and Henley Curl of the other part for the considerations
and and to the use of the said Arthur James Bunting and Henley Curl their heirs and assigns for ever To the use
same might form part of the funds and property of the partnership thenceforth to be carried on by the said
dated the twelfth day of August One thousand eight hundred and eighty and made between John Henry Riggens
hereinafter thirdly described and intended to be hereby released were thereby granted unto and to the use of the said
in the last before recited Indenture formed part of the partnership assets of the firm of "Curl and Bunting" and
disputes having arisen between the said parties an Action was commenced on the ... day of
Plaintiff and the said Henley Curl Defendant praying for a dissolution of the said partnership and a Motion was in
thousand eight hundred and eighty two a judgment or decree was made in the said Action whereby it was orde

And whereas in pursuance of the said judgment. A ... James of Edmonds Street, in the
of January One thousand eight hundred and eighty three, and made between the said Arthur James Bunting of the
otherwise continuing the proceedings in the said Action of Bunting versus Curl the disposal of the business ca
said Action should be stayed **And whereas** at the sale by Auction by Mr Henry Spelman in pursuance
that the said Arthur James Bunting was declared to be the purchasing partner within the provisions of the
in the freehold and leasehold hereditaments and of and in the stock in trade moneys book debts credits and of
payment of certain moneys amounting to the total sum of Nineteen thousand and thirty nine pounds sixteenby the said
the hereinbefore recited Indenture of the eighth day of January One thousand eight hundred and eighty three the said
thereof and the stock in trade moneys credits and effects belonging thereto **And whereas** adventurers duly he
the consideration money for the assignments transfers or other assurances to be made
in pursuance and performance of the provision of the said Indenture of the eighth day of January One thousand eight h
Curl and Edward Curl (which the said Henley Curl doth hereby acknowledge to have been duly paid) and in considera
messuage or dwellinghouse situate in the parish of Saint Andrew in the said City of Norwich with the warehouse a
Benjamin Roe or his undertenants **And also Withal** Hall and ... and buildings situate in
Arthur James Bunting and Henley Curl or their undertenants **All which** said messuage and premises hereby re
messuage in part and on a passage known as the Old Stamp Office Yard in that part on the East on a yard now re
Bransford on the part of the North and which premises formed the Northern part of the hereditaments
thousand eight hundred and thirty mentioned in the schedule to the Indenture of Conveyance dated the twenty
assigns and tenants their tenants servants agents and workmen either with or without horses carts and carria
or any part thereof by and through the present Gateway into and along the said passage known as the Old Stam
being next Saint Stephens Street in the said City of Norwich formerly in the occupation of Reuben Holder then of the
dwellinghouse shop and premises belonging to James Rivans Hardy and now to the said Arthur James Bunting tow
to the said James Rivans Hardy and now to the said Arthur James Bunting towards the West **Together** w
thereby **Al that** messuage or dwellinghouse and shop situate and being next Saint Stephens Street in the
James Bunting and Henley Curl as the same are bounded by a messuage or dwellinghouse and shop formerly in the
towards the East by a way or passage leading from the yard at the back of the said messuage or dwellinghouse an
the West **And also** the privy or watercloset at the West corner of the said yard at the back of the said messua
occupiers for the time being of the said hereditaments and premises expressed to be hereby released to pairs and repair
messuage or dwellinghouse and shop expressed to be hereby released leading from the said yard at the back there
yard and passage the said Arthur James Bunting paying a proportionate part of the expense of keeping the
hundred and eighty mentioned **To have and to hold** the hereditaments and premises hereby rele
free from the right claim share and interest of the said Henley Curl therein and there **In witness** w

... day of January One thousand eight hundred and eighty three **Between** Henley Curl of the ... and Woollen Draper and Manchester Warehouseman of the one part and Arthur James Bunting of the same City and like ... part **Whereas** by an Indenture dated the twenty fifth day of March One thousand eight hundred and seventy four and made ... Curle of the first part Edward Curl and the said Arthur James Bunting and Henley Curl hereinafter referred to as the purchasers ... and James Harcourt of the third part for the considerations therein mentioned the hereditaments hereinafter firstly described and ... released were granted unto and to the use of the purchasers their heirs and assigns **And whereas** by an Indenture dated ... One thousand eight hundred and seventy eight and made between Charlotte Samuel Arnold and Frederick Fox of the first part ... therein mentioned the hereditaments hereinafter secondly described and intended to be hereby released were granted and released unto ... by an Agreement dated the ... day of July One thousand eight hundred and eighty and made between the said Edward Curl Arthur James ... stuff business which had hitherto been carried on by the said Arthur James Bunting Edward Curl and Henley Curl (and of which ... the said Arthur James Bunting and Henley Curl and that the said Arthur James Bunting and Henley Curl should take the business of the said firm ... Indenture dated the ... day of ... One thousand eight hundred and eighty two and made between the said Arthur James ... Woollen Drapers and Manchester Warehousemen under the style or firm of "Curl and Bunting" for the sum of eight years from the first ... **And whereas** by an Indenture bearing even date with the last before recited Indenture and made between the said Edward ... ...ments hereinafter firstly and secondly described and intended to be hereby released were released and confirmed by the said Edward Curl ... and retain and enjoy the same free from the equal claim share and interest of the said Edward Curl therein and therein and that the ... Henley Curl as set forth and provided in the last hereinbefore recited Indenture of Partnership **And whereas** by an Indenture ... Arthur James Bunting and Henley Curl of the other part for the considerations therein mentioned the hereditaments and premises ... and Henley Curl their heirs and assigns forever **And whereas** the hereditaments hereinafter thirdly described and comprising ... Arthur James Bunting and Henley Curl as aforesaid as the said parties hereto do hereby admit and acknowledge **And whereas** ... hundred and eighty two in the Chancery Division of Her Majesty's High Court of Justice in which the said Arthur James Bunting on ... behalf of the said Arthur James Bunting for the appointment of a Receiver **And whereas** on the fourth day of October One ... ...ship should be dissolved as from the date of the said judgment and that certain accounts should be taken and a Receiver appointed ... ...ant was appointed Receiver in the said Action of Bunting versus Curl **And whereas** by an Indenture dated the eighth day ... ...y Curl of the second part and the said Edward Curl of the third part it was mutually agreed that instead of taking the accounts ... ...ted under the style or firm of Curl and Bunting should be effected as in the said Indenture now in recital provided and that the ... ...said recited Indenture held at the Royal Hotel Norwich on Tuesday the ninth day of January One thousand eight hundred and eight ... **Whereas** by the said Indenture of the eighth day of January One thousand eight hundred and eighty three it was provided that upon ... ...g partner should execute to the purchasing partner proper assignments transfers conveyances or other assurances of all his interest ... partnership **And whereas** by an Indenture bearing even date, without executed before these presents in consideration of the ... ...said to the said Edward Curl and Henley Curl respectively as therein mentioned and being the moneys payable by the purchasing partner under ... ...said Arthur James Bunting as therein mentioned all the said business of the said firm of "Curl and Bunting" and the Goodwill ... ...y impressed stamps upon the last below recited Indenture in respect of the said legal sum of ... and thirty nine pounds ... Indenture of the eighth day of January One thousand eight hundred and eighty three **Now this Indenture witnesseth** that in ... ...in consideration of the payment of the moneys by the said Indenture made payable by the said Arthur James Bunting to the said Henley ... Henley Curl as beneficial owner doth hereby release and confirm unto the said Arthur James Bunting and his heirs **Firstly All that** ... ...d Office) yard and offices to the same adjoining and belonging and all those premises as well there in the occupation of the ... ...conveniences and adjoining or near to the said messuage or dwellinghouse as the same are now or late were in the occupation of the said ... ...draw or a messuage formerly of James Bache now or late of the said ... Harcourt on the part of the South on the last mentioned ... ...s or Trustees of Thomas Lickiss deceased on the part of the West and on other premises formerly of the said James Bache and now or late ... ...seised and conveyed by certain Indentures of Lease and appointment and Release respectively dated the seventh and eighth day of October One ... thousand eight hundred and seventy four **And also** full and free right and liberty for the said Arthur James Bunting his heirs and ... and egress to and the public Street called Saint Andrews Broad Street to and from the premises hereby released or intended so to be ... ...es whatsoever **And secondly All that** messuage or dwellinghouse and shop and the two cellars under the same situate and ... ...ning Edward Curl and Henley Curl and now of the said Arthur James Bunting and Henley Curl and bounded by a messuage or ... Public Street called Saint Stephens Street towards the East by a way or passage towards the South and by conveniences formerly belonging ... ...closet situate and being in the Yard next to the said Messuage or Dwellinghouse and Shop hereby released and used therewith **And** ... in the City of Norwich formerly in the occupation of Eliza Hewitt and afterwards of John Henry Pigott and now of the said Arthur ... ...man and now in the occupation of, and belonging to George Reeve towards the South by the said Public Street called Saint Stephens Street ... called Saint Stephens Street towards the North and by the said Yard at the back of the said messuage dwellinghouse and shop towards ... **Together** with the full and free right and liberty to and for the said Arthur James Bunting his heirs and assigns owners and ... ...et called Saint Stephens Street by over and along the said Yard and the said way of passage at the North end thereof of the said ... in common with the owners and occupiers for the time being of other hereditaments and premises having a right to use the said ... and the entrance door inside in repair **Except** as in the hereinbefore recited Indenture of the eighth day of August One thousand eight ... ...unto and to the use of the said Arthur James Bunting in fee simple To the intent that he may hold retain and enjoy the same ... ...to these presents have hereunto set their hands and seals the day and year first above written

Forms that change legal relationships among people and things. Contracts of employment, of sale and assignments

STATE OF NEW YORK, COUNTY OF ss.:	STATE OF NEW YORK, COUNTY OF ss.:
On the day of 19 , before me personally came	On the day of 19 , before me personally came
to me known to be the individual described in and who executed the foregoing instrument, and acknowledged that executed the same.	to me known to be the individual described in and who executed the foregoing instrument, and acknowledged that executed the same.

STATE OF NEW YORK, COUNTY OF ss.:	STATE OF NEW YORK, COUNTY OF ss.:
On the day of 19 , before me personally came to me known, who, being by me duly sworn, did depose and say that he resides at No.	On the day of 19 , before me personally came , to me known and known to me to be a partner in
that he is the of the corporation described in and which executed the foregoing instrument; that he knows the seal of said corporation; that the seal affixed to said instrument is such corporate seal; that it was so affixed by order of the board of directors of said corporation, and that he signed h name thereto by like order.	a partnership, and known to me to be the person described in and who executed the foregoing instrument in the partnership name, and said duly acknowledged that he executed the foregoing instrument for and on behalf of said partnership.

Closing of title under the within contract is hereby adjourned to   19   , at
o'clock, at   ; title to be closed
and all adjustments to be made as of   19
Dated,   19

For value received, the within contract and all the right, title and interest of the purchaser thereunder are hereby assigned, transferred and set over unto
and said assignee hereby assumes all obligations of the purchaser thereunder.
Dated,   19

....
Purchaser

....
Assignee of Purchaser

Contract of Sale

PREMISES

Title No.

Section
Block
Lot
County or Town
TO   Street Numbered Address

Recorded At Request of

RETURN BY MAIL TO:

Zip No.

THE OBSERVANCE OF THE FOLLOWING SUGGESTIONS WILL SAVE TIME AND TROUBLE AT THE CLOSING OF THIS TITLE

The **SELLER** should bring with him all insurance policies and duplicates, receipted bills for taxes, assessments and water rates, and any leases, deeds or agreements affecting the property.

When there is a water meter on the premises, he should order it read, and bring bills therefor to the closing.

If there are mortgages on the property, he should promptly arrange to obtain the evidence required under Paragraph 5 of this contract.

He should furnish to the purchaser a full list of tenants, giving the names, rent paid by each, and date to which the rent has been paid.

The **PURCHASER** should be prepared with cash or certified check drawn to the order of the seller. The check may be certified for an approximate amount and cash may be provided for the balance of the settlement.

would be examples of these. They would appear in pre-printed format in commercial applications and in volume applications in the law office.

2. The price is

Dollars, payable as follows:

Dollars,

on the signing of this contract, by check subject to collection, the receipt of which is hereby acknowledged;

Dollars,

in cash or good certified check to the order of the seller on the delivery of the deed as hereinafter provided;

Dollars,

by taking title subject to a   mortgage now a lien on said premises in that amount, bearing interest at the rate of   per cent per annum, the principal being due and payable

Dollars,

by the purchaser or assigns executing, acknowledging and delivering to the seller a bond or, at the option of the seller, a note secured by a purchase money   mortgage on the above premises, in that amount, payable

together with interest at the rate of   per cent per annum payable   .

3. Any bond or note and mortgage to be given hereunder shall be drawn on the standard forms of New York Board of Title Underwriters for mortgages of like lien; and shall be drawn by the attorney for the seller at the expense of the purchaser, who shall also pay the mortgage recording tax and recording fees.

4. If such purchase money mortgage is to be a subordinate mortgage on the premises it shall provide that it shall be subject and subordinate to the lien   of the existing   mortgage   of $, any extensions thereof and to any mortgage   or consolidated mortgage   which may be placed on the premises in lieu thereof, and to any extensions thereof provided (a) that the interest rate thereof shall not be greater than   per cent per annum and (b) that, if the principal amount thereof shall exceed the amount of principal owing and unpaid on said existing mortgage   at the time of placing such new mortgage or consolidated mortgage, the excess be paid to the holder of such purchase money mortgage in reduction of the principal thereof. Such purchase money mortgage shall also provide that such payment to the holder thereof shall not alter or affect the regular installments, if any, of principal payable thereunder and shall further provide that the holder thereof will, on demand and without charge therefor, execute, acknowledge and deliver any agreement or agreements further to effectuate such subordination.

5. If there be a mortgage on the premises the seller agrees to deliver to the purchaser at the time of delivery of the deed a proper certificate executed and acknowledged by the holder of such mortgage and in form for recording, certifying as to the amount of the unpaid principal and interest thereon, date of maturity thereof and rate of interest thereon and the seller shall pay the fees for recording such certificate. Should the mortgagee be a bank or other institution as defined in Section 274-a, Real Property Law, the mortgagee may, in lieu of the said certificate, furnish a letter signed by a duly authorized officer, or employee, or agent, containing the information required to be set forth in said certificate. Seller represents that such mortgage will not be in default at or as a result of the delivery of the deed hereunder and that neither said mortgage, nor any modification thereof contains any provision to accelerate payment, or to change any of the other terms or provisions thereof by reason of the delivery of the deed hereunder.

6. Said premises are sold and are to be conveyed subject to:

   a. Zoning regulations and ordinances of the city, town or village in which the premises lie which are not violated by existing structures.

   b. Consents by the seller or any former owner of premises for the erection of any structure or structures on, under or above any street or streets on which said premises may abut.

   c. Encroachments of stoops, areas, cellar steps, trim and cornices, if any, upon any street or highway.

Omit Clause 8 if the property is not in the City of New York. Clause 9 is usually omitted if the property is not in the City of New York.

7. All notes or notices of violations of law or municipal ordinances, orders or requirements noted in or issued by the Departments of Housing and Buildings, Fire, Labor, Health, or other State or Municipal Department having jurisdiction, against or affecting the premises at the date hereof, shall be complied with by the seller and the premises shall be conveyed free of the same, and this provisions of this contract shall survive delivery of the deed hereunder. The seller shall furnish the purchaser with an authorization to make the necessary searches therefor.

8. All obligations affecting the premises incurred under the Emergency Repairs provisions of the Administrative Code of the City of New York (Section 564-18.0, etc.) prior to the delivery of the deed shall be paid and discharged by the seller upon the delivery of the deed. This provision shall survive the delivery of the deed.

9. If, at the time of the delivery of the deed, the premises or any part thereof shall be or shall have been affected by an assessment or assessments which are or may become payable in annual installments, of which the first installment is then a charge or lien, or has been paid, then for the purposes of this contract all the unpaid installments of any such assessment, including those which are to become due and payable after the delivery of the deed, shall be deemed to be due and payable and to be liens upon the premises affected thereby and shall be paid and discharged by the seller, upon the delivery of the deed.

10. The following are to be apportioned:

(a) Rents as and when collected. (b) Interest on mortgages. (c) Premiums on existing transferable insurance polices or renewals of those expiring prior to the closing. (d) Taxes and sewer rents, if any, on the basis of the fiscal year for which assessed. (e) Water charges on the basis of the calendar year. (f) Fuel, if any.

Category 2

Forms that are used to gather, sort, and retain information as part of a work product of a lawyer or legal assis-

© 1975 Julius Blumberg, Inc., 80 Exchange Pl., NYC 10004

T 1056— Debtor's Worksheet

LIST OF DEBTS — PRINT OR TYPE

Enter "yes" in appropriate columns.

Name & Address of Creditors Personal loans, rent, banks, finance and loan co.'s, credit cards, contracts, stores, medical, dental, car payments, and any other debt of any kind. Include street address or post office box, city, state, zip code, and name of person at creditor's business who is familiar with debt.	Year Debt Incurred	Total Balance Due	Basis of Debt Goods Sold and Delivered Work, Labor and Services Loan, Guarantee, etc.	I have papers covering debt.	I dispute this debt.	Legal action started on this debt.	Office use only
16							A-1 A-2 A-3 ☐☐☐
17							A-1 A-2 A-3 ☐☐☐
18							A-1 A-2 A-3 ☐☐☐
19							A-1 A-2 A-3 ☐☐☐
20							A-1 A-2 A-3 ☐☐☐
21							A-1 A-2 A-3 ☐☐☐
22							A-1 A-2 A-3 ☐☐☐
23							A-1 A-2 A-3 ☐☐☐
24							A-1 A-2 A-3 ☐☐☐
25							A-1 A-2 A-3 ☐☐☐
26							A-1 A-2 A-3 ☐☐☐
27							A-1 A-2 A-3 ☐☐☐
28							A-1 A-2 A-3 ☐☐☐
29							A-1 A-2 A-3 ☐☐☐
30							A-1 A-2 A-3 ☐☐☐

58

tant. Questionnaires, check lists, time sheets, and accounting records would be examples of these. Most often these
forms are pre-printed and are completed by hand.

T 1056— Debtor's Worksheet

© 1975 Julius Blumberg, Inc., 80 Exchange Pl., NYC 10004

LIST OF DEBTS — PRINT OR TYPE

Enter "yes" in appropriate columns.

#	Name & Address of Creditors Personal loans, rent, banks, finance and loan co.'s, credit cards, contracts, stores, medical, dental, car payments, and any other debt, of any kind. Include street address or post office box, city, state, zip code, and name of person at creditor's business who is familiar with debt.	Year Debt Incurred	Total Balance Due	Basis of Debt Goods Sold and Delivered Work, Labor and Services Loan, Guarantee, etc.	I have papers covering debt.	I dispute this debt.	Legal action started on this debt.	Office use only A-1 A-2 A-3
1								☐☐☐
2								☐☐☐
3								☐☐☐
4								☐☐☐
5								☐☐☐
6								☐☐☐
7								☐☐☐
8								☐☐☐
9								☐☐☐
10								☐☐☐
11								☐☐☐
12								☐☐☐
13								☐☐☐
14								☐☐☐
15								☐☐☐

Category 3

Forms which contain information to be filed as part of public records. UCC financial statements, memorandums of leases, conveyance forms and mortgages would be ex-

Index No.

STATE OF NEW YORK
COUNTY OF

Husband

and

Wife

MEMORANDUM OF AGREEMENT OF SEPARATION

The original Agreement of Separation, duly subscribed and acknowledged, has been exhibited to me this   day of   19

County Clerk

Filed by :

attorney(s) for

amples of these. These forms are usually pre-printed. In some cases there is a monetary penalty for failure to provide the prescribed printed form.

T 190—Memorandum of Agreement of Separation
Domestic Relations Law

COPYRIGHT 1967 BY JULIUS BLUMBERG, INC., LAW BLANK PUBLISHERS
80 EXCHANGE PLACE AT BROADWAY, NEW YORK

MEMORANDUM OF AGREEMENT OF SEPARATION

(a) The names and addresses of each of the parties:

Husband

Wife

(b) The date of marriage of the parties

(c) The date of the Agreement of Separation

(d) The date of the subscription and acknowledgment of such Agreement of Separation

Dated:

....
name signed must be printed beneath

....
name signed must be printed beneath

Category 4

Non-substantive forms used in legal procedures or forms that are used as a part of the work process in courts. Pleadings, subpoenas, summonses, notices of trial would be

B 537—Note of Issue and Statement of Readiness, 1st and 2nd Departments.

COPYRIGHT 1973 BY JULIUS BLUMBERG, INC., LAW BLANK PUBLIS
80 EXCHANGE PL. AT BROADWAY, N. Y. C. 1

NOTE OF ISSUE

This space for Clerk's file st

Index No..

.... Court, ...County, N. Y.

NOTICE FOR TRIAL

Trial By Jury of........jurors demanded ☐

Trial Without jury ☐

Filed by Attorney for...................................

Date summons served...................................

Date issue joined...................................

NATURE AND OBJECT OF ACTION
(Specify for *each cause* of Action)

Plaintiff(s)

against

Negligence

	M.V.	R.R.	Bldg. & Sidewalk	Othe
Personal Injury	☐	☐	☐	☐
Property Damage	☐	☐	☐	☐
Both	☐	☐	☐	☐

Other Tort (specify) ....

Contract (specify) ....

Other Law (specify) ....

Matrimonial (specify) ....

Other Equity (specify) ....

Amount Demanded $...................................

Other Relief ....

Defendant(s)

....

Attorney(s) for Plaintiff(s)
Office & P.O. Address:

Attorney(s) for Defendant(s)
Office & P.O. Address:

Phone No.:

Phone No.:

Preference claimed under... on the ground that...

Note: Statement of readiness on reverse side must be completed

This Note of Issue must be typed or printed. Original and two duplicated originals, with proofs of service required.

62

examples of these. In trial courts with substantial volume these forms should be pre-printed. We will speak more about this later.

STATEMENT OF READINESS

For use in First and Second Judicial Departments

Required by Special Rules respecting Calendar Practice

<table>
<tr><td>FOR CLERK'S USE</td></tr>
<tr><td>N. I. SERVED</td></tr>
<tr><td>ON</td></tr>
</table>

1. All necessary or proper preliminary proceedings allowed by statute and rule applicable to the action (Civil Practice Law and Rules, Article 31, Section 3041 and Rules 3042, 3043 and 3044) and by rules of the Appellate Division applicable to notes of issue.

 *a. have been completed by all parties hereto;

 *b. the plaintiff has completed all such proceedings except

 and the plaintiff does not intend to conduct these proceedings,

 *c. the defendant has completed all such proceedings except

 and the defendant has had a reasonable opportunity to complete such proceedings

2. *a. Settlement of this action has been discussed unsuccessfully — or —

 *b. The reasons why no settlement discussions have been had are:

3. This action is ready for trial.

4. The name of the insurance company, if any, which is acting on behalf of any party either prosecuting or defending the action is*

....
(Date)

* Strike out if inapplicable.

Signature — type name below.

Attorney(s) for........................
Office & P. O. Address

State of New York, County of   ss.:

being duly sworn, deposes and says; that deponent is not a party to the action, is over 18 years of age and resides at

That on the   day of   19
deponent served the within note of issue and statement of readiness on

attorney(s) for
herein, at his office at

during his absence from said office
(a) by then and there leaving a true copy of the same with

his clerk; partner; person having charge of said office.
(b) and said office being closed, by depositing a true copy of same, enclosed in a sealed wrapper directed to said attorney(s), in the office letter drop or box.

Sworn to before me, this
day of   19

State of New York, County of   ss.:

being duly sworn, deposes and says; that deponent is not a party to the action, is over 18 years of age and resides at

That on the   day of   19
deponent served the within note of issue and statement of readiness on

attorney(s) for
at
the address designated by said attorney(s) for that purpose by depositing a true copy of same enclosed in a postpaid properly addressed wrapper, in—a post office—official depository under the exclusive care and custody of the United States Postal Service within New York State.

Sworn to before me, this
day of   19

Admission of Service   Due service of a note of issue and statement of readiness, of which the within is a copy,

admitted this.................day of................................, 19............

....

Attorney(s) for........................

What is a law form?

It is a printed or typed document with blank spaces for insertion of required or requested information. A broader and perhaps more helpful definition would be: words organized in such a way that they can be used on repeated occasions. This latter definition suggests a method of retention. Historically the two major sources or methods of forms retention were the forms book and individual printed or typed law forms. Recently, magnetic memory within word processing equipment has become a third and very useful method. Each has its own advantages and disadvantages and each will continue to be an important segment of law office document production.

"A form book is a research device, intended to furnish a variety of samples for a large number of situations. Consequently its content is broad and varied."[1] These form books are designed as a broad range reference guide and are often annotated by law office staff members. They are useful to the lawyer as a check-list and in researching unfamiliar areas. These forms are most often edited by the attorney in use.

Printed or typed papers are, today, the most commonly used forms in the law office. These forms contain blank spaces in which the variable information is inserted by typewriter. The variable information may be obtained through dictation, check-list or work sheet provided by the form publisher and completed by hand, or on a copy of the form itself completed by hand. The role of pre-printed forms as questionnaires and check-lists is growing. They enable the attorney to delegate responsibility to legal assistants in such areas as initial interview of clients, creating worksheets as input to lengthy document production, scheduling court calendars and appearances.

The proliferation of rule making in both governmental agencies and in the courts has created greater demand for pre-printed forms in two major ways. First, in actually prescribing forms that are to be used and secondly, necessitating standard approaches to the courts' very sophisticated rules and regulations.

Legal forms publishers are able to do the research necessary to create forms that comply with the regulations because they can effectively spread out the forms part of the cost of the compliance throughout the system. Attorneys and their clients would not and should not bear these costs on an individual transaction basis.

In addition to the mandated use of pre-printed forms, there are great practical considerations for using them. For purposes of standardization and reductions of filing costs, forms should be used in their pre-printed versions. Filing fees are generally established based upon length of documents. Penalties are sometimes charged for non-standard documents. Very often, non-standard documents are refused.

[1] Sternin, Bernard, Programmed Approaches to Office Paperwork, Practical Lawyer, June 1975, page 56.

For procedural matters, law forms are preferred for the expeditious handling of legal documents in courts of law. The obvious major advantage to the use of the pre-printed form is that it precludes the necessity to read the entire document. In as much as law clerks are familiar with most of the more commonly presented documents, this standardized pre-printed format allows for scanning the areas already known and understood by the clerk and directs attention to the typewritten inclusions which contain the variables in the proceedings.

More important, if there are any short comings in the way that the form is completed it can be rapidly ascertained and brought to the attention of the filing party. When you are dealing with a totally type-written form, rather than a printed one, an error may not be discerned for several hours or days. The subsequent delay can be very costly to the moving party.

There is a secondary advantage to the use of these forms in that they effect uniformity and, therefore, speed handling which allows for an increased volume of work to be processed in the trial courts.

The role of magnetic memory (on word processing equipment or computers) is developing rapidly. The memory is a word storage facility. The word processor or computer automatically prints the stored material in any planned format that may be programmed or requested manually.

A program book is maintained illustrating forms in memory. The attorney or assistant drafts a document by inserting or dictating the variable information verbatim and makes reference to the appropriate stored forms by use of a reference code. The operator selects the card, tape or disc containing the stored forms, types in the supplied variable information in the applicable spaces. The program book becomes a valuable part of the forms reference library.

When the words are repeated frequently within the same law firm, the value of pre-printed forms and forms in automated memory becomes greater than the forms book. Where it is essential to create a specifically tailored document utilizing many "boiler plate" paragraphs, which are not often combined in the same document, the automatic memory format is excellent.

Where the document is mostly standard "boiler plate" paragraphs repeatedly used together, pre-printed forms make greater sense.

It should be remembered that clients are fairly sophisticated. They do not wish to pay fees for clerical time. Overhead costs should not be built up to the point where a substantial part of an attorney's fee is charged to cover that overhead. Credibility is developed when the client knows that fees are paid for the attorney's expert knowledge and experience rather than for elaborate documentation.

Pre-printed forms may be completed on non-automated typewriters or on word processing equipment. Standard terminology which is complex and lengthy can be placed on word processing memory and programmed to fill in the blank space(s) on the form. This procedure is not advisable for incidental matters and should be reserved for use in lengthy, complicated language. This system allows for the recognition of the pre-printed legal form in the courts and the speed and accuracy of the word processing system. It offers optimum advantages. The key to the effectivity of this method is accurate programming, storing, revision, and retrieval of the information on the word processing memory. "Once a particular form has been programmed it can be done in a fraction of the time formerly required."[2]

This affords considerable time savings for the attorney who can assign a project to an assistant with a minimal amount of instruction. An atmosphere is created in which the assistant is placed in the position of having more meaningful work. This increases the assistant's value in the office and also increases the productivity of the attorney. When the legal assistant has the proper "tools" to complete a challenging work load, a situation develops where a satisfying amount of work can be completed by them almost totally on their own.

The lawyer needs to be relieved of as many ministerial tasks as possible. The lawyer can then direct his efforts to the performance of specialized and professional duties, thereby increasing the quality and quantity of work performed and creating the milieu to be filled by the legal assistant. This need for increased efficiency is now forcing systemization into the practice of law. The use of legal assistants in combination with systemization of law office procedures is the key to the efficient law practice. "When a well organized system is used, including check-lists and procedural outlines, there is little chance of overlooking something that should be done. The work is done systematically with periodic review; thus, mistakes are eliminated"[3] and the possibility of human error decreased.

In studies made by the Utah Law Research Institute it was stated that there are three basic components needed in systems designed to train the legal assistant. These are:

1- A Master Information List (MIL) which is cross-referenced to appropriate forms
2- Procedural outlines and checklists
3- Forms

Therefore, you can see the important role that the legal form and its handling plays in your daily routine and development.[4]

Remember, forms are not rigid nor antiquated. They are the starting point for your final document. As each form is completed with

---

[2] Ibid.

[3] Endacott, Richard R., Systemization and the Legal Assistant in the Law Office, Nebraska Law Review, 54-46-57 '75, pages 46-48.

[4] TRIAL - The National Legal Newsmagazine, Volume 10, Number 5, Sept.-Oct., '74, page 10.

the variable information you supply, it obtains a certain individuality which reflects the image of your office.

How to File Printed Forms

All systems and forms are only as good as the persons using them, and their methods of retaining and retrieving them. There are two basic methods of filing forms, that is, either alphabetically or numerically.

Forms filed alphabetically are arranged in folders, labeled as to the subject title and filed in alphabetical order of these subjects. In offices of broad general practice these subjects may be further subdivided into categories and then alphabetically arranged within the category. Examples of such categories are: litigation forms, real property forms, trust and estate forms and criminal forms.

With this system, as the number of forms filed increases, the retrieval of individual forms becomes difficult and cumbersome. It is laborious to find the folders and it is easy to lose them if they are misfiled.

Filing by subject matter is subjective and depends greatly on the interpretation of the file originator. Therefore, as the staff changes, or as the office grows and thinking becomes more sophisticated, the system is not necessarily kept up with the times. Due to these disadvantages, serious consideration should be given to filing numerically.

The second, more preferred way to file forms, is numerically. This is an indirect filing system, since it must be used in connection with a cross-referencing index. In this system, each form is given a number and is cross-referenced to an indexed sample form book. It is much easier to retrieve forms filed numerically and to maintain a file properly. The index gives a cross-reference between subject matter and file number and becomes a useful implement in itself. The ideal way in which to create this index, is to use a loose-leaf book with a sample of the current form on file. Use only one book or one set of books. Do not have a sample book for each legal assistant or secretary. The use of one book allows for a "total" record to be maintained.

Annotations should be made directly on these samples or on sheets stapled to these samples. This will create the best possible up-dating of information by and for all users. As samples are entered into the book, copyright or printing dates of the form should be circled in red. If the date does not appear on the form, it should be stamped in red with "date received _____" and the proper date. These stamps are available at your stationer and this simple procedure will save hours in checking on whether you have a current or out-dated form on hand. As forms are updated, the old form(s) should be stapled to the back of the new one and can be used for reference regarding revisions and changes in the law. If you are using your pre-printed forms in conjunction with a word processing system, you can indicate the sections of your word processing memory that applies to the completion of each form and ultimately you can cross-reference your word processing program book against this form index retrieval book. This book may be divided into subject headings such as in the sub-divisions of the alphabetical system. It will be continually up-dated as forms are added or deleted. It also becomes a form book for easy access to language used in other documents. If convenient, the index may also be kept on cards such as is done for library books or other indexing methods particularly suited to the requirements of your office.

Advantages of the numerical system are the rapidity and accuracy of refiling and the opportunity for unlimited expansion. The disadvantages are the maintenance of the auxiliary cross indexed file, which necessitates making two searches (one of the index and one of the files). You will find that the advantages far exceed the disadvantages when related to efficiency and, particularly, when related to time savings.

In a filing system, any system, it is imperative to the operation of that system that all parties who will be using it are well versed in its perameters, its purpose, its functions and its maintenance. A written statement to the effect should be posted nearby. It should be referred to and used as a reference. Responsibility for the system should come under the "supervision" of a key legal assistant who will see that all users abide by the rules set forth and share in the responsibility of seeing to the perpetuation of the system.

No matter what system you use, the accuracy with which you file determines whether you will be able to find the desired material without extended searching and fumbling. Remember that a paper misplaced, even temporarily, causes embarrassment to you and to the lawyer, and could mean a lost client. Your filing system should be so well organized that anyone can find papers when needed.[5]

In the final analysis, legal forms play an integral role in the professional activities of the legal assistant. The pre-printed legal form has made a tremendous contribution to the efficiency of the legal office and toward speeding the processing of paperwork in the courts. Forms are a beneficial tool to help you more easily accomplish your job. They should be used to their best advantage. Thought needs to be given in their preparation and retrieval. Remember that word processing used in conjuction with the legal form has a tremendous value and offers great advantages.

As a legal assistant, you must address yourself to the following problem: "How can your office practice law more efficiently and economically?" The solution lies in the employment of efficient tools to assist you in your daily routine.[6] The legal form will be one of your most valuable tools.

[5] Millar, Bessie May, Legal Secretary's Complete Handbook, Prentice Hall, May, 1956.

[6] Endacott, Richard R., Systemization and the Legal Assistant in the Law Office, Nebraska Law Review, Volume 54, No. 1, 1975, pages 46-57.

CHAPTER V

A Survey of the American Legal System

Familiarity with the machinery of the judicial system is a basic requirement for the paralegal who is, after all, going to spend his working life dealing with the legal problems of his office's clients. The legal system, meaning the courts, procedures and remedies, is the machinery that processes the work of a law office. Paralegals should have a basic understanding of which courts handle which kinds of cases and under what circumstances. Beyond that, they should have a broad background for knowing how the courts function. All this means that paralegals as much as their employing attorneys know the meaning of terms like jurisdiction, questions of law and fact, jury selection and the jury system in general, appellate and trial court distinctions, venue, civil and criminal litigation, and a number of other judicial words and phrases. Judicial decision-making and judicial remedies must be understood by the paralegal in order to carry through his work with clients as well as in his assistance to the attorney in charge of the case.

All this is described in this chapter and in its totality the reader will come to realize how close to being a quasi-lawyer one becomes when he or she pursues a paralegal career.

THE JUDICIAL SYSTEM

Courts

A court is a governmental body to which the administration of justice is delegated. In the United States there are fifty-one court systems: each state plus the federal government has established its own. Even though these judicial systems are available, very few of the disputes in our society are ever brought before them. In the usual case, a dispute is settled outside the courtroom, based on a prediction of what a court would do if the issue were brought before it. Both the expense connected with bringing a suit and the time delay in obtaining judicial relief encourage parties to reach an agreement without the use of an organized court system.

Courts are classified by function: there are trial courts and appellate courts. A trial court hears and decides controversies by determining facts and applying appropriate rules. The opposing parties to a dispute argue their positions by presenting arguments on the law and evidence on the facts in the form of documents and testimony from witnesses. This is done before a single judge sometimes in the presence of a jury. In a trial without a jury, the judge controls the entire trial and determines the outcome. In a trial with a jury, the decision-making functions are divided between the judge and jury. A safeguard of checks and balances in the legal process is achieved through this division of responsibility: the judge determines the correct law to be applied and decides the questions of law; the jury decides what the facts are and applies to those facts the law as stated by the judge. The judge controls the entire litigation. His actions and statements are often persuasive in the decision-making process of the jury.

The distinction between questions of fact and questions of law is not easily ascertained. Factual issues, which are decided by the jury, involve a determination based on the special circumstances of each case. A factual issue is presented when reasonable men could arrive at different results in deciding what happened in an actual event. When an inference is so certain that all reasonable men must agree upon and draw the same conclusion, it becomes a question of law for the judge. The jury must resolve all questions regarding the weight of the evidence and the credibility of the witnesses. In a negligence case, for example, the jury would have to decide what really happened (if the facts are disputed), whether the defendant was negligent under the circumstances, and the amount of money damages to be awarded to the plaintiff. In this example, the judge's function of deciding the questions of law would involve the determination of the rule of duty. If there were no dispute over the facts, the judge would determine the law that is applicable and interpret it.

A jury acts as the conscience of the community. Jurors are selected at random from a fair cross section of the community, usually from a list of registered voters, and summoned to the courthouse for jury duty. After a case has been assigned to a courtroom, the judge calls in a group of prospective jurors, who take their seats in the jury box and are asked questions by the lawyers and the judge. A *voir dire* examination is conducted to determine each juror's qualifications for duty under the appropriate statute, and any grounds for a challenge for cause, or information on which to base a peremptory challenge. Securing an impartial jury is the objective of the examination. Attorneys for both sides may make as many challenges for cause as they wish, and it is within the judge's discretion to replace a juror for cause. A challenge for cause may be based on prejudice or bias. A juror's relationship, business involvement, or other close connection with one of the parties or attorneys may also be considered cause for replacing a juror. In addition to the challenges for cause, each party is given a limited number of peremptory challenges which may be exercised at will.

State and Federal Judicial Systems

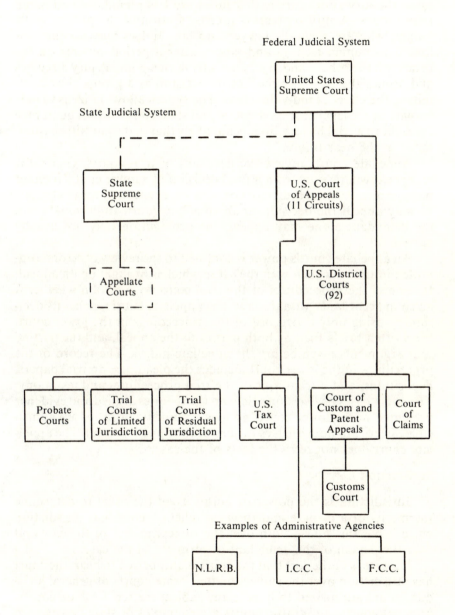

Federal Judicial System

State Judicial System

United States Supreme Court

State Supreme Court

U.S. Court of Appeals (11 Circuits)

Appellate Courts

U.S. District Courts (92)

Probate Courts

Trial Courts of Limited Jurisdiction

Trial Courts of Residual Jurisdiction

U.S. Tax Court

Court of Custom and Patent Appeals

Court of Claims

Customs Court

Examples of Administrative Agencies

N.L.R.B.

I.C.C.

F.C.C.

Although the jury system is an accepted part of our legal process, there is some dispute concerning the advisability of retaining it. It has been argued that juries are arbitrary, unpredictable, and subject to passion. Jury trials are time consuming and contribute to the congestion of court dockets. A jury trial is more expensive. Those who favor the jury system argue that juries are less prejudiced and fairer than judges. A jury represents a cross section of the public, while judges, who are generally lawyers, do not. Judges may become calloused to human feelings and misery after a period of time on the bench; on the other hand, a jury has a fresh viewpoint. A jury discusses and argues the case and reaches its decision as a group, thus minimizing the effect of individual bias. The system allows citizens to participate in the legal process. Federal and state constitutions guarantee the right to a trial by jury, so it is not likely that that right will be eliminated in the near future.

Appellate courts review the decisions of trial courts. Generally, an appeal will lie only from a final decision of a lower court. If either party in a civil action is dissatisfied with the decision of the trial court, he may appeal the decision to an appellate court. In criminal cases the defendant alone may appeal; the prosecution may not usually appeal.

An appellate court's power is confined to the review of errors committed in the court below in the cause which is brought up on appeal. It reviews the proceedings of the trial court to ascertain whether it acted in accordance with the law. The appellate court reaches its decision by using only the record of the proceedings in the lower court, the written briefs filed by both parties to the appeal, and the parties' oral arguments given before the appellate judges. The record of the proceedings in the lower court includes the pleadings, pretrial papers, depositions, and a transcript of the trial proceedings and testimony. The court bases its decision solely on the theories argued and evidence presented in the lower court; no new arguments or proof are admissible. There are no witnesses or jury at the appellate level. The appellate court does not retry the facts of the case.

Jurisdiction

Jurisdiction is the power or authority of the court to determine the merits of a dispute and to grant relief. A court has jurisdiction when it has this power both over the subject matter of the case and over the person of the defendant or property of the case.

If a case is of the sort that the court is authorized to hear, the court has jurisdiction over the subject matter. State courts of general jurisdiction are authorized to handle any subject matter. Probate courts, criminal courts, and traffic courts are examples of state courts with limited subject matter jurisdiction. If, for example, a traffic court decided a controversy involving a probate matter, the judgment would be of no legal consequence, for the court has no jurisdiction over the subject matter. Occasionally, jurisdiction over the subject matter is determined by the amount involved in the controversy.

In personam jurisdiction — jurisdiction over the person of the defendant — may be acquired in one of three ways: by serving process ˒ (giving notice of the hearing) on the defendant in person in the state where the court sits; by serving process to his residence or domicile in the state where he is being sued; or by his voluntary submission or consent to the court's jurisdiction. If a defendant wished to challenge the court's jurisdiction over his person, he enters a special appearance for that purpose. If he makes a general appearance by arguing the facts of the case, he is giving implied consent to jurisdiction over his person. A defendant is considered to have given consent to the court's jurisdiction if the cause of action arises from his transacting business in the state or from a tort he has allegedly committed in the state. A nonresident motorist gives consent to suit in the jurisdiction where he has an automobile accident.

A state court has jurisdiction over property and can render a decision *in rem* only over property located within the state. An *in rem* decision operates directly against a particular thing, whereas a decision *in personam* imposes liability directly upon a person and binds him personally.

There is a difference between jurisdiction, which is the power to adjudicate, and *venue,* which refers to the place where judicial authority may be exercised. A court may have jurisdiction over a controversy, yet venue in that particular district may not be proper. A party wishing to challenge the venue must assert his objection promptly, or he may waive it. Venue in both civil and criminal cases may be considered not proper for several reasons. Fear of local prejudice, convenience for litigants and witnesses, and interests of justice are reasons for a court to decline to hear a case.

In a civil case the most common reason given for a court to decline to exercise jurisdiction is that it believes the case can proceed more conveniently in another court. This is known as the doctrine of *forum non conveniens.* This is an exception to the general rule that a court with jurisdiction has not only the right but the duty to exercise it. The doctrine is applied with caution and discretion. One frequent ground for applying the doctrine occurs when the event which gave rise to the suit took place somewhere other than in the forum state. The difficulties of securing the attendance of out-of-state witnesses and applying foreign law make decision making inconvenient.

The Federal Court System

Article III, section 1, of the federal Constitution is the basis of our federal court system. It provides that "the judicial power of the United States shall be vested in one supreme court, and in such inferior courts

73

as Congress may, from time to time, ordain and establish." Congress has the power to establish courts inferior to the Supreme Court of the United States, to regulate their procedure and practice, and to prescribe their jurisdiction. Congress first exercised this power by passing the Judiciary Act of 1789, which has been amended and supplemented many times in order to establish the various federal courts, their jurisdiction, and procedure.

The federal court system consists of the district courts exercising original federal jurisdiction, courts of appeal exercising intermediate federal jurisdiction and the United States Supreme Court sitting as the highest court for both federal and state matters. Alongside these courts of general jurisdiction, there are the Court of Claims, which decides non-tort claims filed against the United States; the Customs Court, which reviews the rulings and appraisals of customs collectors; the Court of Customs and Patent Appeals, which reviews decisions of the Customs Court and the Patent Office; and the Tax Court, which decides federal tax matters.

The United States District Courts

There are ninety-four federal district courts — at least one in each state and territory of the United States. They are courts of original jurisdiction which serve as the trial court in the federal court system. The federal district courts are given jurisdiction by the Constitution and by Congress. In criminal cases these courts have original jurisdiction, exclusive of the state courts, of all violations of federal laws.

In civil actions the district courts have subject matter jurisdiction over the following categories:

1. Diversity of citizenship cases in which the amount in controversy exceeds $10,000 and is between citizens of different states or between a citizen of a state and an alien. The diversity of citizenship must be complete—meaning that in a multiple-party suit no one plaintiff and one defendant can be citizens of the same state. Suppose a citizen of New York brings a suit against two defendants, one a citizen of Ohio and one a citizen of Michigan: there would be diversity of citizenship. A federal district court would have jurisdiction over the subject matter if the plaintiff is suing in good faith for over $10,000. If, however, one of the parties being sued was a citizen of New York, there would not be complete diversity of citizenship necessary for jurisdiction. For purposes of these suits, a corporation is considered a citizen in the state where incorporated and in the state of its principal place of business. For example, a corporation incorporated in Delaware with its principal place of business in New York cannot sue or be sued by citizens of either of the two states in a diversity case in a federal district court.

2. Federal question cases, in which the amount in controversy exceeds $10,000 and arises under the Constitution, laws, or treaties of the United States.

3. Cases in which the controversy involves a question arising under numerous federal statutes that have no money requirement. Some of these are cases involving suits by the United States, civil rights, patents, copyrights, trademarks, unfair competition, bankruptcy, and admiralty.

In order for a district court to hear a civil case, it must have, in addition to jurisdiction over the subject matter, jurisdiction over the property in an *in rem* proceeding or over the person of the defendant in an *in personam* proceeding. Jurisdiction over the person is normally acquired by service of a summons within the territory. In an ordinary civil action the summons may be properly served anywhere within the territorial limits of the state in which the district court is located.

Except in those areas where federal courts have exclusive jurisdiction, a suit does not have to be brought in a federal district court just because it has jurisdiction over the subject matter and over the person or property. A plaintiff may bring his dispute in any state or federal court that has jurisdiction.

Any civil action brought in a state court may be moved by the defendant to a federal district court if the district court has jurisdiction. In other words, if the suit is one which could have been initiated in the district court, it is removable. When any of the defendants to a suit are citizens of the state in which the action is brought, it is not removable unless it is a claim arising under the Constitution, treaties, or laws of the United States.

Quite often the litigants have a choice of bringing their suit in a federal court or in a state court. Will a federal court follow different rules of law than a state court when adjudicating state matters? Section 34 of the Judiciary Act of 1798 states:

> The laws of the several States, except where the Constitution treaties, or statutes of the United States otherwise require or provide, shall be regarded as rules of decision in trials at common law, in the courts of the United States, in cases where they apply.

Originally, the federal courts held that "the laws of the several states" meant statutes only. In the absence of any state statute the federal courts followed their own common law.

The United States Court of Appeals

The United States is divided into eleven circuits with one court of appeals sitting in each circuit. These appellant courts hear appeals on questions of law from decisions of federal district courts in their circuits and review findings of federal administrative agencies. For most litigants they are the ultimate appellate tribunal of the federal system. Appeal to the court of appeals is a matter of right, not discretionary, so long as proper procedures are followed in bringing the appeal.

When an attorney wishes to appeal the decision of a lower tribunal, he must follow the proper procedures to get the case before the court of appeals. Then he must persuade the judges that the lower tribunal committed errors which resulted in injustices to his client. Notice of appeal must be filed within thirty days from the entry of judgment and sixty days when the United States or an officer or agent thereof is a party. A cost bond (in civil cases), the record on appeal, and a brief must also be filed. On appeal the court of appeals will not substitute its judgment for that of the lower tribunal's finding of fact; it will reverse the lower court's decision if its determination was clearly erroneous.

The United States Supreme Court

The Supreme Court has existed since President Washington appointed its first justice. Today the court consists of a chief justice and eight associate justices. It exercises both appellate and original jurisdiction. Its chief function is to act as the last and final court of review over all cases in the federal system and some cases in the state system. It occupies a singular position within the dual system of federal and state courts to the extent that it reviews certain decisions of the states' highest courts as well as decisions of lower federal courts.

The greatest majority of cases that reach the Supreme Court come from the United States Courts of Appeals on *certiorari*. A review by *certiorari* is not a matter of right but of sound judicial discretion and will be granted only where there are special and important reasons for so doing. The Court thus controls its docket, reserving its time and efforts for the cases which seem to the justices to deserve consideration. Only in a few circumstances can one appeal a decision to the Supreme Court as a matter of right.

Unlike the other federal courts, the Supreme Court of the United States is named and has its jurisdiction specified in the Constitution. After defining the judicial power of the United States, article III, section 2, granted original jurisdiction to the Supreme Court in certain cases:

> In all cases affecting ambassadors, other public ministers and consuls, and those in which a state shall be party, the Supreme Court shall have original jurisdiction. In all the other cases before-mentioned, the Supreme Court shall have appellate jurisdiction, both as to law and fact, with such exceptions, and under such regulations as the Congress shall make.

Original jurisdiction means the power to take cognizance of a suit at its inception, try it, and pass judgment upon the law and the facts of the controversy. In addition to the appellate jurisdiction of the Supreme Court, the Constitution has given it the power to perform the function of a trial court in cases affecting ambassadors, public ministers, and counsels, and in controversies in which a state is a party. The power is not exclusive.

State Court Systems

The power to create courts is an attribute of every sovereignty. The various states of the United States have exercised this power either by constitutional provisions or by statutory enactments. The power to create courts includes the authority to organize them, including the establishment of judgeships, and to regulate their procedure and jurisdiction.

It is beyond the scope of this presentation to describe adequately the court systems of fifty states, because the judicial systems vary considerably from state to state. A general structure pattern does exist among the states even though the terminology and structures differ. A state court system usually consists of probate courts, a large number of courts with limited jurisdiction, courts with residual jurisdiction, and appellate courts.

Courts of limited jurisdiction, inferior courts, are limited as to subject matter and territory. For example, the justice of the peace court administers justice in minor matters at the local level. A justice of the peace with little or no legal training conducts trials in civil cases involving small sums of money and in minor criminal matters. A state judicial system usually includes a probate court to handle deceased persons' estates. Local courts, such as municipal, city, and county courts, have their jurisdiction limited to a specified territory. Small claims courts have their jurisdiction limited to relatively low maximum amounts. Representation by attorney and ordinary court procedure may be dispensed with in small claims proceedings.

Trial courts of residual jurisdiction in the state court system may bear the name of Common Pleas, District, Superior, Circuit, or even - in New York State - Supreme Court. These courts have the power to hear all types of cases. The primary function of trial courts is to exercise original jurisdiction: generally, they also exercise appellate jurisdiction over decisions of courts of limited jurisdiction.

A state's judicial system may provide an intermediate appellate court analogous to the court of appeals in the federal system. Not all states provide this intermediate step. A final appellate court, analogous to the United States Supreme Court, serves as the highest court of the state. It reviews appeals of major questions emanating from the lower state courts, and its decision is final at the state level.

JUDICIAL DECISION MAKING

Stare Decisis

A rule of law that has been decided by judicial decisions is generally binding on the courts and should be followed where applicable in later cases. This principle is referred to as the doctrine of *stare decisis;* it is a policy, not a rule of law. Judge-made law, or case law or common law is created by judicial decisions. The doctrine of *stare decisis* is the basis of common law. It originated in England and was used in the colonies as the basis of their judicial decisions.

A decision on an issue of law by a court will be followed in that jurisdiction by the same court or by a lesser-ranked court in a future case presenting the same issue of law. A court is not bound by decisions of courts of other states, although such decisions may be considered in the decision-making process. A decision of the United States Supreme Court on a federal question is absolutely binding on state courts as well as on lower federal courts. Similarly, a decision of a state court of final appeal on an issue of state law is binding on federal courts dealing with that issue. The decisions of lower federal courts are generally not binding.

Courts are bound to follow the common law as it has been judicially declared in previously adjudicated cases. Prior decisions on a point of law are binding on a future case only if the same or substantially the same issue is involved. In order to determine whether the issues are the same or substantially the same, the precedent must be considered in the light of the facts. Where the facts are substantially different, the principle of *stare decisis* does not apply.

Predictability and certainty are promoted in our legal system by the adherence to previous decisions as precedent. Where a sufficient reason exists, the court may decide not to follow a previous decision. Courts do not over-rule a precedent lightly, especially where it has been followed for many years. Changing economic, political, and sociological conditions and viewpoints can constitute grounds for overruling precedents.

Rule of the Case

Under the doctrine of *stare decisis* only a point of law necessarily decided in a reported judicial opinion is binding on other courts as precedent. A question of fact determined by a court has no binding effect on a subsequent case involving similar questions of fact; the facts of each case are recognized as being unique. The authority of a previous decision as precedent is therefore limited to the rule of law as applied to the particular facts of that case. For the rule of law expressed in a previous case to apply, the factual situations in both cases must be nearly alike. A decision which applies a rule of law to a set of facts different from those in the case in question may not serve as a precedent for that case.

Those points of law decided by a court to resolve a legal controversy constitute the holding of the case. In other words, the court holds that a certain rule of law applies to the given factual situation of the case and renders its decision accordingly. The rule of law as applied to the facts of the case express the rule of the case. Under *stare decisis,* the rule of the case will be applied to decide future cases with the same or closely analogous factual situations. The rule of the case as expressed in a court's holding becomes a precedent which guides courts in their decisions and is generally considered to be the law.

Sometimes courts make comments in their opinions which are not necessary to support the decision. These extraneous judicial expressions are referred to as *dictum* and have no value as precedent because they do not fit the facts of the case. Even though *dictum* is not binding under the doctrine of *stare decisis,* it is entitled to consideration as being persuasive. Other judges and lawyers can determine what the decision makers are thinking and gain an indication of how the problem may be handled in the future.

Conflict of Laws

Each of the fifty-one states is an individual sovereignty that creates its own common and statutory law. Frequently there are inconsistencies among the laws of the various states. A conflict of laws problem is presented whenever a legal controversy arises in which there is a foreign element. When the facts of a case under consideration have occurred in more than one state or country, and it becomes necessary for a court to make a choice between the laws of the different states or nations, a conflict case is presented. Another type of conflict of laws case involves a situation in which an event occurred in one state and the suit is brought in another state. In this situation the court must decide whether to apply its own substantive law, the law of the state where the events occurred, or possibly the law of some other state. A court always follows its own procedural law.

Conflict of laws rules have been developed by each state to assist its courts in determining whether and when foreign substantive law should be given effect within the territory of the forum. A lawyer uses these rules to predict the outcome of his case. The rules afford some assurance that a case will be treated in the same way under the appropriate law no matter where the suit is brought.

Full Faith and Credit

Article 4, section 1, of the federal Constitution provides that "full faith and credit shall be given in each state to the public acts, records, and judicial proceedings of every other state." A judgment of a sister state valid on its face must be given full faith and credit, providing that the court had jurisdiction over the parties and over the subject matter of the case, and providing that the judgment is not against the public policy of the home state.

JUDICIAL REMEDIES

Equitable Remedies

In American jurisprudence, the remedies that courts award in civil cases are classified either as equitable remedies or as common law remedies. Common law remedies are generally limited to the court's determination of some legal right and the awarding of money damages. Equitable remedies generally consist of the court's command directed to a person requiring him to do or refrain from doing something. The command ordering one to do a certain act is called a mandatory injunction, or specific performance. A prohibitory injunction, which is the most common injunction, is a command of the court ordering one to refrain from doing something. Equity makes use of the injunction to prevent a threatened injury or wrong, or to repair an injury.

Injunctions are classified by the stage of the case when they are issued, and by their duration. A preliminary or interlocutory injunction is issued in order to keep everything unchanged until the parties' rights have been finally decided. A preliminary injunction is temporary and continues only until a further order of the court is made. Only when the final decision of the court is in the plaintiff's favor is a permanent injunction issued in his favor.

The equitable remedy of reformation is granted when a written agreement fails to express accurately the parties' agreement because of mutual mistake, fraud, or the draftsman's ambiguous language. Today, most courts in the United States are empowered to grant both equitable and legal relief as required to achieve justice.

Development

The distinction between equity and common law is a historical one. Equity in the United States is that portion of remedial justice which was formerly administered in England by the court of chancery. English equity was a system of justice administered by a tribunal apart from the common law courts. The common law system of justice in England was deficient in that its procedural requirements were highly technical. These requirements confined the courts to redressing wrongs by awarding money damages to an injured party. In situations where a common law remedy either did not exist or was inadequate to redress the wrong, the king referred the matter to the Lord High Chancellor. This practice became institutionalized to the point where the chancellor, presiding over a court of chancery, issued decrees on his own authority. The court of chancery, or equity court, came into being in order to provide a forum for granting relief in accordance with broad principles of right and justice in cases where restrictive technicalities of the common law prevented giving relief.

For centuries, common law and equity were administered in England by two separate sets of courts, each applying its own system of jurisprudence and following its own system of procedure. Equity furnished a remedy only when the common law procedure was deficient or the remedy at common law was inadequate. The underlying concepts of law and equity have been retained in the United States, although the formalism that historically distinguished the two has largely disappeared.

One of the principle deficiencies of the common law system is that it generally awarded only money damages as relief to an injured party. Since equity granted relief only when the common law system's remedy was inadequate, equitable relief was obtainable when damages were not capable of rectifying the injustice. Even today in our legal system equitable remedies are granted only when the common law remedies are inadequate.

Jury Trial

Cases are normally tried before a jury only if the parties have a right to a trial by jury and when one of the parties takes the required steps necessary to assert this right. In cases in equity the parties have no right to a jury trial. Jury trial was not a part of chancery procedure.

For the most part, trial by jury is a constitutional right. Litigants are guaranteed a jury trial in federal courts by the seventh amendment to the United States Constitution which provides: "In suits at common law, where the value in controversy shall exceed twenty dollars, the right of trial by jury shall be preserved...." Most state constitutions make similar provisions for a jury in suits at common law. There is no constitutional right to a jury trial in equity cases.

Common law and equitable remedies may be sought in the same action in most American courts. The parties do not give up their rights to a trial by jury when legal and equitable issues are joined in the same suit. In this situation the legal and equitable issues should be separated. The legal issues are determined by the jury, and the equitable issues are for the judge sitting as a chancellor.

Common Law Remedies

Common law remedies are generally limited to the court's determination of some legal right and the award of money damages. There are some exceptions; for example, when parties want the court's opinion concerning their legal rights, without seeking legal damages or injunctive relief, they seek a declaratory judgment. The action of ejectment is a common law remedy brought by a party who wants possession of his land and damages for the unlawful detention of its possession. Another common law remedy, replevin, is brought to recover possession of goods unlawfully taken.

Usually, a common law court grants relief in the form of damages, a sum of money awarded as compensation for an injury sustained as the consequence of either a tortious act or a breach of a legal obligation. Damages are classified into (1) compensatory damages, (2) punitive damages, (3) nominal damages, and (4) liquidated damages.

Compensatory Damages

Compensatory damages are awarded to compensate the plaintiff for those pecuniary losses which resulted from the defendant's wrong. These losses may have resulted from either tortious conduct or breach of contract. Future losses are recoverable also. Compensatory damages may be awarded for loss of time or money, bodily pain and suffering, permanent disabilities or disfigurement, injury to reputation, and mental anguish. Recovery is not allowed for consequences which are remote, indirect or speculative.

In awarding compensatory damages, the court's objective is to put the plaintiff in the same financial position he was in prior to the commission of the tort; or, in a contract case, in the financial position in which he would have been had the promises been fulfilled. In the absence of circumstances giving rise to an allowance of punitive damages, the law will not put the injured party in a better position than he would be in had the wrong not been done.

Sometimes the defendant's wrongful act may cause a benefit as well as an injury to the plaintiff. In this case, the damages resulting from the suit should be the difference between the value of the injury and the value of the benefit. This is called the benefit rule.

Putting a dollar value on the plaintiff's loss in order to compensate him often becomes a difficult task. Since the amount of damages is a factual question and decisions on factual issues do not create precedent, previous case decisions are not binding. The amount of damages is decided by a jury unless a jury trial has been waived.

CIVIL PROCEDURE

Civil procedure is the name given to the sum total of rules, forms, doctrines, and devices which govern the conduct of most noncriminal judicial proceedings. Rules of procedure govern the conduct of the law suit; they exist so that substantive law can be implemented. The principal objective of procedural law is to give each party to a dispute an equal and fair opportunity to present his side of the case before a non-prejudiced and convenient tribunal. If procedural rules are correctly drafted and effectively implemented, both parties to the dispute should feel that they have been treated fairly. At another point in this volume the reader will be provided with a general explanation of the procedures that govern a civil suit from the time the litigant decides to sue until final court judgment. The legal system in the United States is composed of fifty-one different court systems, each with its own procedures. Indispensable to the understanding of these systems is a familiarity with the various stages and terms that are encountered in a civil proceeding.

CRIMINAL PROCEDURE

A crime is an offense against a sovereign. An act is not a crime unless it has been made so by statute or by common law. In many jurisdictions there are no common law crimes. There are no common law crimes against the United States.

The objective of criminal law is to regulate the conduct of individuals in order to maintain public order. Criminal law provides punishment for those who deviate from the defined social norms and protection for society from the consequences of antisocial behavior. The preservation of the integrity of the community is of paramount importance in determining what conduct is antisocial.

Crimes traditionally have been classified as treason, felonies, and misdemeanors. Whether a crime is considered to be a felony or a misdemeanor depends upon the character of the punishment prescribed for it, not upon the nature of the act. Offenses punishable by death or by imprisonment in a state penitentiary are felonies. All others, including those that are punishable by imprisonment in a county jail are misdemeanors. Less serious misdemeanors are often referred to as petty offenses.

Criminal procedure is that area of the law which deals with the judicial process in criminal cases. It is concerned with the administration of criminal justice, from the initial investigation of a crime and the arrest of a suspect, through trial, sentence, and release. The goal of criminal justice is to protect society from anti-social activity without sacrificing individual rights, justice, and fair play.

The court referees the confrontation between the interests of society and the rights of the accused. The judge and jury determine the guilt or innocence of the accused by evaluating facts properly presented in open court. Ideally, the truth emerges from an adversary proceeding conducted in a manner consistent with constitutional guarantees. The due process guaranty of the fifth and fourteenth amendments requires reasonable notice of the charges and an adequate opportunity to defend oneself at a fair hearing before a competent and impartial tribunal. The guaranty applies whether the crime charged is a felony or misdemeanor.

It is a fundamental principle of criminal procedure that one is presumed to be innocent until proved guilty beyond a reasonable doubt. The purpose of this principle is not to protect the guilty but to prevent the conviction of one who may be innocent. The prosecution has the burden of producing evidence and proving guilt beyond a reasonable doubt. The presumption of innocence is not specifically guaranteed by the Constitution, yet it has remained unchallenged by the courts of the United States.

Since the integrity of the judicial system must prevail, criminals must occasionally be freed when their constitutional guarantees have been abrogated at some step in the criminal justice process. The guaranties that deal with criminal procedure are defined primarily in the Fourth, Fifth, Sixth, Eighth, and Fourteenth Amendments to the Constitution. They are delineated in general language, the practical meaning of which is interpreted by the courts. In the 1960's the trend of the Supreme Court was an expansive one, tending to increase the scope of the rights of persons accused of crimes. In the present decade of the 1970's there has been a contracting of this scope of the rights of the accused.

CHAPTER VI

The Educational Training of the Paralegal

There is at the present time a great amount of healthy experimentation going on in paralegal training. Some believe that the best training for paralegals is to show them systematically how to handle every step of a particular kind of case. This is the "systems" approach. Others believe that short-term intensive training is the most appropriate, and have designed courses which run anywhere from one week to three months, producing a paralegal knowledgeable and skilled in one substantive law area. Still another approach is commonly found among the community colleges which prepare so-called "generalists." Finally, there are those who contend that on-the-job training for paralegals is the most effective approach.

At least in the opinion of this author who has had many years of both working experience as an employer of paralegals and academic experience as Director of one of the largest university-connected paralegal institutions, that the training institutions, university as well as proprietary, are the sources most employing law firms and businesses turn to for hiring purposes because they recognize their commitment and expertise to such training.

Accreditation and Certification Issues

Accreditation remains one of the major issues in paralegal education. This is the process by which an agency or organization (public or private) evaluates and recognizes a program of study as meeting certain predetermined qualifications or standards. Whether paralegal training programs should *now* be subject to accreditation; how such an accreditation agency should be established; and who should control it, are all pending dimensions of this issue. A possible approach which at some future time may be adopted would be to establish a broadly representative accrediting body, including paralegals themselves as well as lawyers, legal and paralegal educators, and public representatives.

Certification, on the other hand, is the voluntary process by which a non-governmental agency or association recognizes an individual who has met certain predetermined qualifications specified by that agency or association. Thus the National Association of Legal Assistants has made recommendations for the certification of paralegals which may very well be effectuated in the foreseeable future. The Certifying Board, of which this writer is a member, has made a recommendation that certification should be given following completion of minimum education requirements, work experience and an examination indicating the proficiency of the applicant. The Board believes that a certification program would establish a high standard of proficiency and competency. Upon completion of formal training and after accumulation of the stated amount of practical experience as a legal secretary, legal assistant, or legal administrator, a graduate of an accredited program should be eligible for certification by a certifying board of the American Bar Association.

This Association sees the difference between a legal secretary and paralegal as follows: a legal secretary must be able to type and take dictation, while a paralegal need not have any typing skills. The legal secretary maintains appointment schedules for the attorney, while the paralegal works independently and makes and keeps his own appointments. The legal secretary works in an office at all times, while the paralegal assists the attorney in and out of the law office. The legal secretary maintains the attorney's time records, while the paralegal maintains his own time records and bills for his own time. The legal secretary knows how to cite cases, but the paralegal knows how to research cases and points of law. Finally, the legal secretary need not have any analytical skills, while the legal assistant must be capable of analyzing and summarizing documents, depositions, and other kinds of legal instruments.

The first state certification examination was given by the Oregon State Bar Association in June of 1975. The requirements for taking the examination to be certified as a paralegal in Oregon require completion of ninety hours of credit, including fifteen hours in five basic sections:

> 1. Introduction to the law, including role and function of law assistant (paralegal) and the ethics relating to their relationship to clients.
> 2. The psychology of dealing with clients, lawyers, witnesses and colleagues.
> 3. Legal research.
> 4. Interviewing and investigation techniques.
> 5. Law office operation and management principles, including accounting, timekeeping, billing, etc. Thirty hours are required in a specialty and forty-five hours in general educa-

tion which include English, accounting, philosophy, et al. In addition, two years experience in law offices are required.

The examination is divided into three sections. The first tests the five basic requirements, the second covers the elective or special field that the paralegal is most interested in, and the third section is a practical application of the knowledge (as distinguished from the skills) which the Board believes a paralegal should have in order to deal with a variety of factual situations or settings, including an interview with the Board, observation of a dramatized interview followed by a written response, defining the problem and recommending procedures to follow, or, in the alternative, written problems to solve. Since this certifying examination may become a model adopted or adapted by other states it is felt by the author here that it is useful to give its details to the prospective student of a paralegal program.

An American Bar Association report published in 1974 revealed that a group of law firms employing paralegals found that English, business administration courses, research writing, ability to analyze and organize ideas were the most useful studies and skills they looked for in their paralegals.

Paralegal Training Institutions

At this point it would seem to be appropriate to speak about where paralegals can obtain the training required to take on the skills and knowledge just described.

More than seventy community colleges around the country offer paralegal training. The curricula are almost entirely geared to private, not public, law jobs. The colleges take no responsibility for placement of students, and the programs are so new that employment success has not been measured. Common elements of community college curricula are law office administration, legal writing, and legal research. Beyond that, most offer a potpourri of courses designed to produce a generalist: corporations, tax, real estate and family law.

Many paralegal training programs are offered at the community college level, but an increasing number of colleges and a very few law schools offer them. Several universities offer paralegal training programs as part of their continuing education offerings. A small number of proprietary schools also offer paralegal courses. Some proprietary schools, however, tend to be general-career-vocational institutions offering short courses. On the other hand, one of the largest and most successful of such paralegal training institutions is a proprietary school.

The best of the paralegal training schools, including both the university-related and the proprietary schools, place great emphasis of job placement for their graduates. Many of them maintain full-time placement service staffs. Such staffs do much more than send out promotional literature and inquiries. In some cases they meet with lawyers in their offices to describe and explain the training their institutions have provided prospective paralegal job applicants. Institutional representatives attend bar association conventions, advertise in the professional journals, and provide speakers on request especially from local city bar groups. The placement effort and investment are important factors to be investigated before committing yourself to any paralegal training institution program.

What The Paralegal Should Be Taught

Let us now turn to a statement of the understandings and skills which paralegal training institutions generally aim to offer their students. This will then be followed by an example or model of the curricula typical of recognized institutions offering paralegal training.
In broad terms, the paralegal should have:

1. An understanding of the history, principles and purposes of legal institutions, the operation of those institutions in the modern world, and the ability to relate the individual to those institutions.

2. An understanding of and appreciation for the role of the lawyer and legal tribunal in the administration of justice.

3. An extensive knowledge of several fields of law. The degree of competency and depth of understanding should be sufficient to enable the individual to establish successful rapport with lawyers by whom employed and to do detailed legal work as outlined in general procedures or instructions. This requires individual judgment, initiative and resourcefulness in the use of techniques, procedures, written information and legal practice.

Given here now is a detailed summary of the functions which should be performed by graduates of a paralegal program under the supervision and control of a lawyer. For the purpose of using a single legal specialty, Real Estate Law is presented as our model:

A. **Interviewing.**
   Obtain and record basic information from the client on the real estate transaction contemplated (usually after the lawyer has spoken to the client), *e.g.,* for a real estate sale, the paralegal, using a checklist, asks the client the names and addresses of present mortgage holders, the date of original purchase, the capital improvements made on the structure, *etc.*

B. **Title Work**
   1. Conduct title search in the records office
   2. Prepare a preliminary abstract of title for attorney who will then write the opinion on the title
   3. Arrange for the purchase of title insurance

C. Mortgage Work
1. Assist an office client in obtaining mortgage financing
2. Review mortgage applications for office clients that sell mortgages (mortgage reviewing)
3. Assist in the recording of mortgages

D. Taxation
1. Assemble tax receipts
2. Allocate property taxes for closing
3. Record capital gain or loss in client's file for later preparation of client's income tax return
4. Keep abreast of latest tax law through loose-leaf services and bring such developments to the attention of the office attorneys

E. Drafting
1. Preliminary abstract of title
2. Preliminary opinion on title
3. Property tax returns
4. Preliminary draft of purchase and sale agreement

F. Closing
1. Arrange for closing date
2. Notify all parties involved in closing
3. Record minutes of closing
4. Be general aid to attorney at closing
5. Notarize documents at closing

G. Liability Insurance
1. Assist the client in obtaining liability insurance (*e.g.*, homeowner's policy)
2. Coordinate the office's handling of insurance claims of the client

H. Litigation
1. Legal research: shepardizing cases
2. Legal research: brief writing
3. Factual research: *e.g.*, compile a list of the number of commercial mortgages a bank client issues in a certain year
4. Legislative history: check on the past and present history of certain legislation dealing with real estate law
5. Draft preliminary answers to written interrogatories
6. Draft preliminary written interrogatories to be addressed to attorney of the other side
7. Read trial depositions; summarize them; point out common themes, point out inconsistencies

I. **Office Management**
   1. Maintain office "tickler" system
   2. Maintain individual attorney's calendar
   3. Be in charge of the entire client's file (opening it, keeping it up to date, knowing where parts of it are at all times)
   4. Training other office staff in the office system of handling real estate transactions

Paralegal Curricula Designed to Meet Above Skills and Understandings

Now it would be appropriate to present at this point the full curricula of a "typical" paralegal training institution. And we will start with the Real Estate Curriculum first so that you can most immediately see what kind of training you can expect to receive in order to carry out the functions of that specialty which were just described.

Real Estate Curriculum

1. **Introduction to Real Property.** - Students will be introduced to background concepts relating to the ownership, sale, leasing, financing, and governmental regulation of improved and unimproved land.

2. **Survey and Legal Description.** - The paralegal will learn to order and read surveys and to prepare legal descriptions for insertion in deeds, mortgages, and other documents.

3. **Recording Statutes.** - Statutes providing for the recording of documents relating to real estate will be studied. The paralegal will be trained to understand what types of documents must be recorded and to carry out the actual recording.

4. **Title Abstracting.** - The paralegal will learn the elements of searching title to real estate and preparing an abstract to be used at the time of a purchase, mortgage or lease. In addition, students will be trained to read title reports and abstracts prepared by title companies or lawyers for the purpose of obtaining documents necessary to clear title at a settlement or closing.

5. **Title Holder.** - Individual, partnership, joint venture, straw and corporate ownership of real estate will be examined. The student will train to form title-holding corporations and to prepare the documentation required where title is held by a straw party or corporation.

6. **Deeds.** - Students will learn to prepare the various types of deeds in common use. Deed forms used in several states will be examined and the differences analyzed.

7. **Mortgages.** - The paralegal will study mortgage financing with an emphasis on learning to prepare mortgages, notes and the

multitude of supporting documents required for construction and permanent loan closings, such as security agreements, declarations of no set-off, performance bonds and corporate resolutions. In addition, students will be trained to prepare and title the documentation involved in mortgage foreclosures.

8. **Government Control Over Land Use.** - Students will be trained to assist the lawyer in applying for and obtaining zoning, building, occupancy and other similar permits required by local governmental authorities.

9. **Leasing Real Estate.** - Students will review the provisions of standard residential, commercial, shopping center and net leases in great detail. They will be trained to draft a variety of leases, from simple residential leases to more complex commercial and shopping center leases.

10. **Buying and Selling Real Estate.** - Students will learn the steps necessary to buy and sell real estate by examining purchases and sales of properties ranging from homes through multi-million dollar industrial and commercial properties. They will be trained to prepare agreements of sale covering certain of the transactions studied.

11. **Partnership and Joint Venture Agreements.** - Students will study the Uniform Partnership and Limited Partnership Acts. They will learn to prepare an initial draft of general and limited partnership agreements as well as joint venture agreements.

12. **Construction Contracts.** - The paralegal will learn to prepare simple construction contracts with an emphasis on A.I.I. and bank forms.

13. **Settlements and Closing.** - The events which take place at a settlement or closing for the purchase and/or mortgaging of real estate, as well as the role of the paralegal in preparing for the closing, will be the subject of the final topic of the course. Students will be trained to obtain or perhaps prepare, as the case may be, tax receipts, lien clearances, corporate resolutions, pay-off statements, etc. In addition, they will be trained to prepare a binder of the transaction.

Corporate Law Curriculum

1. **Introduction to the Corporation.** - The Model Business Corporation Act and selected state corporate laws will be examined in order to familiarize the student with the concept of a corporation as well as the basic law governing its formation and operation.

2. **Formation and Structure of Corporations.** - The paralegal will learn to prepare initial and amended articles or certificates

of incorporation, satisfy state filing and advertising requirements, draft pre-incorporation subscriptions and draft or modify by-laws.

3. **Shareholders and Directors Meetings.** - Students will receive instruction and practice in preparing initial incorporators' or directors' minutes, waivers and notices of meetings, repetitive resolutions whether in the form of written consents or actual meetings, agenda, scripts and ballots for directors' and shareholders' meetings.

4. **Corporate Equity and Debt Securities.** - This section of the course will focus upon the characteristics of debt and equity securities as well as the variety of securities within each category. Students will learn to prepare stock certificates, maintain stock ledgers and books and prepare drafts of securities.

5. **Corporate Dividends.** - The student will learn to draft resolutions authorizing cash and stock dividends and stock splits as well as resolutions relating to spin-offs, liquidations and dissolutions. In addition, the student will prepare the forms required by the state and by the Internal Revenue Service in connection with the liquidation and dissolution of corporations.

6. **Qualification in Foreign Jurisdictions.** - There will be an introduction to the concept of "doing business." Students will learn to draft qualification papers, withdrawal from qualification and special reports.

7. **Employment Agreements.** - The paralegal will learn to draft an employment agreement containing frequently used terms including "non-competition," "trade secrets" and "stock option" provisions.

8. **Stock Options.** - Students will analyze and draft qualified stock option plans and stock option agreements.

9. **Stock Restriction Agreements.** - A typical buy-sell agreement will be reviewed paragraph by paragraph. Students will be trained to draft a comparable agreement and to draft the corporate resolutions necessary to approve the transaction.

10. **Regulation of Public Sale of Securities.** - The paralegal will be trained to prepare blue sky memoranda and supporting material and forms for the registration of securities under blue sky laws. In addition, the paralegal will assist in compiling information and documents required for Registration Statements under the Securities and Exchange Act.

11. **Additional Documents Relating to the Public Sale of Securities.** - Students will learn to draft an underwriting agreement,

as well as powers of attorney and resolutions authorizing the sale of securities, registration with the various regulatory agencies and the execution of the underwriting agreement.

12. **Securities and Exchange Act of 1934.** - Paralegals will be trained to know when and how to prepare Form 3 and 4 reports, Form 8-K, 10-K and 10-Q reports and the Form 10. In addition, they will be trained to draft proxy materials for a shareholders' meeting at which certain routine events occur, such as the election of directors, adoption of a stock option plan, selection of auditors and amendments to the articles or certificate of incorporation or by-laws.

13. **Listing Application to Stock Exchanges.** - Students will prepare drafts of corporate resolutions relating to listing of securities. In addition, they will review the listing application itself and various supplemental forms required by the exchanges.

14. **Acquisition and Merger Agreements.** - Paralegals will learn the different types of acquisitions and merger, the statutory requirements of such a transaction (including procedures required to comply with Bulk Sales Acts), and the customary range of provisions that appear in the agreement, including affirmative covenants, representations and warranties, indemnifications and escrow provisions, deferred pay-outs and registration rights. They will be trained to prepare a closing agenda and papers and prepare the necessary corporate resolutions.

15. **Closing Papers and Closing Binders.** - Paralegals will be aware of the various closing documents necessary to consummate each of the transactions covered in the course. They will be able to prepare or obtain the officers' certificates, certified resolutions, encumbency certificates, good standing certificates, tax lien certificates, etc. They will also be able to prepare closing agenda, closing papers and a binder for the transaction.

Estates and Trusts Curriculum

1. **Introduction to Estates and Trusts.** - Students will be introduced to the basic concepts of intervivos trusts, testamentary trusts and estates and how they are created and administered.

2. **Probate.** - The paralegal will learn to prepare for probate in both formal and informal jurisdictions. They will learn to gather the necessary information and draft and file applicable documents for both testate and intestate estates.

3. **Asset Accumulation and Payment of Debts.** - Students will be trained to aid the lawyer in discovering, gathering and valuing the assets of a decedent. This will include instruction in such

tasks as changing record ownership of property to the executors, obtaining social security, medicare and veteran's benefits, etc. In addition, the paralegal will be trained to prepare the inventory of assets and aid the executor in the payment of the decedent's debts.

4. **Preparation of Federal Estate Tax Return.** - A major part of this course is devoted to teaching students to prepare a Federal Estate Tax return. Many basic concepts of property law and federal estate taxation will be explored through a schedule by schedule study of the return.

5. **Preparation of Federal Income Tax Returns.** - Students will be introduced to the preparation of individual income tax returns. Special emphasis will be placed on the preparation of the final lifetime return and fiduciary income tax returns for both estates and trusts. The paralegal will be familiar with the interrelationships among the federal estate tax, the fiduciary income tax and the income tax of beneficiaries.

6. **State and Local Taxation.** - Students will be introduced to the returns required for state gift, inheritance and estate taxes. To a lesser extent, this section of the course will also deal with state income taxes and real and personal property taxes.

7. **Formal Accounting.** - The paralegal will be introduced to the process of fiduciary accounting. The concepts of principal and income, disbursements and distributions and reconciling an account with the assets on hand will be covered. Students will explore the procedures of a court accounting in both formal and informal jurisdictions.

8. **Settlement by Agreement.** - Students will be prepared to draft a family agreement and distribute assets in cases where no court accounting is desired.

9. **Distribution of Assets.** - Students will learn how to take all the steps necessary to accomplish the actual physical distribution of assets from an estate or trust. This section will also teach students to prepare whatever court filings are necessary to terminate the administration of an estate or trust.

10. **Gifts and Federal Tax Return.** - Paralegals will learn the legal elements involved in a gift. They will be taught to prepare the documents required to transfer property by gift and to prepare and file, when necessary, federal gift tax returns.

11. **Estate Planning and Drafting.** - Students will be prepared to help lawyers in estate planning and drafting by assembling relevant information, making estimated tax calculations, and calculating liquidity requirements. Students will learn the fun-

damentals of will and trust drafting so that they will be able to assist lawyers in preparation and periodic review of these documents.

12. **Estate Record Keeping and Office Systems.** - The paralegal will be prepared to keep filing systems and accounting records for both large and small estates. Students will be introduced to modern office systems aimed at assuring that work is accomplished at the appropriate time, that both the lawyer and the client are informed of progress, and that billing is kept current. In addition, students will learn to install and monitor systems for the periodic review of estate plans.

Litigation Curriculum

1. **Introduction to Litigation.** - Students will be introduced to the differences between civil and criminal litigation. While there will be references throughout the course to criminal litigation, the emphasis will be on civil litigation. The student will be exposed to the basic framework or rules which govern the lawsuit, the manner in which legal principles are developed by precedent and the types of relief that are available.

2. **Courts and their Jurisdiction.** - Students will learn of the variety of state and federal courts and the differences in the scope of their jurisdiction. By the use of selected federal and state laws and rules, they will be exposed to such concepts as "in personam", "in rem" and "subject matter" jurisdiction. In this and other parts of the course, particular emphasis will be placed on the Federal Rules of Civil Procedure and the Judicial Code.

3. **Substantive Law.** - In order to prepare the student to assist a lawyer in a lawsuit, a rudimentary understanding of certain major areas of substantive law is essential. This course will expose the student to the broad outlines of law in the areas of anti-trust, contracts, negligence, shareholder derivative actions and fraud (with particular reference to Rule 10b-5 under the Securities and Exchange Act).

4. **Investigation of Facts.** - Students will learn how to assist lawyers in the initial interview and how to take the client's "history." The student will also be taught techniques for reviewing the client's documents and cataloging the information obtained.

5. **Commencement of the Lawsuit and the Preparation of Pleadings and Motions.** - Students will learn how to assist lawyers in the commencement of lawsuits by ascertaining the correct names of the parties, helping to gather facts which establish that jurisdiction exists, assisting in drafting simple motions and pleadings and providing defendants with the required notice.

6. **Discovery.** - Students will develop an appreciation for the kinds of information sought through discovery and will learn how to gather the relevant information, prepare certain types of interrogatories and answers to interrogatories, arrange depositions and medical examinations and make requests for document inspection.

7. **Preserving Facts and Preparation for Trial.** - A significant portion of the course will be devoted to training students to digest and index depositions, interrogatories and documents so that information within these materials can be made readily available for the lawyer. The student will also be introduced to techniques for preparing chronologies of the facts as well as charts and other visual-aids useful in lawsuits, such as anti-trust litigation, involving significant amounts of data.

8. **Trial.** - To help the paralegal in undertaking work for an attorney and to give an overview of the litigation process, students will learn the various phases through which a trial proceeds.

9. **Decisions and Settlement.** - Paralegals will learn to draft releases and prepare and record settlement agreements, and will study how to assist lawyers in the collection of judgments.

10. **Post Trial Motions and Appeals.** - Students will review the mechanics of challenging a court decision and the procedure for staying the judgment of the court until an appeal is filed.

11. **Techniques of Legal Research.** - In order to assist lawyers who are preparing briefs or memoranda of law, students will learn how to use various legal research tools such as indexes, digests, Shepards, treaties and the West "key number system." Students will also be able to do "cite checking" and "proof checking" of the legal citations.

12. **File Maintenance and Docket Control.** - For a busy litigation lawyer who represents many different clients in a wide variety of lawsuits, it is essential that he have a systematic procedure for maintaining all of the documents, paperwork and evidence which are involved in each case. Students will learn various techniques for keeping track of the paperwork as well as the court dockets.

What follows is a comprehensive presentation of Course Outlines covering *all* the subject or topic areas which are offered in the typical paralegal training institution. These Outlines are offered in addition to those described up to this point in this chapter. Following this material is an example of a Probate and Trusts examination which is typically given in a paralegal training institution.

COURSE OUTLINE
REAL ESTATE

I. **General Introduction**

   A. Substantive and Adjective Law Concepts
   B. Equity Law Distinguished and Defined
   C. Court Structure
   D. Legal History
   E. Real and Personal Property Distinguished

II. **Estates and Real Property**

   A. Various Forms of Estates

III. **Liens and Encumbrances**

   A. Nature and Examples of Various Liens

IV. **Transfer of Title to Real Property**

   A. Types
   B. Methods

V. **Mortgages**

   A. Background and History
   B. Kinds of Mortgages
   C. Bonds and Notes
   D. Drafting Mortgages - Types of Clauses
   E. Truth-in-Lending
   F. Real Investment Trusts (REITS)

VI. **Leases**

   A. Study of Contracts
   B. Types of Leases
   C. Lease Clauses

VII. **Deeds**

   A. Basic Types and Forms

VIII. **Zoning**

   A. Constitutional Police Power
   B. Environmental Protection Acts
   C. Variances

IX. **Real Estate Brokers**

   A. Role as a Fiduciary
   B. Kinds of Agreements
   C. Compensation

X. **Contract of Sale or Real Estate**

   A. Options
   B. Contract Clauses

C. Types of Contracts
D. Vendor's - Vendee's Returns

XI. **Real Estate Closings**

A. Preparation
B. Examination of Instruments and Other Documents
C. Title Company
D. Computation of Adjustments
E. Conveyance, Mortgage and Deed Recording Taxes
F. Closing Statement

XII. **Title Holder**

A. Types
B. Multiple Ownership

XIII. **Descriptions of Real Property**

A. Meets and Bounds
B. Diagraming
C. Maps
D. Prior Deeds
E. Drafting

XIV. **Surveys**

A. Purpose
B. Preparation
C. Reading the Survey
D. Standards of Measurement

XV. **Recordings**

A. Recording Offices
B. Failure to Record
C. Recording Special Instruments
D. Form of Record
E. Recording Books and Indices
F. Statutory Requirements
G. Preparation of Instruments for Recording

XVI. **Title Searches**

A. Use to Search Titles

XVII. **Abstracts**

A. Shorthand
B. Abstracting Instruments and Returns

XVIII. **Title Reports**

A. Reading the Abstract
B. Checking Unrecorded Information
C. Certificate of Ownership and Exceptions

Part I - **Substantive**

I. **Overview**

   A. Business Concepts
   B. Business Publications
     1. Wall Street Journal
     2. Business Week
     3. New York Times
     4. Miscellaneous Publications
   C. Business Organizations: (Forms of Business Ownership)
     1. Sole proprietorship
     2. Partnership
     3. Corporation
   D. Closely Held Businesses
   E. Basic Business Accounting
     1. Income statement
     2. Balance sheet
   F. Assets - Types of property
     1. Definition
     2. Types - in depth analysis
       a. cash
       b. tangible
       c. real property
       d. stocks
       e. bonds
       f. notes
       g. life insurance
     3. Types of asset ownership
       a. sole ownership
       b. joint ownership
         1. definition
     4. Valuation of Assets

II. **The Will**

   A. Definition and Types
   B. Purpose
   C. Law of Wills
     1. Testamentary Capacity
     2. Age
     3. Execution
     4. Witnesses
     5. Executor
     6. Commissions
     7. Types of bequests

8. Dispositions
9. Types of Will Clauses
10. Codicils
11. Lapsed dispositions
12. Abatement
13. Common Disaster
14. Illusory Transfers
15. Charitable Dispositions
16. Divorce
17. Revocation
18. Renunciation
D. Drafting Wills
E. Elections against Estate
F. Testamentary Substitutes

III. Intestate Succession

A. Intestacy - defined
B. Distributees
C. Family Tree
D. Division of Assets

IV. Probate Proceedings

A. Probate - defined
B. Letters Testamentary
1. why necessary
C. How to probate a will
1. Petition
2. Fees
3. Citation
a. who must be cited
4. Waiver of citation
5. Notice of probate
6. Jurisdiction
7. Affidavit of attesting witnesses
8. Depositions of attesting witnesses
D. Objections to Probate - Will Contest
1. Improper execution
2. Lack of testamentary capacity
3. Fraud
4. Undue influence
E. Posting Bond by Executor
1. Bond - defined
2. When needed
F. Renunciation of appointment by fiduciary

V. Administration Proceedings

A. Intestacy
B. Who may qualify as an administrator
  1. Priority
  2. Joint administration
C. Letters of administration
  1. Petition
  2. Fees
  3. Citation
    a. who must be cited
  4. Waiver of citation
  5. Notice of application for letters of administration
  6. Renunciation of right to letters
  7. Jurisdiction
D. Bond of Administrator
  1. Amount of Bond
  2. How calculated

VI. Ancillary Administration

A. Rules
B. State of domicile
C. Location of Assets
D. Avoidance of Ancillary Administration

VII. Temporary Administration & Preliminary Letters Testamentary

A. Defined and Distinguished
B. When to apply for
C. Who may apply
  1. Qualifications
D. Powers of temporary fiduciary
E. Accounting of temporary fiduciary

VIII. Estate Administration

A. Fiduciary's responsibilities
  1. Determine if Will exists
  2. Make funeral arrangements
  3. Arrange for probate if Will is found
  4. Arrange for administration if no Will
  5. Search for assets and records of decedent
    a. Take control, if possible
    b. Make sure property insurance is adequate
  6. Obtain Letters of Administration or Letters Testamentary
  7. Collect Assets
    a. Insurance Policies
    b. Bank Accounts

  c. Stocks & Bonds

  d. Other assets

 8. Obtain Tax Waivers

 9. Arrange for Safe Deposit Box opening if one exists.

 10. Start raising cash for estate needs

  a. start liquidating brokerage accounts

 11. Determine debts of decedent

  a. Investigate all claims to determine if debt is valid

  b. Pay those claims as local law may allow

 12. Arrange to have any business run properly until proper disposition is determined

 13. Valuation of assets

  a. Securities

  b. Closely held businesses

  c. Real property

 14. File Tax Returns

  a. Personal

  b. Fiduciary Income Tax Returns

  c. Estate Tax Returns

 15. Prepare for Tax Audits

 16. Pay Legacies and distribute bequests

 17. Fund any trusts established under Will

 18. Distribute residuary estate

 19. Prepare final accounting

IX. Powers of Fiduciary

 A. Distinguished from duties

 B. EPTL 11-1.1

 C. Additional powers granted by Will

X. Accounting

 A. Petition on Accounting

 B. Accounting

 C. Citation

  1. Who must be cited

 D. Waiver of Citation

 E. Objections to account

  1. Surcharge

 F. Decree on accounting

 G. Voluntary accounting

 H. Compulsory accounting

 I. Judicial account

 J. Receipt and release

XI. Trusts

 A. Trust - defined

    B. Types
       1. Intervivos
         a. revocable
         b. irrevocable
         c. funded
         d. unfunded
       2. Testamentary
    C. Elements of a Trust
    D. Reasons for establishing Intervivos Trusts
       1. Save taxes
       2. Check fiduciary's handling of assets
       3. Personal satisfaction of transfer of wealth
       4. To facilitate handling of various assets
       5. To avoid probate
       6. Clifford Trusts
         a. Income Tax Savings
    E. Testamentary Trusts
    F. Estate Tax consequences of establishing trusts

Part II - **Taxation**

I. **Estate, Income Gift Taxation - History & Background**

II. **Federal Estate Tax**

    A. The Federal Estate Tax Return - Form 706
    B. Form 706 - Schedules
       1. Schedule A - Real Estate
       2. Schedule B - Stocks & Bonds
       3. Schedule C - Mortgages, Notes & Cash
       4. Schedule D - Insurance
       5. Schedule E - Jointly owned property
       6. Schedule F - Miscellaneous property
       7. Schedule G - Transfers on Decedent's life
       8. Schedule H - Powers of appointment
       9. Schedule I - Annuities
      10. Schedule J - Funeral expenses & expenses incurred on administering property subject to claims
      11. Schedule K - Debts of Decedent and mortgages and liens
      12. Schedule L - Net losses during administration and expenses incurred in administering property not subject to claims
      13. Schedule M - Bequests, etc., to surviving spouse (marital deduction)
      14. Schedule N - Charitable, public, and similar gifts and bequests
    C. Gross Estate
       1. What's includible

D. Deductions from Gross Estate
   1. Funeral Expenses
   2. Administration Expenses
   3. Debts
   4. Mortgages & notes payable
   5. Miscellaneous deductions
E. Concept of Adjusted Gross Estate
F. The Marital Deduction
G. Charitable Deduction
H. Specific Exemption
I. Taxable Estate
   1. Estate Tax Rates
      a. 3% to 77% depending on size of estate
J. Credits against the federal Estate Tax
   1. State Estate or Inheritance Tax
   2. Gift Taxes
   3. Foreign Death Taxes
   4. Federal Estate Tax on Prior Estates
K. Alternate Valuation
L. Gifts in Contemplation of Death

III. **New York Estate Tax**

A. Article 26 of the Tax Law
B. Procedure to determine tax for New York State
   1. File with Surrogate's Court
      a. Petition
      b. Notice of motion
      c. An order
C. Temporary Payment
D. Comparison - New York Estate Tax Return v. Federal Estate Tax Return
E. New York Gross Estate
   1. Personal Exemptions:
      a. Spouse - $20,000
      b. Children - $5,000
   2. Insurance
      a. Spouse
      b. Family members
      c. Dollar Limitation
   3. Marital Deduction

IV. **The Gift Tax**

A. Gift defined and analyzed
B. Federal Gift Tax
   1. History & background
   2. Gift Tax Rates
      a. Cumulative nature of tax
      b. 3/4 of Federal Estate Tax Rate

3. Lifetime Exemption
4. Annual Exclusion
5. Gift Splitting
6. Marital Deduction
7. Penalties for failure to file
8. Payment of tax by donee - effect of
C. Valuation of Gifts
D. Types of Gifts
E. Gifts to Minors

V. Fiduciary Tax Return - Form 1041

A. Who must file
1. Executors
2. Trustees
B. Simple Trusts
C. Complex Trusts
D. Distributable Net Income (DNI)
E. Fiscal Year
F. Types of Income
1. Dividends & Interest
2. Capital gains & losses
3. Section 303 Redemptions
4. Depreciation
5. Amortization of Premiums
6. Throwback Rules

VI. Decedent's Final Income Tax Return (Form 1040)

A. Allocation of Income
B. Income in respect of a decedent
C. Elections
D. Life Insurance proceeds
E. Joint Return

CORPORATIONS

EMPLOYEE BENEFITS

I. **Types of Plans**
   A. Basic Description of Pension and Profit Sharing Plans
   B. Special Types of Plans

II. **Requirements for Qualification**
   A. Key Elements in Qualified Plans
   B. Covering Requirements of Qualified Plans
   C. The New Vesting Rules
   D. Limitations on Benefits to Participants
   E. Payment of Benefits — Settlement Options
   F. Integrating Pension and Profit Sharing with Social Security
   G. Application of Integration Rules to Particular Types of Plans
   H. Integration on the Basis of the Employer's Contributions
   I. Amendments, Curtailments and Terminations

III. **Deductions and Taxation**
   A. Advantages of a Tax Qualified Retirement Plan
   B. Employer's Deductions for Contributions to the Plan
   C. Tax Treatment of Distributions to Employees Covered by Qualified Retirement Plan
   D. Retirement Plans of the Subchapter S

IV. **Administration of Plan**
   A. Submission of Plan for Qualification
   B. Reports and Disclosures
   C. Fiduciary Responsibility: Prohibited Transactions Investment in Employer Securities and Realty

Funding
   A. New Funding Standards Under the Employee Retirement Income Security Act of 1974 (ERISA)
   B. The Role of the Trust Company in Qualified Plans
   C. The Role of Life Insurance and the Life Insurance Company in Qualified Plans
   D. Plan Termination Insurance

VI. **Self-Employed**
   A. Qualified Plans for the Self-Employed Individual
   B. Individual Retirement Plans

NEGLIGENCE AND LITIGATION

I. **Describe PI office**
   A. Direct and of counsel cases
   B. Economics important-expense of file
   C. Fee arrangements
   D. Insurance company offices

II. **Types of negligence**
   A. Define negligence-carelessness-prudent man
   B. Products liability
   C. General liability
   D. Auto liability
   E. Medical malpractice

III. **No fault**
   A. $500 in medical
   B. Permanent injury to system
   C. Fracture-more than simple

IV. **Contributory negligence**
   A. Effect on "fault" states
   B. Dole vs. Dow

V. **Take file and trace it**
   A. Original history
   B. Physical examination
   C. Pleadings
   D. Bill of particulars
   E. Depositions
   F. Place case on calendar
   G. Calendar practice
   H. Trial procedure

VI. **Civil practice in U.S. District and New York State Courts**
   A. Introduction
   B. History of New York procedure
   C. Use and structure of the CPLR
   D. Various courts of New York

VII. **Statute of Limitations**
   A. Nature of statute
   B. Applicability of statute
   C. Accrual of cause of action
      1. Malpractice
      2. Negligence-breach of warranty
      3. Libel
      4. Wrongful death
   D. Interruption in running of statute

VIII. **Concept of jurisdiction**
   A. Jurisdiction in personam, in rem & quasi in rem

E. Verification of pleadings CPLR 3020 (a)

F. Extention of time to plead CPLR 2004, 2104

XV. **Motion practice**
   A. Contested motions
   B. Ex-parte motions
   C. Who may make motion
   D. Notice of motion and supporting affidavits CPLR 2214
   E. Notice of opponent CPLR 2103 (b) (2) and 2214 (b)
   F. Opponents answering affidavits
   G. Moving party's reply affidavit CPLR 2214 (b)
   H. Cross-notice of motion by opponent CPLR 2215
   I. Placing motion on motion calendar
   J. Hearing of motion by submission of oral argument
   K. Order to show cause
   L. Corrective motions

XVI. **Provisional remedies**
   A. Arrest CPLR 6111
   B. Attachment CPLR 6201
   C. Sequestration in matrimonial actions DRL 233
   D. Preliminary injunction CPLR 6311
   E. Notice of pendency CPLR 6501
   F. Temporary receiver CPLR 6401
   G. Recovery of chattel CPLR 7101

XVII. **Pre-trial preparation**
   A. Bills of particulars CPLR 3041 and 3042
   B. Disclosure
      1. Examination before trial CPLR 3101
      2. Written interrogatories CPLR 3130 and 3134
      3. Discovery and inspection CPLR 3120
      4. Physical or mental examination CPLR 3121
      5. Notice to admit
      6. Subpoenas CPLR 2301
         (a) Issuance by attorney, court
         (b) Quash, modify or alter subpoena on CPLR 2304
         (c) Service and fees CPLR 2303
         (d) Attendance of witness CPLR 2305
         (e) Disobedience of subpoena, penalties CPLR 2308
      7. Notice to produce original documents

XVIII. **Trial practice**
   A. Notice of issue CPLR 3402
   B. Trial preferences CPLR 3403
   C. Call of calendar
   D. Unrestored cases deemed abandoned CPLR 3404
   E. Right to jury trial CPLR 4101
      1. Demand
      2. Waiver CPLR 4102
      3. Jury size CPLR 4104

F. Non-jury trial
1. Reference to determine CPLR 4211 and 4317
2. Advisory jury CPLR 4015 and 4212
3. Referee to report CPLR 4214
G. Empanelling jury CPLR 4105
Voir dire
H. Challenges to prospective jurors
1. To array CPLR 4108
2. Preemptory CPLR 4109
3. For cause CPLR 4110
4. To the favor CPLR 4108
I. Jury sworn in CPLR 4105
J. Opening statements CPLR 4016
K. Right to open and close CPLR 4016
L. Presentation of evidence and testimony
M. Objections
N. Defendant's motions for judgment at end of evidence CPLR 4401
O. Summation
P. Charge of jury
Q. Jury deliberations
R. Verdict
S. Motions after verdict
XIX. **Accelerated judgment**
A. Default judgment CPLR 3215
B. Dismissal of action on neglect to prosecute CPLR 3216
C. Judgment by confession CPLR 3201
D. Action on submitted facts CPLR 3222
E. Simplified procedure CPLR 3031
XX. **Judgment CPLR 5011**
A. Entry CPLR 5016
B. Judgment roll CPLR 5017
C. Relief from judgment CPLR 5015
D. Satisfaction CPLR 5001
E. Enforcement CPLR 5105
1. Judgment creditor's rights CPLR 5205
(a) Presonalty CPLR 5205
(b) Realty CPLR 5203
(c) Exempt property CPLR 5205
(d) Restraining order CPLR 5222
(e) Disclosure CPLR 5223
(f) Payment—delivery CPLR 5225
(g) Installment payment order CPLR 5226
(h) Receiver CPLR 5229
(i) Income executions CPLR 5231
(j) Property CPLR 5232 and 5235
(k) Arrest CPLR 5250

XXI. **Costs CPLR 8108 - 8110**
    A. Amount CPLR 8201
    B. Security for costs CPLR 8501
XXII. **Special proceedings**
    A. Habeas corpus CPLR 7003
    B. Proceeding against body or officer CPLR 7801
XXIII. **Appeals**

GENERAL PRACTICE - CRIMINAL

  I. **Pre-Trial Procedure**
    A. The Initial Interview
    B. Bail
    C. Arraignment
    D. Preliminary Hearing
    E. The Grand Jury
    F. Pre-Trial Motions
    G. Discovery
    H. Preparation for Trial
  II. **Trial of a Criminal Case**
    A. Selection of the Jury
    B. The Opening Statements
    C. The Prosecution's Case
    D. Presenting the Defense
    E. Summation
    F. Charge to the Jury
  III. **Procedure Subsequent to Trial**

GENERAL PRACTICE - MATRIMONIAL

    I. The Marriage Contract
   II. Spouse's Rights and Obligations
  III. Void Marriage
  IV. Voidable Marriage
   V. Annulment
  VI. Separation
 VII. Divorce
VIII. Support - Alimony
  IX. Custody of Children

Typical Final Examination
Probates and Trusts

ABC UNIVERSITY

Paralegal Education Program

Instructions:

1. Answer any four out of the five essays. Write on a separate sheet of paper. Each essay will count for 12½%. This represents a total of 50% of the examination.

2. Space is provided for answers to the objective questions next to each of the questions. Each objective question has a value of 1/2% for a total of 37.5% of the examination.

3. All five mathematical essays should be answered on a separate sheet of paper. Each of these essays is valued at 2½% for a total of 12½% of the examination.

4. All questions have been prepared so that all facts necessary to formulate an answer are available. If, however, an assumption must be made, be certain to state such assumption or assumptions clearly so that the Instructor may grade your paper accordingly.

ESSAY QUESTION NO. 1

T properly executed a holographic will during 1965 by the terms of which he distributed his entire estate in the following manner:

"First: I bequeath my Patek-Phillipe watch to **X**.

Second: I give $3,000 to **Y**.

Third: I give, devise and bequeath the rest, residue and remainder of my estate to **Z**."

In 1969, T properly executed a new will in the following terms:

"First: I give $3,000 to **Y**.

Second: I give, devise and bequeath the rest, residue and remainder of my estate to **B**."

In 1970, T properly executed a codicil to his 1965 will by the terms of which he increased the legacy to **Y** to $5,000 and in all other respects, he said, he ratified, confirmed and republished that will.

T died in 1971. In a probate proceeding, the evidence established that:

1. T was drunk when he executed his 1965 will and lacked testamentary capacity because of his intoxication. He was perfectly sober when he made his codicil in 1970.

2. T sold his Patek-Phillipe watch in 1968 but had acquired a new one in 1971 shortly before he died.

3. The 1970 codicil was prepared by his attorney, **A**, who kept the original and gave an executed copy to **T**. The original could not be found by **A** who testified that it might have been lost or destroyed by his secretary when he moved his office. The executed copy was found among **T**'s effects after his death.

What are the rights of **X**, **Y**, **Z** and **B** in the estate of **T**?

ESSAY QUESTION NO. 2

T and W, residents of Albany, New York, were married in 1940. A son, S, was born to them in 1941. In 1966, T became enamored of a younger woman, G. In December 1967, W instituted an action in Supreme Court against T for a separation based on his adultery with G.

On February 1, 1968, T duly executed a will, the dispositive provisions of which provided:

"1. I give the sum of $10,000 to my son, S."

"2. I give all my remaining personal property to my friend G."

In March 1968, **W** obtained an uncontested judgment of separation from **T**. The following month **T** purchased a home in Albany for $75,000 placing the property in the names of **T** and **G** as joint tenants with right of survivorship.

On November 15, 1968, **T** made a gift of $10,000 to **S**, his son, so that **S** could begin his own business. In March 1969, **T** opened an account in the XYZ Bank in the name of "**T**, in trust for **G**" and deposited $14,500 of his own funds in the account.

Shortly thereafter, **T** and **S** had a violent quarrel concerning **T**'s personal life. At **T**'s direction, **T**'s attorney prepared the following written instrument: "April 1, 1969, I hereby declare that the $10,000 gift which I made to my son, **S**, on November 15, 1968, shall be treated as an anticipatory distribution in complete satisfaction of **S**'s legacy under my February 1968 will". This statement was signed by **T** and witnessed by his attorney.

T died suddenly on November 1, 1969, survived by **W**, **S** and **G**, and his February 1969 will was duly admitted to probate. At the time of his death the balance in the account of XYZ Bank was $20,000. Apart from that account and the Albany property, **T**'s net probate estate after payment of debts and funeral and administration expenses amounted to $175,000.

What are the rights, if any of **W**, **S** and **G** in **T**'s estate? (Disregard) any question of estate taxes.)

ESSAY QUESTION NO. 3

H and **W** were married in New York in 1962. Shortly thereafter, in the same year, **H** made his will and by the terms thereof he left everything he owned to **W**. In 1963 **H**, with his own funds, purchased a one-family home and took title in the names of "**H** and **W**, his wife."

In October, 1966 **H**, who was then financially solvent, deposited $15,000 in a savings bank account in the name of "**H** in trust for **M**." **M** was his mother. Later that month, he deposited $15,000 in another savings bank account in the names of "**H** and **W**, payable to either or the survivor."

In April, 1967 **H** suffered serious business reverses which went unanticipated. His financial difficulties caused considerable marital friction. In September, 1967 **H** made a codicil to his 1962 will. By the codicil he revoked the disposition in favor of **W** and left everything to **P**. He did not, however, change the bank accounts before he died of a heart attack in October, 1967. **H** had no children and was survived by **W**, **M** and **P**. His probate estate after debts, administration and funeral expenses amounted to $170,000. The one-family home had a fair market value at death of $35,000. **W** has timely served and filed her notice of election.

What are the rights of **W**, **M** and **P**?

ESSAY QUESTION NO. 4

In 1964, **A**, who was not then domiciled in New York, executed a will in State **X**. The will was in writing and signed by **A** and otherwise executed in accordance with the local law of **X**. In 1965, **A** became a domiciliary of New York. Shortly thereafter, **A** made a new will which was validly executed in accordance with the law of New York and which expressly revoked all prior wills and codicils. Pursuant to its terms, **A** left everything he owned to his wife, **W**. In October, 1966, **A** deposited $10,000 in a savings bank in an account entitled "**A** or **B**, payable to either or the survivor." In April, 1967, **A** duly executed a codicil to his 1964 will which named **B** as the executor of his estate in place of the person originally named and which in all other respects ratified, confirmed and republished the 1964 will. Pursuant to the terms of the 1964 will and codicil thereto, **A** left $100 to his wife, **W**, and the residue of his estate to his friend, **B**.

A died in April, 1968 survived only by **W** and **B**. His testamentary net estate is $150,000. The capital value of the joint bank account at the time of **A**'s death is $10,750. The will of 1965 and the will of 1964 together with the 1967 codicil are offered for probate.

What are the rights, if any, of **B** and **W**?

ESSAY QUESTION NO. 5

In 1963, **H** married **W1** one month after **C1**, their child was born. In 1965, **W1** divorced **H** in New York for adultery. The divorce judgment incorporated and ordered performance of a valid separation agreement, previously entered into by them. By its terms, **H** bound himself and his estate to pay to **W1** $10 weekly for **C1**'s support, and $35 weekly "for the life of **W1**" for **W1**'s support. Both sums are conceded to be fair and reasonable. In 1968, **W1** married one **Z**, and she is still married to him. **Z** duly adopted **C1** in 1968. As soon as **W1** remarried, **H** stopped making any payments for **W1** and **C1**. **H** met and married **W2** in 1969. Shortly after their marriage, **W2** and **H** separated on mutual consent. In 1970, **H** discovered that **W2** was living openly with another man. In 1971, **H** married **W3**, concealing his prior marriages, and a child, **C2**, was thereafter born to them. In 1972, **H** died intestate, survived by all of the above. In administration proceedings in the Surrogate's Court, five claims have been filed. Pass on the merits of each.

(I) **W1**, both for herself and as guardian of **C1**, filed a claim for payments under the separation agreement for the period since her marriage to **Z** in 1968. (2) **C1**, by **W1** as his guardian, claims an intestate share as a surviving child of **H**. (3) **W2** claims an intestate share as the surviving spouse of **H**. (4) **W3** claims an intestate share as the surviving spouse of **H**. (5) **C2**, by **W3** as his guardian, claims an intestate share as a surviving child of **H**.

ANSWER TO ESSAY QUESTION NO. 1

X will take **T**'s Patek-Phillipe watch.
Y will take $5,000.
Z will take **T**'s residuary estate.
B will take nothing.

The will of 1965 was revoked by the will of 1969. Although the will of 1969 does not expressly revoke the will of 1965, it does so by implication. As a general rule, a later will which is entirely inconsistent with a prior will, or a later will which makes a complete disposition of the testator's property will be deemed to have revoked the prior will by implication. The will of 1969 is not only inconsistent with the will of 1965, but also makes a complete disposition of **T**'s entire estate and therefore, in accordance with the foregoing principle, revoked the will of 1965.

When **T** in 1970 executed a codicil to his 1965 will he republished that will and made it speak as of the date of the codicil. The fact that **T** was drunk when he executed his will in 1965 does not adversely affect its effective republication in 1970 when he was sober. A properly executed codicil operates as a republication of a will which is, in form, properly executed, despite the fact that it may have been invalid for want of testamentary capacity. **T** suffered from no testamentary infirmity when he executed his codicil in 1970.

The 1965 will and the 1970 codicil together constitute the last will and testament of **T** and since these instruments make a complete disposition of his estate and are inconsistent with the 1969 will, the latter will is deemed revoked by implication. The testamentary instruments which must be given effect as the last will and testament of **T** are, therefore, the 1965 will and the 1970 codicil, if they can be probated.

The question as to whether they can be probated is prompted by the fact that the codicil was executed in duplicate original copies and one copy was lost. If a will or a codicil is shown to have been in the testator's possession and cannot be found after his death, a rebuttable presumption arises that it was destroyed by the testator with the intention to revoke it. In the case of duplicate wills, the same rebuttable presumption arises as to both copies, where one of them cannot be found and is shown to have been in the testator's possession when he died. The copy which could not be found was the one retained by his attorney. In such a case, no presumption of revocation arises and the copy retained by the testator will be admitted to probate. In accordance with the terms of the 1965 will and the 1970 codicil, **Y** takes $5,000, **Z** takes the residuary estate and **B** takes nothing.

Whether X will take T's Patek-Phillipe watch, depends upon whether that specific bequest was adeemed when T sold the watch in 1968. As a general rule, unless the subject of a specific legacy exists unchanged in substance at the death of the testator, an ademption results. Had T sold his watch in 1968 and never replaced it, the bequest to X would have been adeemed. However, in this case, T purchased another Patek-Phillipe watch in 1971 and owned it at the date of his death.

The rule is that, as to personal property, the will of a testator speaks as of the date of death and that any article of personal property, which the testator owns at the time, which answers the description of an article bequeathed, passes under his will to the legatee named, although such article was not the identical article owned by the testator at the time he executed his will. Applying this rule to the facts, X takes the watch. (There are some N.Y. cases to the contrary, holding that such a disposition refers to the specific article possessed by the testator at the time of the execution of the will. If the rule of these cases is applied, the bequest of the watch, of course, is adeemed.)

ANSWER TO ESSAY QUESTION NO. 2

W is entitled to elect against the will. A judgment of separation defeats the right of election only where it is rendered against the surviving spouse.

Because T died after 9/1/66, and because the joint tenancy and the Trotten trust were created after that date and after marriage, both are testamentary substitutes, to the extent of the balance in the Totten trust account at T's death, and the amount of the consideration furnished by him to purchase the jointly held realty.

Hence, W may elect against the net probate estate ($175,000) plus the amount paid for the Albany property ($75,000) plus the balance in the Totten trust at T's death ($20,000), a total of $270,000. The elective share is 1/3, since T is survived by issue. The amount of W's elective share is, therefore, $90,000.

The disposition to S is effective notwithstanding the instrument executed on 4/1/69. No advancement is effective unless proven by a writing reflecting an intent to make an advancement, signed by the donor or donee of the intervivos transfer, and signed contemporaneously with the transfer.

W's elective share will be contributed ratably by S from his testamentary disposition, and by G from the residuary disposition and the aforementioned testamentary substitutes.

ANSWER TO ESSAY QUESTION NO. 3

W may exercise her right of election. The estate subject to W's elective right will include not only the probate estate, but also the joint account and the Totten trust, both of which were effected by H after the marriage and after September 1, 1966. The additional requirement — a will executed on or after September 1, 1966 — is also satisfied. When, in September, 1967, H executed a codicil to his 1962 will, he republished that will and made it speak as of the date of the codicil. The real property held by H and W will not be included because the tenancy by the entirety was created prior to September 1, 1966. There being no issue surviving H, W's elective share is one-half of the net estate of H, computed as follows: The probate estate, joint bank account and Totten trust equal $200,000. W's elective share is one-half of that amount, or $100,000 reduced by the joint bank account which passed to W as survivor. W's elective share, therefore, is $85,000 which shall be contributed ratably by P and M.

P will be permitted to take under H's will, less the sum she will be required to contribute toward the elective share of W.

M will take the balance on deposit in the Totten trust, less the sum she will be required to contribute toward the elective share of W.

ANSWER TO ESSAY QUESTION NO. 4

The 1964 will and the codicil thereto should be admitted to probate and W has a right of election.

The will of 1964, executed by A while domiciled in State X and in accordance with the local law thereof was admissible to probate in New York because it was in writing, signed by the testator and otherwise executed in accordance with the local law of the jurisdiction in which A was domiciled at the time of execution. That will was expressly revoked by the will of 1965 which was duly executed in accordance with the law of New York. The 1967 codicil revived and republished the 1964 will and together made a complete disposition of A's property. Although the codicil did not expressly revoke the 1965 will, that will was revoked by implication. The general rule is that a later will, which makes a complete disposition of the testator's property and is inconsistent with a prior will, revokes the prior will by implication. Upon the death of A, therefore, the 1964 will and the 1967 codicil to it constituted the last will and testament of A and were admissible to probate.

W, not being adequately provided for by A's last will is entitled to elect to take a share of his estate. Since A was not survived by issue, W's elective share is one-half of A's net estate which is derived at by deducting from the gross estate debts, administration and reasonable funeral expenses but not estate taxes. The net estate is stated to be $150,000.

Since the 1967 codicil republished the 1964 will, **A** is deemed a testator who executed a will after August 31, 1966. The joint bank account, effected after his marriage and after August 31, 1966 is a testamentary substitute and the capital value thereof at the date of death of **A** is included in the net estate and is subject to **W**'s elective right. The net elective estate, therefore, is $160,750 and one-half thereof is $80,375. **W**'s elective share is reduced by the value of property passing to her under **A**'s will ($100) and is, therefore, $80,275, which she may receive from **B**. **W** must exercise her right of election within six months from the date of issuance of letters testamentary and must serve written notice of such election upon the personal representative of **A**'s estate.

ANSWER TO ESSAY QUESTION NO. 5

(1) The claim of **W1** for herself is valid until she dies; the claim for **C1** is valid until the date of **C1**'s adoption by **Z**. While by statute **H**'s obligation to support **W1** under the order of the divorce court ended on **W1**'s remarriage, his obligation under the separation agreement was expressly agreed to be "for the life of **W1**". Such duration is not against public policy even where **W1** is being supported by **Z**, for it is akin to a property settlement. Whether or not the agreement contained an express non-merger clause, the Surrogate should find a clear intent that the agreement survive incorporation into the divorce judgment, and even survives **H**'s death, for by its terms (a) **W1** was to receive payments until an event not affected by divorce, and (b) **H** bound both himself and his estate. As to the claim for **C**'s support: The parental obligation of child support is not affected by a divorce; however, it wholly ends on an adoption away. Therefore, since the agreement cannot be equated to a property settlement with a baby, the Surrogate should hold that the claim is valid only for unmade payments prior to **C1**'s adoption by **Z** in 1968.

(2) **C1** may not recover an intestate share. Although illegitimate on birth, he was made legitimate by the subsequent inter-marriage of his parents. But his adoption by **Z** cuts off his right to inherit from his natural father.

(3) The fact that **W2** had been living openly with another man would have entitled **H** to sue her for divorce. However, this remedy is personal to the wronged spouse, and may not be collaterally raised by another than the spouse. Also, adultery forecloses neither intestate rights nor right of election. While abandonment does foreclose both rights, abandonment cannot be predicated on a separation by mutual consent, as here.

124

(4) **W3** may not recover an intestate share. Since **H**'s marriage to **W2** was in full force when **H** married **W3** (as has already been shown above), the marriage to **W3** was bigamous and void. Had **W3** obtained a declaration of nullity prior to **H**'s death, the Supreme Court would have had authority to award her temporary and permanent alimony in its discretion. However, this past possibility is of no relevancy where she makes a claim in the Surrogate's Court. One married to a decedent by a void marriage is not a surviving spouse entitled to an intestate share.

(5) **C2** should receive an intestate share. By statute, so long as its parents have entered into a marriage in a manner authorized by the law of the place of such marriage, a child is legitimate as to both parents notwithstanding that such marriage is void or voidable or has been annulled or judicially declared void.

MATHEMATICAL ESSAYS

1. Assume that in 1967 a childless testator died leaving a will executed in November, 1966, in which he bequeathed to his cousin **X** his entire estate amounting to $200,000. He also left Totten trusts of $100,000 in trust for **Y** and joint accounts of $80,000 with his wife. The accounts were opened in October, 1966, with his own funds. Debts, funeral and administration expenses amount to $50,000, so that the net estate for the purpose of election is $330,000.

   What is the widow's elective share?

2. Assume that a man made a will in December, 1966, in which he disinherited his wife and when he died his testamentary net estate amounted to $75,000. He also left an insurance policy of $100,000 and United States savings bonds of $15,000 purchased in 1967, both payable on death to his daughter by a previous marriage.

   What are the widow's rights?

3. Assume that in January, 1967, the decedent with her own funds opened joint accounts with and trust accounts for her brother in the sum of $50,000. In March, 1967, she married and in April she died intestate leaving this $50,000.

   Does her husband have a right of election?

4. Assume that in August, 1967, a man died intestate, survived by his wife as his sole distributee. In July, 1967, he opened a $50,000 joint account with his brother. His widow contends that the account was entirely the decedent's funds and the brother contends that he contributed $20,000 towards the account.

   Who has the burden of proving the decedent's contribution and what is the widow's elective right?

5. Assume that a testator made a will in 1967 in which he left $20,000 to his wife. He had opened joint savings accounts with her after August 31, 1966, amounting to $80,000, $30,000 of which she claims she had contributed. He died in 1967 without issue. His net testamentary estate amounts to $140,000.

   Does the widow have a right of election?

126

ANSWERS TO MATHEMATICAL ESSAYS

1. The widow's share is one-half of $330,000 or $165,000, less the $80,000 in joint accounts payable to her. The balance of $85,000 will be paid by **X** contributing 60% or $51,000 and by **Y** contributing 40% or $34,000. EPTL 5-1.1(c)(1).

2. Under EPTL 5-1.1(c)(1) she would have a right to elect to take one-third of $75,000, the net testamentary estate, or $25,000, since there is a descendant surviving. She is not entitled to share in the other property since under EPTL 5-1.1(b)(2) neither the insurance proceeds nor the United States savings bonds are includible in the estate to determine her elective share.

   Where a provision is made for the surviving spouse of a testator in his will executed after August 31, 1966, in the form of a trust with income for life, such spouse has the limited right to withdraw from the trust the sum of $10,000 or the elective share to which she is entitled, whichever is less. Such sum, however, is inclusive of any absolute testamentary provision or intestate share to which she is entitled and is payable from the principal of any trust, legal life estate or annuity created by such testamentary provision the terms of which remain otherwise effective.

3. NO. Under EPTL 5-1.1(b) the husband would have no right of election as against the $50,000 in the joint and trust accounts, for the reason that the transactions took place before the marriage.

   Where a person dies leaving a joint account opened or deposits made after August 31, 1966, in which both tenants had contributed, it shall be treated as a testamentary substitute "in the proportion that the funds on deposit were the property of the decedent immediately before the deposit or the consideration for the property held as joint tenants or as tenants by the entirety was furnished by the decedent."

4. Under EPTL 5-1.1(b)(3) the widow has the burden of establishing the proportion of the account contributed by the decedent. If she can prove that the account was entirely his funds, she will be entitled to one-half of $50,000 or $25,000. EPTL 5-1.1(c)(1)(B).

   If the widow is unable to prove that the account was entirely the decedent's funds, the widow will be entitled to one-half of $30,000 or $15,000, since the brother has admitted that he contributed only $20,000.

5. YES. If she can establish that she contributed $30,000 to the joint accounts, then for the purpose of EPTL 5-1.1(c) the estate amounts to $190,000 (the balance of $50,000 in the joint accounts plus $140,000 net testamentary estate). One-half of $190,000 is $95,000. Since the widow will receive $20,000 under the will and $50,000 from the joint accounts, under EPTL 5-1.1(c)(1)(B) she is entitled to a limited right of election of $25,000, i.e., the difference between $70,000 and $95,000.

In the event she cannot establish that she contributed $30,000 or any part thereof to the joint account, she would still have a right of election to receive $10,000 in addition to the $20,000 that she is receiving under the will and the $80,000 from the joint account. For the purpose of her election the estate amounts of $220,000, one-half of which is $110,000. Since she is receiving $100,000, as stated, her elective share is $10,000.

OBJECTIVE QUESTIONS

Please do not refer to any source materials in order to answer any of the following questions. The following questions should be answered with either "yes" or "no" in the space provided:

T died on May 1, 1964. By his will executed in 1952 he devised Blackacre to his brother **B**. He devised Whiteacre to his brother **B**, "but if **B** should die without issue then to my sister **S**." He left the bulk of his personal property, totalling over one-half of his estate after payment of debts, to the **M** Missionary Society. **T** was survived by only his father, **F**, his sister, **S**, and **D**, an adopted daughter of **B** who had been adopted in 1954. **B** had predeceased **T**.

1. Q. Can S contest any part of the bequest to the **M** Missionary Society? _____

2. Q. A will is revoked if:
   The testator executes another will expressly revoking the prior will. _____

3. Q. If S had been one of the two witnesses to the will, would the will have been, for that reason, invalid? _____

4. The testator, with the intent to revoke, writes "Cancelled" across the face of the will. _____

5. Q. Can F contest any part of the bequest to the **M** Missionary Society? _____

6. The testator, with the intent to revoke, directs a friend to burn the will and the friend does this. _____

7. Q. Does **D** take Whiteacre? _____

8. Q. Does **D** take Blackacre? _____

9. The testator executes a notarized certificate of revocation of the will. _____

B and S are brother and sister. S is unmarried and B is a widower with one daughter **D**. S executed a will in which she left all her property to **B**. **B** died in January 1970, and S died in March 1970. S was survived by her niece **D** and another brother **A**.

10. Would the answer to question 11 differ if **D** were adopted by **B**? _____

11. Is **D** entitled to any part of the estate left by **S**? _____

12. Would the answer to question 11 differ if **B** were the cousin of **S**? _____

13. Is **A** entitled to any part of the estate left by **S**? _____

T died on June 1, 1971, leaving a net probate estate of $110,000 and no interest in any other property and no powers of appointment. Pursuant to a will duly executed on October 1, 1968, **T** bequeathed $40,000 to **W**, his wife, $10,000 to **S**, his son, $10,000 to **F**, a friend, and the residue to **X** University. **S** and **F** are the only witnesses to the will. **T** is survived by **F**, **W**, and **S**.

14. Is **F** entitled to $10,000 only? _____

15. If **T** had died intestate, would **W** be entitled to take one-third of the net estate? _____

16. Is **X** University entitled to the residue? _____

17. If the will is admitted to probate, is **W** entitled to take $55,000? _____

18. Is **S** entitled to $55,000? _____

19. Is **S** entitled to $10,000 only? _____

20. May **S** and **F** testify as witnesses, regarding the execution of **T**'s will? _____

21. Q. In a contested probate proceeding is the burden of proving fraud on the proponent of the will? _____

22. Q. Does the failure to appoint an executor make a will void? _____

23. Q. When a testator has been prevent by fraud from revoking a will must the will be denied probate? _____

24. Q. Where a will was executed outside New York and was valid where executed, can it be admitted to probate in New York if it is in writing and subscribed and there is only one witness? _____

25. Q. Would a wife have a right of election against a husband's will where the will was executed by the husband in 1929 and where he executed a codicil in 1931 changing the executor and otherwise reaffirming the will? _____

26. Q. Can a will be validly executed when the witnesses do not see the testator sign the will? _____

27. Q. When a will has been lost can it be admitted to probate? _____

28. Q. When a will is last known to be in the possession of the testator is it presumed to be revoked if it cannot be found? _____

29. Q. May a document, executed with testamentary formalities, be admitted to probate, if its sole dispositive provision merely states that the maker's son is not to inherit "one penny of my estate"? _____

30. Q. Can a will be partially revoked by a writing of the testator executed with the same formalities as a will? _____

31. Q The priority order for qualification as a voluntary administrator is the same as that for Letters of Administration? _____

32. Q. If the decedent left a will, the estate cannot be settled under Article 13? _____

33. Q. A spouse with 2 children of the decedent would receive $10,000 plus one-half of the estate in an intestate distribution? _____

34. Q. A spouse with no issue or parents of the decedent would take the entire estate in intestate distribution? _____

35. Q. Real property is not subject to intestate distribution? _____

36. Q. Persons who cannot read or write the English language cannot qualify as voluntary administrators? _____

37. Q. A distribution to all the issue of the decedent in equal shares is known as a *per stirpes* distribution? _____

38. Q. In order to meet the $3,000 limitation under Article 13, Totten trusts, jointly owned property and U.S. Savings Bonds payable on death are not included? _____

39. Q. A creditor may become a voluntary administrator under the Article 13 SCPA procedure for settlement of small estates? _____

40. Q. The voluntary administrator must act without compensation? _____

Define the following terms on a separate sheet of paper. Please be as brief as possible.

41. Concurrent Jurisdiction

42. Exclusive Jurisdiction

43. Personal Jurisdiction

44. *In rem* Jurisdiction

45. General Jurisdiction

Describe briefly where Jurisdiction over the following items would be proper. (Proper Location)

46. Life insurance policy of a non-domiciliary

47. Shares of stock of a non-domiciliary

48. A debt of the decedent

49. Negotiable instrument

50. A suit against a corporation

Please list the following in the proper order of priority for eligibility to receive Letters of Administration (Insert the letter in Column B in the proper place in Column A.)

51.	(a) Brothers & Sisters
52.	(b) Children
53.	(c) Father and Mother
54.	(d) Surviving spouse
55.	(e) Creditors
56.	(f) Grandchildren
57.	(g) Other distributees preference to largest share.

58. In order to collect most assets, a fiduciary must normally obtain _____ from the New York State Tax Commission.

59. The order by the Surrogate granting Letters of Administration is called a _____ .

60. The person requesting Letters of Administration must cite all those having a right to letters _____ to that of the person so requesting.

61. The proceeding for Letters of Administration is initiated by the filing of a _____ .

62-64. Briefly describe the Anti-Lapse Statute as it is now used in New York State.

65. One of the glaring features of a tenancy in common when compared to joint tenancies is the absence of _____.

66. The rule described in question 73 is commonly called the _____ .

67. In order for a power of appointment to meet one of the prerequisites for validity, the property passing under the power must vest within _____ years after the death of the last measuring life.

68. One type of "testamentary substitute" is _____.

69. Property passing to a Husband and Wife as joint tenants with right of survivorship is known as _____.

70. In order to legally make a will, a person must be at least _____ years of age.

In New York State the will should be executed as follows:

71. signed at the physical _____ by the testator.

72. in the presence of at least _____ witnesses.

73. declared by the testator in the presence of the witnesses to be his
_____ .

74. Property devised to two or more persons with a right of survivorship is known as _____ .

75. In order to properly execute a will, a testator must have _____
_____ at the time of execution of the will.

OBJECTIVE QUESTIONS --- ANSWERS

1. No - EPTL 5-3.3. A sister cannot contest an excessive gift to charity.

2. Yes.

3. No - EPTL 3-3.3. The interest of a witness in a will as legatee or devisee does not invalidate the will.

4. Yes.

5. Yes - EPTL 5-3.3. Surviving issue or parents can, where the gift to charity exceeds one-half of estate, after debts.

6. No - Unless will is burned by friend in the presence and by the direction of the testator and proved by at least two witnesses, neither of whom was the said friend.

7. Yes - EPTL 2-1.3. An adopted child takes as a natural child would.

8. Yes - Child of deceased legatee or devisee brother or sister takes. EPTL 3-3.3. An adopted child is a child within 3-3.3.

9. No.

10. No - "Issue" under EPTL 3-3.3 includes adopted children.

11. Yes (see comments to #13.)

12. Yes - EPTL 3-3.3 prevents lapse only of dispositions to testator's predeceased siblings or issue.

13. No - The disposition to S's predeceased brother **B**, does not lapse, but vests in **D**, his issue that survived S. (EPTL 3-3.3 (a))

14. No - **F**'s disposition is voided and he is not a distributee.

15. No - **W**'s intestate share is $2,000 plus 1/2 of the residue EPTL 4-1.1

16. Yes - Although the residue ($60,000) exceeds 1/2 the estate, only parents and issue are qualified to contest. **W** is neither. S cannot contest because, under the limitations explained in (17) above, a successful contest will not produce a pecuniary benefit to him EPTL 5-3.3.

17. No - **W** may take $40,000 under the will as a maximum. Her elective share, 1/3 of the net estate, is $36,666.66 EPTL 5-1.1.

18. No - S's Disposition is voided because he is a beneficiary witness. As a distributee, he can take so much of his intestate share as does not exceed the voided disposition ($10,000). EPTL 3-3.3. In any event, $54,000 and not $55,000 is S's intestate share. EPTL 4-1.1. (See 15 Above)

19. Yes - (See 18 Above)

20. Yes - A beneficiary - witness is competent, and may be compelled to testify regarding execution. EPTL 3-3.2.

21. No -'The burden of proof is on the contestant on issues of undue influence, fraud and duress.

22. No - If no person is named executor in a will, an administrator with the will annexed (c.t.a.) will be appointed (SCPA 1418).

23. No - A constructive trust may be raised in favor of those persons who were intended to be benefitted by revocation.

24. Yes - EPTL 3-5.1.

25. Yes - The codicil republished the will.

26. Yes - EPTL 3-2.1 (a) (2)

27. Yes - SCPA 1407

28. Yes - There is a rebuttable presumption that he destroyed it with intent to revoke it.

29. Yes - EPTL 1-2.18

30. Yes - EPTL 3-4.1 (a), (1), (A), (B)

31. No.

32. No.

33. No.

34. Yes.

35. No.

36. Yes.

37. No.

38. Yes.

39. No.

40. Yes.

41. Jurisdiction of Surrogate's Courts of two or more counties in the same state.

42. Jurisdiction of one Surrogate's Court as to another in a different County in the same state.

43. Jurisdiction over the person.

44. Jurisdiction obtained because situs of property is within the county.

45. Jurisdiction to hear all subject matters.

46. County where policy is located.

47. County where shares of stock are located.

48. Domiciliary county of decedent or county where two or more domiciliaries (parties to the debt) reside.

49. Situs of instrument.

50. Place of principal office.

51. a

52. f

53. e

54. d

55. b

56. g

57. c

58. Tax Waivers

59. Decree

60. Equal or prior

61. Petition for Letters of Administration

62-64. See EPTL 3-3.3.

65. Right of survivorship.

66. Rule against Perpetuities.

67. Twenty One

68. Any one of: Totten Trust
Joint Account
Joint Tenancy
Tenancy by the Entirety
Gift-Causa Mortis

69. Tenancy by the entirety

70. Eighteen

71. End

72. Two

73. Will

74. Joint Tenancy

75. Testamentary capacity

CHAPTER VII

Obtaining Employment As a Paralegal

Every attorney is a prospective employer of a paralegal. But it is the large or so-called "major" firms, consisting of at least fifteen attorneys to more than one hundred in a single firm, which are the prime target for the paralegal seeking employment. Such firms exist throughout the United States, but it is in the larger cities where these firms have the resources to employ paralegals in great numbers.

As a matter of fact, the big law firms have been active in the training of paralegals many years before the paralegal concept became attractive to the formal training institutions, the universities and the proprietary business schools. Firms of this size are so set up that a paralegal operating under the supervision of an attorney can serve as an efficient and viable force in reducing the work load of the member attorneys. Although a reluctance to delegate still prevails to some degree in some of the largest firms, more and more attorneys are realizing that the use of paralegals saves them both time and money. Many tasks formerly performed by junior associates in large law firms are now being delegated to paralegals. To repeat some examples given earlier in this guide, paralegals are assigned substantive factual research in non-legal areas, digesting and summarizing depositions and transcripts, digesting documents, indexing documents, and drafting interrogatories. The performance of these tasks by paralegals is more profitable to the large firm: attorneys are freed to take on more substantive, purely "legal" work and a larger case load. The availability and the reduction in cost of legal services is an even more important and relevant issue in the public sector, where the low-income consumer is forced to seek legal redress free of charge. Nevertheless, the use of paralegals in the private sector is also relevant because it reduces the cost to the client: paralegal services are billed at lower rates than are attorney services.

The success of the paralegal movement among the large law firms is well known, and the paralegal is well-advised to seek out the largest firm in any geographical area when seeking employment. The interviews conducted by the large law firms are very different from those conducted by a small firm or by a single practitioner. When seeking

137

employment the paralegal should review the sample interviews at the end of this chapter and help himself be prepared for the type of law firm that is conducting the interview.

Preparing for a Job Interview

Before the actual interview, you should find out as much as you can about the firm either by a direct phone call or by using the lawyer directory which the central branch of a public library system is likely to shelve, and learn how many attorneys are in the firm and if the firm presently employs paralegals. If in fact the firm does employ paralegals it will not be necessary for you to devote any of your preciously limited interview time "selling" the need and advantage of the paralegal. A firm that has had experience with paralegals does not require an explanation for the role and use of paralegals!

On the other hand, the small law firm or the individual practitioner is frequently hostile to the paralegal movement and so they have not been a ready source of employment for the paralegal. And the irony of this is that the individual practitioner stands to gain the most economically from the presence of a paralegal in his office! It is known that the individual practitioner must gross approximately $40 an hour in order to make $30,000 a year. The significant factor in the gross income requirements is the limited hours per year that an attorney can work. The American Bar Association has determined that the average attorney has only 1,385 billable hours. If the attorney realized that his time is worth anywhere from $40 to $75 per hour and even more, then it is in the attorney's best interest to get assistance in the mechanical work in order to open up more billable hours for the attorney. The sample interviews conducted in the small office will indicate clearly the different approaches the paralegal job seeker must pursue.

The paralegal training institutions for the most part maintain placement services as a feature of their programs. The procedure of these placement offices is to send several resumes to the law firm which has expressed interest in employing a graduate of the program. After selecting a few of these resumes the law firm conducts personal interviews with the applicants.

Given the competition among students going to the same law firm for an opening, the applicant would be well advised to determine the nature of the specialty of the firm. A paralegal who has worked in a hospital for two or three years would not be offering the background that would interest say, a strictly corporate practice firm. But a litigation firm specializing in personal injury work would be very interested in a paralegal who has a medical vocabulary and familiarity with medical procedures.

The Resume

The resume is an all-important element in the job search. A resume is meant to be a summary of the student's personal, scholastic and business experience. It must present the kind of information which will encourage the prospective employer to interview the student and perhaps ultimately employ him. The resume should be a thoughtfully and even creatively worded document which cries out to the employer, "Hire me!" The following information should be included:

1. Personal information—name, address, and marital status.
2. The applicant's educational background, including specific courses which are related to the job being offered.
3. Present position if it includes a course of study or employment.
4. Honors or publications, if any.

Again, we emphasize the importance of ascertaining the type of law practice or specialty of the firm before submitting a resume or going for an interview. In any case, the resume should relate to your expertise. Feature any factor which will favorably impress the reader of your resume. If the firm specializes in tax matters and you have published a paper dealing with taxation you certainly want to emphasize that fact. Should you have been listed in *Who's Who in American High Schools* (or colleges and universities) provide for a "professional listing" in your resume. Any activity in charitable or "Pro Bono" work should be listed under a heading of "community endeavors" or "volunteer work."

The resume, in short, must reflect a personalized approach meaning that it should be altered to suit the particular recipient.

Of course, your main source of employment will be attorneys. Unfortunately, many if not most attorneys are not yet in favor of the paralegal program and position so that you must be prepared to discuss both the professional and especially the economic advantages such a prospective employer can expect from employing you as a paralegal.

Seeking Out Sources of Employment On Your Own

Wherever and whenever possible, you should attend meetings and social events where attorneys are likely to be present so that you can come to make as many "contacts" as possible with attorneys. If you are unable to get an interview with an attorney, you might ask that same attorney to recommend someone who he thinks, or even knows, might have an office which would be suitable for a paralegal. The fact is that a resume or a telephone call from a person who knows the attorney will be received with more respect than a cold canvass call.

Relatives and close friends are potential sources of paralegal employment. Very often, a relative or friend operates a substantial business enterprise. People in control of large business organizations are always in need of legal services. A recommendation from someone who has a business relationship with the attorney will not fall on deaf ears. Many attorneys are eager to engage someone who has a personal relationship with an important client, present or potential. It would not be surprising that a major client recommending a paralegal would be pleased to deal with that paralegal who was under the control and supervision of the attorney. Ask friends and relatives if they are acquainted with an attorney on the chance that this may put you in the position just described.

Advertisements placed in legal journals, bar association bulletins, or law school publications may lead to employment and should be considered. It is incumbent upon the paralegal to read all of the local law publications and law bulletins. Many law firms advertise for assistance through the use of these journals.

The employment of paralegals is not restricted to the law offices. The paralegal should contact local insurance companies, district attorneys' offices, public prosecutors' offices, government agencies, banks, and title companies to name a few of the types of offices that are in need of paralegals or at least should consider the employment of paralegals.

Sample Interviews

The interviewing technique employed by the large law firm is totally different from the interviewing technique of the individual practitioner or small law firm. The major law firm knows precisely in what area the paralegal will serve, and it is not necessary for the paralegal to convince the interviewer of the need of a paralegal. The small or individual practitioner will ask questions which generally indicate that they are not certain in which capacity a paralegal will be most useful. The following illustrations will bring some of these problems to light:

Fact Pattern: Interviewer is a major Houston law firm with twenty-three partners, forty associates, and several paralegals.

Interviewer: Well, Miss Jones, it is nice meeting with you. Are you familiar with our firm?

Paralegal: Yes, I had the opportunity to look at the *Martindale-Hubbell**, and I noticed that your firm processes a great deal of anti-trust work with a specialty in litigation and admiralty.

Interviewer: It is the practice of our office to assign a paralegal to one of the partners, and the paralegal will be required to

_____
* A standard lawyer's directory.

Paralegal:	specialize in one particular field. Do you feel that it would be any problem for you if you are not working in your specialty?
Paralegal:	I did specialize in litigation; however, the program that I graduated from did have a complete legal research course together with an introduction to law. I do not think it would be difficult for me to learn the work. I would like the opportunity to do so.
Interviewer:	Could you tell me why you entered the paralegal field instead of continuing into law school?
Paralegal:	Law school would require a three-year study program, together with additional time in order to pass a bar examination. I am not in a financial position to wait four years to earn a living. I do feel that the paralegal position would be challenging if I had the opportunity to work with a firm as highly regarded as yours.
Interviewer:	Could you tell me what traits you have which you feel would be suited toward working in an office such as ours?
Paralegal:	I was assistant editor of my high school newspaper and continued writing when I attended college. Despite the fact that I was unable to complete my college education, I nevertheless was working in areas which required research and study and independence of thought.
Interviewer:	Where do you see yourself in five years?
Paralegal:	It is difficult to answer that question, but at the present time I feel that my position as a paralegal should be challenging and interesting, and I trust that it will result in a long-time relationship with a law firm such as yours.
Interviewer:	I have enjoyed talking with you, and I still have one or two other interviews. I would like to call you if I make a decision within the next few weeks.
Paralegal:	*If it is permissible, I would like the opportunity to call you in about a week or so, and in that way I will have a better idea of whether it will be necessary to seek employment in other areas.*

If at all possible, the paralegal should try to call the employer rather than have the employer call the employee. It is possible that the interviewer is not able to decide which applicant to accept, and very often a telephone call at a propitious time will seal his choice. Let us try the following line of questioning in the same interview:

Interviewer:	I notice that you are not a college graduate, and it is the practice of this office to hire only college graduates.

Paralegal: I respect that opinion. However, I would like to point out to you that during the time I left high school I was involved in a job experience which would perhaps be more suited to the legal profession than a college education. I served as a social worker in the Department of Welfare and had the opportunity over the past four years to deal with people on a highly personal level. My position mandated that I record a careful history of each person and conduct investigations into their finances, and part of my job required a personality evaluation. I did not drop out of college because of grades; however, it was a financial necessity which required me to seek employment.

Take the converse of this situation:

Interviewer: I understand that you were recommended by one of our clients. I must point out to you that it has been the practice of this office to train our legal stenographers and put them to more efficient use as paralegals. I notice that you do not have any experience in the law office field.

Paralegal: I have completed a study course as a paralegal and I am a graduate of Long Island University. My studies at LIU included courses in philosophy, history, government, communications, and English. I feel that my diversified training would permit me a broad perspective in the performance of a position such as the one you are looking to fill. I do not feel that the lack of law office training would be a disadvantage, and I would welcome the opportunity to prove this to you.

Fact Pattern: The Interviewer is an individual practitioner with one law associate and has never hired a paralegal before.

Attorney: Mr. Jones, I understand that my good friend, Bob Smith, asked you to give me a call. How can I help you?

Paralegal: Mr. Smith thought that perhaps you might be in a position to find use for a qualified paralegal. Mr. Smith tells me that you are a very busy attorney and perhaps I could be of assistance to you.

Attorney: How many words a minute can you type?

Paralegal: My training is more sophisticated than that of a secretary and I do not do any typing. I do dictate to a secretary or to recording equipment, and I feel that I will be in a posi-

Attorney:	How can you help me in my legal work? You are not an attorney.
Paralegal:	That is true. However, I have had extensive study in legal research and I am certain that if you give me the opportunity, you will see that I will be in a position to save you many research hours. I also will be able to draft documents and prepare legal pleadings.
Attorney:	I see on your resume that you specialized in estates and wills. A great deal of my practice is in contracts.
Paralegal:	The training that I had in estates and wills was broadly based, and I noted that many problems in contracts did come up in wills and estates. Take, for example, a will which is to some extent a contract. Many of the basic rules of law would apply equally to both.
Attorney:	How much does a paralegal make?
Paralegal:	In the major cities, the large law firms start a paralegal for $10,000 or more. I know that here in Ann Arbor you probably would not be interested in starting a paralegal at that salary. I would like to start in the neighborhood of $8,500, and I think that in a short period of time I will be able to prove my value to you.
Attorney:	Are you also familiar with office equipment common to law offices, and can you undertake law office administrative duties?
Paralegal:	I have some training in law office management. While it was not a major part of my specialty, I have had enough instruction in this area to readily carry out whatever management functions you will require.
Attorney:	Let me think about my need for a paralegal, and I will get back to you.
Paralegal:	Thanks so much for giving me this opportunity to meet with you. I will look forward to hearing from you. Thanks again.

The difference between the large and small office becomes clear. The attorney in this latter setting is not certain what a paralegal can or should do so that considerable discussion is necessary to fill him in and arouse his interest, something that will happen if he can be convinced that it is in his interest to employ a paralegal.

It will no doubt be helpful for the reader to review the model resumes which we reproduce to conclude this chapter. A careful study of these samples will reveal a pattern of repeated similarities which suggest what your own resume should reflect.

SAMPLE RESUMES

GEORGE FORBES
345 Lakeland Ave.
La Junta, Colorado 81050
(303) 589-2275

Synopsis: Seeking a position with a Banking or Finance Corporation in a Para-Legal or Management position. Have received extensive training in Real Estate and Mortgages and have had previous office experience in a supervisory capacity.

Education: Long Island University Graduate School of Business, Brooklyn, New York. Presently pursuing M.B.A. (evening division)

May 1975 Lawyers Assistance Program. Intensive twelve week program in Real Estates and Mortgages (150 hours) and Legal Research (46 hours).

Marist College, Poughkeepsie, New York. June 1969 B.A. in Business Administration. Honors: Business Seminar.

Experience: *General Motors Distributors Corp.,* Smithtown, NY. July 1969-January 1975 Credit Representative.

Supervision and coordination of field and office personnel in area of consumer loans and dealer inventories.

I.B.M., Poughkeepsie, New York. September 1968-May 1969 Computer Operator.

Operation and programming of accounting department computer model 360 mod 65.

State Park Commission, Hempstead, N.Y. Summer 1966-1968 Landscaper.

Maintenance and operation of golf course and its equipment.

References upon request.

SARA R. BROWN
25 Hemptor Road
Plymouth, New Hampshire 03264
(603) 634-1112

SYNOPSIS

Young woman seeking career in the legal field. Completed an intensive Lawyer's Assistant Program sponsored by Long Island University, specializing in Litigation. Perceptive and willing to learn.

EDUCATION

Spring 1975 - Lawyer's Assistant Program, Long Island University, Brooklyn, New York, co-sponsored by the National Center for Paralegal Training. Intensive 12 week 200 hour course, including 46 hours Legal Research.

B.A. 1972 - University of Bridgeport, Bridgeport, Connecticut. Psychology major with minor in Sociology.

Fall 1971 - University of Copenhagen, Denmark. Studied Social Sciences.

WORK EXPERIENCE

1972-1974 - Law firm of Smith, Block, Karsh, Morton and Harrington, 128 Broadway, New York. Duties included indexing documents, reception and client charges.

VOLUNTEER WORK

Worked on many Tutorial Programs for problem children in the Bridgeport area throughout Junior and Senior years in college.

SPECIAL INTERESTS

Have traveled throughout Western and Eastern Europe and Middle East during summers of 1969, 1970, and Fall of 1971.

Avid art collector of original signed lithographs and etchings by Boulanger, Dali, and Miro.

LAUNA D. HELLER
680 Morning Terrace Rd.
Livingston, New Jersey 07039
(201) 992-4456

Objective: To obtain a challenging paraprofessional position in law. Can offer recent intensified legal training with diversified academic and extracurricular background.

Education: *Long Island University,* Brooklyn, New York Lawyers' Assistance Program, May 1975. Specialty in Litigation. Supplemented by techniques of Legal Research, i.e.: preparation of briefs, memoranda and source material bibliographies.

Cedar Crest College, Allentown, PA 18104. Bachelor of Arts Degree in American Studies, May 1974. Concentration is American Politics. Women's Athletic Association Award Recipient.

Activities: *Current Alumnae Representative.* Women's College Study Consortium sponsored by Douglass College.
Senior Class President. Senior Class Pledge Fund initiator and co-chairperson.
Junion Class Vice-President. Annual All-College Spring Weekend Chairperson.
Sophomore Class Secretary.
Admissions Aide/Recruiter for Cedar Crest College.
Varsity Tennis Team, four years.
Team Manager and *Intramural Coordinator,* two years.
Politics Club.

Employment:

Livingston Board of Education 11 Foxcroft Drive Livingston, NJ 07039	September 1974-February 1975: Substitute Teacher 1970-1973 (college vacations): Gal Friday; Receptionist
Gatewood Motel Route #35 South Mantoloking, NJ	May 1974-September 1974: Switchboard Operator; Hostess Cashier; Reservationist
Cedar Crest College Allentown, PA 18104	1970-1974 (academic years): Library Assistant; Professional Aide for Doctoral Study

JOSEPH T. SCELLFO
56 Forrest Avenue
Whitman, Massachusetts 02382
(617) 447-9132

Synopsis: Recent college graduate seeking an opportunity to work as a legal assistant. Concentrated training in the fields of Estates, Trusts, Wills, and Legal research. Very interested in the field of law, with a willingness to learn.

Education: *Long Island University,* Brooklyn, New York. Spring 1975 - Lawyer's Assistant Program. Estates, Trusts and Wills (150 hours). Legal research (46 hours). Program included estate planning, preparation of wills and trusts, and Federal and State tax returns.

Boston College, Chestnut Hill, Massachusetts. B.A. 1974. Major in Biology, Minor in Political Science.

Work Experience: May 1974-January 1975 and Summers of 1971, 72, 73: Town of Whitman, Department of Public Works, Water Department. Construction worker.

1968-1974: Great North Supermarket, Abington, Massachusetts. Part-time bundle boy, cashier, assistant night manager.

Summer 1970: Whitman Foundry, Whitman MA.

1971-1974: Part-time work for Seaside Food Services while attending college. Cook.

References: Furnished upon request.

FRANCIS BEDELL
111 Broadview Avenue'
Jacksonville, Florida 32211
(904) 632-3670

Synopsis: Recent college graduate with Political Science and Business background desires job in the legal or financial community utilizing training obtained at a university sponsored Paralegal Program. Can offer specialized training in Estate, Trusts and Wills, legal research and previous office experience.

Education: *Long Island University,* Brooklyn, New York. Spring 1975, Lawyer's Assistant Program. Intensive program with specialization in Estates, Trusts and Wills (150 hours) and Legal Research (46 hours).

Ohio University, Athens, Ohio 45701. 1974-B.A., Government. Concentration in Business with courses in Business Law, Economics, and Accounting.

Honors: Dean's List, Recipient of University and President's Award Scholarship

Activities: Member of the Ohio University Pre-Law Club.

Work Experience: January 1975, The Reader's Digest Association, Inc., Pleasantville, New York. Worked on annual sweepstakes promotion.

June 1974, Mylott temporary services, White Plains, New York. Various office duties in the following companies: I.B.M., Frank B. Hall Co., Inc., General Foods Corp., Kane-Miller Corp., Pepsico Corp. and Technicon Corp.

Summers 1972-1974, Macys, New York, New York. Sales.

Academic Year 1972-73, Ohio University. Worked with Audio-Visuals in the Learning Resource Dept.

Summers 1967-1971, Greenport Summer Day School, Mamaroneck, New York. Counselor at summer camp.

References: Furnished Upon Request.

LEONARD P. MATUOZZI
245 William Street
Albany, N.Y. 12201
Phone: (518) 485-6985

Synopsis: College graduate with specialized training in Estates, Trusts, Wills, and Legal Research seeking a challenging position as a legal assistant. Can offer an enthusiastic interest in law and a willingness to learn.

Education: *Long Island University,* Brooklyn, New York - Lawyer's Assistant Program. Intensive 12 week program including Estates, Trusts, and Wills (150 hours) and Legal Research (46 hours). May 1975.

State University of New York at Albany, Albany, New York - B.A. in Sociology, minor in History. May 1975.

Work July-December 1974: Merrill Lynch, Pierce, Fenner and Smith,
Experience: Inc., New York, New York. Responsibilities included reviewing and processing of expense reports of company employees.

1970-1973: Various Summer Work while attending college including stock clerk for supermarket chain and factory work.

References: Furnished upon request.

WENDY S. WARREN
100 Clinton Avenue Apt. 4B
Columbus, Ohio 43211
(614) 651-4821

Objective: College graduate interested in position as a legal assistant with a legal department of an investment house or private law firm. Can offer specialized training in Corporations, Legal Research, and a desire to learn.

Education: Long Island University, Brooklyn, New York. May 1975, Lawyer's Assistant Program. Intensive 12 week program with specialization in Corporate Law (150 hours) and Legal Research (46 hours).

Ohio State University, Columbus, Ohio. December 1974, B.A. Social Sciences. Concentration in Sociology with minors in Psychology and Economics.

Experience: January 1975, December 1973. Part-time volunteer work for *Judge John P. Fredlund,* Albany, New York. Duties included assistance in case work.

Summer 1973, *City Engineers Department* - Bureau of Safety Inspection, Syracuse, New York. Duties included making out building contracts, clerical and secretarial work.

Summers 1970-1972, *Onondaga Community College,* Syracuse, New York. Secretary.

Skills: Experienced office worker.

References: Furnished upon request.

WILLIAM A. RYDER
15 Paulding Avenue
Chicago, Illinois 60622

Synopsis: Disciplined college graduate with Literary and Research background desires a position in the legal or financial community. Recently completed a recognized Paralegal Program specializing in Real Estate and Mortgages.

Education: Long Island University
Brooklyn, N.Y.
Lawyer's Assistant Program, Spring 1975
Certificate of Real Estate and Mortgages, 150 hours in course study and 50 hours in legal research.

Loyola University of Chicago
Chicago, Ill.
M.A. Program, 30 completed graduate credits, area of concentration: Greek.

Iona College
New Rochelle, N.Y.
B.A. *cum laude,* 1971.
Area of concentration: Classical and Modern Languages.

Honors: Dean's List, all semesters, Iona College Honors Program, Member, Sigma Delta Epsilon National Honor Society.

Languages: Fluent in French and Spanish; for research purposes, German and Latin.

Work Experience: 1967-Present, Have financed college and graduate school in restaurant service - Howard Johnson Restaurant, 460 South Broadway, Tarrytown, N.Y. Through the years, have performed in all aspects and functions of a small but lucrative business: Worked and supervised fellow employees as a waiter, host and cook in addition to various day-to-day supply, ordering, and bookkeeping duties.

MICHAEL MILONE
28 Main St. - Box 3
Danbury, Conn. 06810
(203) 743-8660

Objectives: Recent graduate of Lawyer's Assistant Program, seeking work as a paralegal, preferably in the field of Estates, Trusts and Wills. Able to perform in a diligent, responsible manner.

Work Experience:

Jan. 1975-April 1975 - *Income Tax Preparer* for Kenneth H. Danielson, Inc., Hempstead, N.Y. Familiar with Federal, State and City tax forms.

Oct. 1974-Dec. 1974 - *Salesman* for Whitmore House Corp., Danbury, Conn. Employed in the sporting goods department.

June 1970-June 1974 - *Salesman/Supply Controller* for Frank Lane Auto Parts, White Plains, N.Y. Duties included working in a supervisory capacity.

Education:

Spring 1975. Long Island University - Brooklyn, N.Y. Lawyer's Assistant Program (co-sponsored by the National Center for Paralegal Training). Specialization in Estates, Trusts and Wills with training in Legal Research.

Sept. 1974-Dec. 1974. H & R Block's course on income tax preparation. Danbury, Connecticut.

June 1973. Adelphi University - Garden City, N.Y. B.A. Cum Laude, Biology.

Honors: National Historical Honor Society - Phi Alpha Theta - Zeta Delta Chapter.

ROBERT E. FASANO
887 E. 36 St. Apt. 4
Portland, Maine 04104
(207) AL4-8767

Synopsis: Veteran interested in management training program in bank with goal of working in corporate finance section.

Education: Long Island University, Brooklyn, New York
Spring 1975 - Lawyer's Assistant Program
Intensive 12 week program with specialization in Corporation Law (150 hours) and Legal Research (46 hours). Corporation study included thorough familiarization with New York Business Corporation Law and Going Public procedures along with extensive outside assignments.

University of Miami, Coral Gables, Florida 33134
June 1968 B.A. Psychology, Minor in French
Member Pi Delta Phi French Honor Society.

Work Experience: May 1971 - February 1975, Taxicab Driver, 161 W. 212 St., New York, New York 10011 (212) WA9-3676.

While in college worked part time as bus boy during school year and room clerk during summers.

Military Experience: December 1968 - December, 1970, United States Army SP/5, Medical Company. Worked in Preventive Medicine Division as Assistant Researcher.

References: Furnished upon request.

SUSAN GOLDSTEIN
443 Cedar Lane
Marion, Kansas 66861

Synopsis: Enthusiastic legal assistant seeking employment in a private law firm or a corporation. Proficient in corporate law and legal research.

Education: Long Island University, Brooklyn, New York, 11201. Lawyer's Assistant Program. Corporations (150 hours), Legal Research (46 hours). 1975.

New York External Degree Program, B.A., History. 1975.

Experience: Winter 74 - Brandy's Restaurant, Athens, Ohio - Waitress.

Winter, Spring 73 - Kappa Delta House, Athens, Ohio - Cook.

Winter, Spring 73 - S.T.E.P. Program, Athens, Ohio, - tutored Appalacian Underprivileged children.

Spring 72 - campaigned Presidential elections.

Summer 72 - Abraham & Strauss, Hempstead, New York - salesgirl.

References Furnished upon Request.

KATHLEEN EVANS

46-28 286th Street
Greenpoint, NY 11222

Telephone
(212) 928-0029

CAREER OBJECTIVE

Seek position as a legal paraprofessional utilizing intense training in corporations and legal research; previous office experience; and an enthusiastic interest in Law.

EDUCATION

2/75-5/75   Long Island University
Lawyer's Assistant Program
200 hour course including extensive training in Corporations (150 hours) and Legal Research (46 hours).

9/72-2/75   New York University - Bachelor of Arts
Majored in Journalism, specialized in Public Relations, minored in History. (2½ year graduate) (3.4 cumulative index)
Sigma Delta Chi (Professional Journalistic Society) Pre-Law Society, Secretary and Treasurer of the Public Relations Student Society of America - New York Chapter; Kappa Tau Alpha (National Society Honoring Scholarship in Journalism).

WORK EXPERIENCE

7/74-9/74   American Telephone & Telegraph Company - Public Relations Assistant
Conducted a research project which involved: researching the topic, writing a questionnaire, conducting over 50 interviews, coding the results, writing a descriptive report on my findings, writing an article for the *Bell Telephone Magazine* on my findings.

2/74-4/74   Hibbert & Daniels
Receptionist

ACTIVITIES

Promotions-(9/74)

One of five NYU students to form our own public relations organization. Engaged in volunteer public relations for non-profit clubs and companies:

Cabal, NYU theater group
University Christian Foundation
Jewish Culture Foundation
Hospital Audiences, Inc.
Symphony of the New World

Children's International Summer Village-(2/74-6/74)

Publicity campaign:
wrote news releases, put together a press kit, contacted editors of newspapers and magazines.

Extensive Writing Experience-

Wrote articles for the *Washington Square News,* NYU yearbook staff, Editor of *HAI Highlights,* Hospital Audiences Newsletter.

CHAPTER VIII

Most Often Asked Questions

In this chapter we attempt to answer the kinds of questions which are most often asked by men and women who are thinking about a career as a paralegal.

Question: How does the paralegal position differ from the job carried out by a secretary?

Answer: The secretary is trained to take shorthand and transcribe it quickly and correctly on a typewriter. The secretary is not trained in the legal concepts, legal procedures, and legal research. In all three of these areas the paralegal has become expert as a result of a paralegal training program. Since the job requirements of a legal secretary and a paralegal are completely different, their training and their qualifications are completely different from each other. Dictation and typing are not the hallmarks of the paralegal as they are of the legal secretary.

Question: Can a paralegal's position be used as a stepping stone toward law school admission?

Answer: Not in a significant way, yet it might prove somewhat helpful. Certainly, if you are able to gain acceptance at a credited law school in the first instance, you should do so. Almost all law schools now require impressive college grades together with relatively high law board scores. This probably eliminates a majority of the applicants. Most states do not recognize paralegal training as a prerequisite for taking bar examinations. Nevertheless, there is small doubt that time devoted to training in the law in any area, including, if not especially, paralegal programs, will impress law school admission boards to the extent that it may play at least a small part in their acceptance considerations.

Question: Must you be a college graduate to become a paralegal?

Answer: It is not necessary to have a college degree or college background without a degree. However, many of the universities which offer paralegal programs do require a four year college degree for admission. At least the major law firms in the larger cities also have a preference for paralegals who are also college graduates.

Question: Is typing ability or skill necessary for a paralegal?

Answer: It is our opinion that a paralegal not offer herself/himself as a typist and deny being able to type! There are, however, still many attorneys who will prefer, if not insist upon, typing from the paralegal. Our own judgment in the matter is that the job requirement for a paralegal does not include secretarial skills.

Question: What is the lawyer's reaction to paralegals?

Answer: The multi-partner law firms which employ large numbers of people have been using paralegals for many years. They are committed to the paralegal movement and are the major source of employment for paralegals. The American Bar Association itself has enthusiastically endorsed the use of paralegals and the various organized bar associations throughout the country are slowly beginning to acknowledge their utility. Individual practitioners and small law firms, especially in the rural areas, are still essentially opposed to the paralegal movement.

Question: I note in the newspaper advertisements that legal secretaries make more money than paralegals. What, then, is the economic advantage of becoming a paralegal?

Answer: Careful reading of those same ads will reveal that a legal secretary with several years of *experience* earns more money than a *starting* paralegal. A beginning legal secretary will demand and receive substantially less salary than a starting paralegal. Beyond that, the opportunity for financial advancement is far greater for the paralegal.

Question: What is the highest salary figure a paralegal can expect?

Answer: Since the paralegal profession has not been in existence very long it is quite difficult to give an accurate figure. However, it is not unusual for a paralegal with five to seven years of experience to be earning between $15,000 and $20,000. Salary figures also reflect the size of the firm and the size of the city. Large firms in large cities generally pay higher salaries to their paralegals.

Question: What characteristics are essential for one to succeed as a paralegal?

Answer: For one thing, all the qualities which are important in any field where you are dealing with people are crucial here! Clients, employers, and colleagues are all part of your life as a paralegal. Diligence, trustworthiness, sensitivity and imagination are all important personal characteristics which will contribute to the success of a paralegal as he/she works with people and problems.

Question: Does the client resent a non-lawyer handling his case?

Answer: In the first place, the paralegal does not actually "handle" the case. The paralegal may assemble information, conduct legal research and remain in constant communication with the client. It has been our own experience that the client is pleased to have someone give him enough time and attention to deal with the many questions which emerge during the processing of the file. Most clients do realize that the time of the attorney is valuable, and therefore expensive, so that the use of a paralegal is a saving to him in fee charges without any diminishment of services.

Question: Most paralegal programs appear to offer specialty training. What happens if you specialize in real estate and the only available job is with a firm which is a general practice operation but does no real estate work?

Answer: To begin with, most paralegal training, even in the specialized program, is general or basic. Most law firms will be aware that if you are trained in real estate, and not in wills or some other branch of the law, you will nevertheless be able to make the transitions necessary. Law books are always available and a review of the files will quickly enable a paralegal to "change specialties." The law has certain basic principles which run through all the so-called specialties. In short, the study of one specialty will not preclude entry into another legal specialty.

Question: Is there any future for the paralegal in the small law firm?

Answer: There are already a large number of law firms which are just beginning to hire paralegals and the trend is increasing in that direction. It is very probable that in the foreseeable future positions in the small firms will be as plentiful as they are in the large ones.

Question: How can I get a job when I have completed a paralegal study program?

Answer: Hopefully, the institution you were enrolled in for your course of study has an active placement service. Most, if not all, institutions offering paralegal programs do in fact have such a service. In any event, relatives and friends who have a business or social relationship with attorneys are a good "contact" source. Advertisements appear in local law journals and in bar association publications which should be utilized. Resumes sent to the attorney or to the personnel person in a firm may also produce results. Contacting local insurance companies, banks, and governmental agencies are all sources for paralegal employment. And of course there is the most obvious place, in the classified sections of newspapers. You should look under the categories of both "legal assistant" and "paralegals."

Question: I do not think that I would make a good paralegal. But the course looks interesting to me. Would you recommend the program just for general knowledge?

Answer: A good paralegal course is geared toward a job oriented situation. You could and should make better use of your time, energy and, not incidentally, funds, in other kinds of educational programs.

It makes little sense to take a paralegal course unless you are in the legal field or would want to be employed in that field.

Question: If I take a paralegal course of study, is it necessary for me to devote any additional time to the program or are the classwork hours themselves enough?

Answer: While every program is different, one can be certain that most university programs require anywhere from at least one to four hours a day of preparation.

Question: Will my training as a legal secretary help in studying in the paralegal program?

Answer: There is a great deal of difference of opinion about this. Our own judgment is that the familiarity with legal terms and legal proceedings will be helpful. There is no substitute for working law office experience. But it should be noted that many of the large law firms prefer a college graduate with a paralegal certificate rather than a legal secretary with moderate experience and the same degree.

Question: Can a paralegal go to court?

Answer: A paralegal in most jurisdictions may answer calendars, conduct research, and assist in courtroom proceedings. Generally, there are no courtroom privileges given to a paralegal that are not given to a lay person.

Question: Is there any difference between a paralegal and a legal assistant?

Answer: No.

Question: Is a legal administrator the same as a paralegal?

Answer: They are two separate jobs. A paralegal is a legal assistant and works in the capacity of assisting the attorney as described before. The administrator is a ministerial function related to the operation and business aspects of the law office.

Question: How do you tell your boss that the office is very inefficient?

Answer: Very carefully. I think it may be easier to tell your employer that the office could perhaps be run more efficiently if certain procedures and guidelines were followed.

Question: Will automatic typewriting equipment and computers have any effect on the future of the legal secretary or paralegal?

Answer: Automatic equipment, which is becoming a standard part of every law office, will increase the need for the paralegal and decrease the need for the legal secretary. Sophisticated dictating equipment permits the use of a typist rather than a legal secretary. Typists earn substantially less than legal secretaries and therefore, will be an economic advantage when used with a piece of equipment. An employer realizes that automatic equipment with legal information stored away and used in conjuction with a paralegal will make that task easier and more efficient. The knowledge and experience of the legal assistant, in many cases, will be merged into the computer and the memory banks of the automatic typewriters.

Question: What is the advantage of a Mag-Card typewriter?

Answer: The Mag-Card typewriters have a memory storage bank which will permit brief, legal memoranda, letter opinion, all types of forms, pleadings, wills, leases, deeds, collection letters, security agreements and time keeping records to be reproduced at a rate faster than any typist can type.

Question: What is word processing?

Answer: Word processing is merely a Madison Avenue term used to describe a concept which examines the total cost of producing text rather than just the cost of the equipment and the cost of the secretarial time involved. Using an office typewriter, the average secretary types approximately 1000 lines a day, spending about 1/3 of her productive hours doing this work. If she is earning only $105 a week or $21 a day, the net secretarial time cost for this typing is $7 a day or 7¢ a line. Word processing centers attempt to reduce this cost.

Question: What is text processing?

Answer: Text processing is the use of a digital computer and associated input and output equipment to prepare, correct, revise, store, and print out reports, letters, and other information. These computers may cost between $500 and $3,000 a month and nevertheless, may be less expensive than a pool of legal secretaries.

Question: Is dictating equipment cheaper to use than dictating to a secretary personally?

Answer: There is no dispute as to the efficiency of dictating equipment. Secretaries type at a much quicker rate from a tape or cassette than they can one to one. The major advantage is that the time of the attorney or the paralegal can be planned. The attorney can prepare work prior to going to court or going into a conference and the secretary can type it without interference from telephone calls, meetings, etc.

Question: What is a WATS line?

Answer: WATS is the Bell System's wide area tele-communication service. Businesses with geographically dispersed interests have come to depend upon WATS to help them keep in touch with clients, suppliers, and sources of information. This type of service is widely used in the business world. A law firm that makes numerous long distance telephone calls during a monthly period may wish to consider the WATS system.

Question: Should a paralegal use a speed letter or a memo type letter instead of a personally drafted letter?

Answer: Some attorneys believe that all letters should be individually typed in the interest of good taste and form. I believe that the cost of an attorney's or paralegal's time is paramount and it is in his client's best interest to reduce the time spent on correspondence. These memos are printed forms carrying the law firm's letterhead and space for a short handwritten note. They are enclosed in a window-type envelope which obviates the necessity of addressing them. The use of these letters avoids the necessity of calling in a secretary, composing and dictating a simple letter. The time of the secretary is also conserved and the end result is to obtain more billable hours. I believe these letters can be selectively used by all members of the law firm to good advantage.

Question: Do any law firms have more than 100 lawyers?

Answer: Chicago, Cleveland, Houston, Los Angeles, Philadelphia, San Francisco, Washington, and New York all have law firms with more than fifty partners. The total of partners and associates in most of these firms is in excess of 100 people.

Question: Is a paralegal included as part of "overhead?"

Answer: Yes. Overhead applied to a law office generally is all expenses excluding a partner's draw in the gross income.

Question: Can a paralegal actually prepare pleadings?
Answer: Yes.

Question: May an employee of a law firm who is not admitted to practice attend a real estate closing with a client of a law firm and close title without the actual presence of a supervising attorney?

Answer: No. A legal assistant may not engage in the unauthorized practice of law. Representing a client and closing title at a real estate closing would affect a client's legal rights and would be considered practicing law.

Question: Is it easier for a female paralegal to obtain employment than a male?

Answer: It has been our experience that there is no discernible difference between the male or female paralegal applications to a law firm. I am certain that there is some individual preference on the part of any given lawyer, however, this can either favor the male or female.

Question: Is it permissible for a paralegal to receive a percentage of a fee for referring a legal matter to the firm that employs the paralegal?

Answer: An attorney is not permitted to share a fee with a non-attorney. The paralegal clearly falls within this category. Any business referred to the attorney by the paralegal cannot be compensated for. If a paralegal is doing an excellent job then the attorney most probably would increase the salary of the paralegal or be considerate when a seasonal bonus time arrives. If the bonus is disproportionate to the salary, it could be construed as payment for the referral of a client and would be violative of the code of professional responsibility.

APPENDICES

APPENDIX I

NEW YORK STATE BAR ASSOCIATION
COMMITTEE ON PROFESSIONAL ETHICS
Subcommittee on Legal Assistants

GUIDELINES FOR THE UTILIZATION
BY LAWYERS OF THE SERVICE
OF LEGAL ASSISTANTS*

PREFACE

The abbreviations employed herein refer to the following citations:

EXAMPLE   *REFERENCE*

The Association or NYSBA = New York State Bar Association.

Code = Code of Professional Responsibility of the NYSBA effective January 1, 1970, as amended.

Canon 8 = Canon 8 of the Code.

EC 2-6 = Ethical Consideration 2-6 of the Code.

DR 2-106(A) = Disciplinary Rule 2-106(A) of the Code.

N.Y. State 603 (1968) = New York State Bar Association Unlawful Practice of Law Opinion 10 issued in 1968.

N.Y. State 603 (1968) = New York State Bar Association Ethics Opinion 603 issued in 1968.

---

*It will be noted that the term "legal assistant" is used by the organizations which sponsored the ethical codes presented here. The term is, nevertheless, inter-used with "paralegal," and it is this latter term which this Guide has adopted and used throughout. It is our belief that in time this will be the standard term used in the profession. (Printed with permission of the New York State Bar Association)

U.P.L. 10 (1968) = New York State Bar Association Unlawful Practice of Law Opinion 10 issued in 1968.

N.Y. City 603 (1968) = The Association of the Bar of the City of New York Ethics Opinion 603 issued in 1968.

N.Y. County 603 (1968) = New York County Lawyers' Association Ethics Opinion 603 issued in 1968.

In conformity with the language of the Code, the words "he" and "his," as used in these Guidelines, are to be construed as referring to lawyers and legal assistants of both sexes.

TABLE OF CONTENTS

tivities consists of the practice of the law, nor shall a lawyer share his legal fees with his legal assistant.

Guideline VI   The letterhead of a lawyer shall not include   8
the name of his legal assistant. A lawyer may permit his name to be stated on his legal assistant's business card, provided the legal assistant's capacity is clearly indicated.

Guideline VII   A lawyer shall require that his legal assistant   9
when dealing with his client, disclose at the outset that he is not a lawyer. He shall also require such disclosure at the outset when his legal assistant is dealing with a court, an administrative agency, attorneys or the public if there is any reason for their believing that he is a lawyer or associated with a lawyer.

Guideline VIII Except as otherwise provided by statute,   10
court rule or decision, rule or regulation of administrative agency, the propriety of the utilization by lawyers of the services of legal assistants shall be governed by opinions of the Committees on Professional Ethics and Unlawful Practice of the Law having Jurisdiction.

References to Opinions

Judiciary Law Section 478 and 484

Opinions.

PRELIMINARY STATEMENT

Value of Legal Assistants

The availability of legal services to the public at a price the public can afford is a goal to which the Bar is committed, and one which finds its support in Canons 2 and 8 of the Code. The employment of trained lay assistants furnishes a means by which lawyers may expand the public's opportunity for utilization of their servies at a reduced cost, while preserving more time for attention to purely legal questions and thus improving the quality of their services. With proper direction and supervision, legal assistants can perform a wide range of delegable tasks which do not require the independent exercise of a lawyer's judgment on the client's behalf. As of October 17, 1975, the New York Bar Foundation sponsored "Equal Justice Under Law Conference" and concluded:

> "Definitional niceties aside, it is clear that appropriately trained and supervised non-lawyers can be enormously helpful in assisting lawyers in fact-gathering, preparation of documents, organizing files, providing information and status reports to clients, and in a myriad of other tasks which are necessary to the efficient operation of a law office which do not require the independent exercise of an attorney's judgment. Particularly in the context of law office systems, paralegals can perform many duties which have traditionally (and for little more reason than tradition) been carried out by lawyers."

Purpose of These Guidelines

Although legal assistants have assumed roles in law-related work for some time, serious attempts to define their responsibilities and to establish suitable educational facilities have only recently been undertaken.

The rapid growth in the employment of legal assistants makes it important that both the lawyer-employer and the lay assistant be aware of the parameters within which the services of the latter may be utilized by lawyers. It is to this end that these Guidelines are directed. They are not intended to stifle the proper development and expansion of acceptable paralegal services and go no further than to state certain general principles and their applicability to particular situations as presently expressed in the Code of Professional Responsibility, various statutes, court rules and decisions, rules and regulations of administrative agencies, and opinions heretofore rendered by the Committees on Professional Ethics and on Unauthorized Practice of Law. It is recognized that the Guidelines are not static but are subject to modification from time to time as questions arise, or because of changes in statutes, rules or regulations, or by reason of new opinions of courts or relevant Bar Association committees.

While the responsibility for compliance with approved standards of professional conduct rests primarily upon members of the Bar, a legal assistant should understand what he may and may not do. The burden rests upon a lawyer who employs a legal assistant to educate the latter with respect to the duties to which he may be assigned and then to supervise the manner in which the legal assistant carries out such duties. However, this does not relieve the legal assistant from his independent obligations to refrain from illegal conduct. See, e.g., Guideline I. Additionally, and notwithstanding that the Code is not binding upon laymen, the very nature of a legal assistant's employment imposes an obligation upon him to use his best efforts not to engage in conduct which would involve his employer in a violation of the Code.

Scope of These Guidelines

These Guidelines are intended to apply to the employment and utilization by lawyers of the services of those lay persons now often designated as legal assistants, paralegals, law specialists, law secretaries, law clerks, qualified law students, and lawyers who are not admitted to practice law in the state of New York but who are employed by lawyers within the state. They are not intended to refer to laymen who are not acting as employees of lawyers, but who engage in activities permitted by statute, court rule or administrative rule or regulation.

GUIDELINE I

A LAWYER SHALL NOT PERMIT HIS LEGAL ASSISTANT TO ENGAGE IN THE UNAUTHORIZED PRACTICE OF THE LAW.

Commentary

Sections 478 and 484 of the Judiciary Law prohibit individuals who are not licensed members of the Bar of the State of New York (with certain exceptions hereinafter noted) from engaging in the practice of the law. Any person, including a legal assistant, who violates the statute may be punished for criminal contempt and his conduct may be enjoined. See Judiciary Law, Sections 750(B), 476-a and 476-b.

Canon 3 provides that:

"A lawyer should assist in preventing the unauthorized practice of law."

DR 3-101(A) mandates that:

"A lawyer shall not aid a non-lawyer in the unauthorized practice of law."

There is no all-inclusive definition of the phrase "practice of law." It has occasionally been referred to as an act requiring the exercise of "independent professional legal judgment." N.Y. State 304 (1973). It has also been defined as the performance of functions which involve the "application of legal principles to factual situations and thus requires the interpretation of statutes, administrative rules and decisional law." U.P.L. 15 (1972); U.P.L. 10 (1968). However, such language is imprecise and does not provide a universal standard for evaluating innumerable situations where the problem arises.

It has been left to the courts to determine, on a case by case basis, whether or not particular acts constitute the unauthorized practice of law. See Drinker, *Legal Ethics,* at page 66.

EC 3-5 treats the subject as follows:

"It is neither necessary nor desirable to attempt the formulation of a single, specific definition of what constitutes the practice of law. Functionally, the practice of law relates to the rendition of services for others that call for the professional judgment of a lawyer. The essence of the professional judgment of the lawyer is his educated ability to relate the general body and philosophy of law to a specific legal problem of a client; and thus, the public interest will be better served if only lawyers are permitted to act in matters involving professional judgment. Where this professional judgment is not involved, non-lawyers, such as court clerks, police officers, abstracters, and many govern-

mental employees, may engage in occupations that require a special knowledge of law in certain areas. But the
services of a lawyer are essential in the public interest
whenever the exercise of professional legal judgment is
required."

The rule is stated in ABA 316 (1967) and quoted in N.Y. County
641 (1975):

" . . . we do not limit the kind of assistants the lawyer can
acquire in any way to persons who are admitted to the
Bar, so long as the non-lawyers do not do things that lawyers may not do or do the things that lawyers only may
do."

Thus, members of the Bar, besides being subject to relevant statutory provisions, are obligated by their profession to make certain
that their paralegal employees do not transgress the rules governing
the practice of law.

For the underlying rationale see EC 3-1 through EC 3-6.

GUIDELINE II

A LAWYER MAY PERMIT HIS LEGAL ASSISTANT TO PERFORM CERTAIN FUNCTIONS OTHERWISE PROHIBITED WHEN AND ONLY TO THE EXTENT AUTHORIZED BY STATUTE, COURT RULE OR DECISION, OR ADMINISTRATIVE RULE OR REGULATION.

Commentary

Notwithstanding the restrictions imposed upon non-lawyers with respect to engaging in the practice of the law, certain exceptions exist by virtue of statute, court rule or decision, or administrative rule or regulation. Where such exceptions are created they of course prevail.

For example, the Judiciary Law provides that the prohibition against practicing law does not preclude certain law students in their senior or final year of law school or to certain law school graduates from performing various functions normally restricted to members of the bar provided they are performed under supervision of an attorney, pursuant to an approved program. Such individuals are permitted to act under supervision of an approved legal aid organization, or a corporation counsel or county attorney in family court proceedings, or a district attorney, provided designated conditions are met. Judiciary Law, Sections 474, 484.

Also, the General Rules of the United States District Court for the Eastern District of New York permit eligible law students who have completed legal studies amounting to at least two semesters to practice before those courts under certain stated conditions, among which are that the court approve the student, the person served consents in writing, an attorney supervises, assists and in court proceedings appears with the student, and the student receives no compensation from the person on whose behalf he renders services. General Rules of the United States District Courts for the Southern and Eastern Districts of New York, Rule 4.1. See, also, Rules Supplementing Federal Rules of Appellate Procedure, United States Court of Appeals, Second Circuit, Part II. Sec. 46(e).

In addition, the rules or regulations of certain administrative agencies permit laymen to appear in behalf of parties to proceedings before such agencies. For example, the Federal Administrative Procedure Act, Title 5, U.S.C. §555(b) authorizes federal administrative agencies to permit representation by non-lawyers.

GUIDELINE III

EXCEPT AS OTHERWISE PROVIDED BY STATUTE, COURT RULE OR DECISION, ADMINISTRATIVE RULE OR REGULATION, OR BY THE CODE OF PROFESSIONAL RESPONSIBILITY, A LAWYER MAY PERMIT HIS LEGAL ASSISTANT TO PERFORM SERVICES FOR HIM IN HIS REPRESENTATION OF A CLIENT, PROVIDED THE LAWYER:

A. Retains a direct relationship with the client;

B. Supervises his legal assistant's performance of his duties;

C. Remains fully responsible for such representation, including all actions taken or not taken in connection therewith by the legal assistant.

Commentary

EC 3-6 recognizes the value of utilizing the services of legal assistants, but provides certain conditions to such employment, viz:

"A lawyer often delegates tasks to clerks, secretaries, and other lay persons. Such delegation is proper if the lawyer maintains a direct relationship with his client, supervises the delegated work, and has complete professional responsibility for the work product. This delegation enables a lawyer to render legal service more economically and efficiently."

As stated in N.Y. County 641 (1975), quoting N.Y. County 420 (1953):

"What an employee, who is not a lawyer, does in the course of his employment by the law office is deemed a professional service by the law firm for which it is charged with full responsibility. Consequently, his work must be done under the supervision and direction of one or more lawyers in the firm; . . . "

In order to retain a "direct relationship" with the client, a lawyer need not be in contact with the client with any specified degree of regularity or frequency, nor is the language of EC 3-6 to be construed as contradicting any statutes, rules or administrative regulations which permit representation by persons who are not attorneys. The lawyer should, however, at all reasonable times be available for consultation by the client, and whenever in the course of supervising the legal assistant's work it appears that communication with the client is desirable he should act accordingly in the client's interest.

Of course, the obligations imposed upon a lawyer with respect to the services of his legal assistant do not in any way relieve the latter from his personal obligation to obey the law and his employer's instructions.

GUIDELINE IV

THE LAWYER SHOULD EXERCISE CARE THAT HIS LEGAL ASSISTANT PRESERVES AND REFRAINS FROM USING ANY CONFIDENCES OR SECRETS OF A CLIENT, AND SHOULD INSTRUCT THE LEGAL ASSISTANT NOT TO DISCLOSE OR USE ANY SUCH CONFIDENCES OR SECRETS.

Commentary

DR 4-101(D) provides, in part, that:

"(D) A lawyer shall exercise reasonable care to prevent his employees, associates, and others whose services are utilized by him from disclosing or using confidences or secrets of a client, . . . "

This obligation is emphasized in EC 4-2:

" . . . It is a matter of common knowledge that the normal operation of a law office exposes confidential professional information to non-lawyer employees of the office, particularly secretaries and those having access to the files; and this obligates a lawyer to exercise care in selecting and training his employees so that the sanctity of all confidences and secrets of his clients may be preserved."

See also N.Y. County 641 (1975) and N.Y. City 884 (1974). It should be noted that CPLR, Section 4503, provides that unless a client waives the right to assert the attorney-client privilege, neither the attorney nor his employee may disclose in evidence a confidential communication made between the attorney or his employee and the client in the course of professional employment.

GUIDELINE V

A LAWYER SHALL NOT FORM A PARTNERSHIP WITH A LEGAL ASSISTANT IF ANY PART OF THE FIRM'S ACTIVITIES CONSISTS OF THE PRACTICE OF LAW, NOR SHALL A LAWYER SHARE HIS LEGAL FEES WITH HIS LEGAL ASSISTANT.

Commentary

This Guideline is based upon the express provisions of DR 3-102 (A) and DR 3-103. In accordance with these rules, the compensation of a legal assistant may not include a percentage of the fees received by his employer, nor may the legal assistant receive any remuneration, directly or indirectly, for referring matters of a legal nature to his employer. Cf. N.Y. State 302 (1973); ABA 316 (1967).

DR 3-103 provides that:

> "(A) A lawyer shall not form a partnership with a non-lawyer if any of the activities of the partnership consist of the practice of law."

A lawyer may, however, include his legal assistants in a retirement plan, even though the plan is based in whole or in part on a profit-sharing arrangement. This is provided in the exception to DR 3-102 (A), above noted, which reads as follows:

> "(3) A lawyer or law firm may include non-lawyer employees in a retirement plan, even though the plan is based in whole or in part on a profit-sharing arrangement."

See also, N.Y. State 282 (1973); N.Y. City 884 (1974); ABA 325 (1970).

GUIDELINE VI

THE LETTERHEAD OF A LAWYER SHALL NOT INCLUDE THE NAME OF HIS LEGAL ASSISTANT. A LAWYER MAY PERMIT HIS NAME TO BE STATED ON HIS LEGAL ASSISTANT'S BUSINESS CARD, PROVIDED THE LEGAL ASSISTANT'S CAPACITY IS CLEARLY INDICATED.

Commentary

DR 2-102(A) (4) specifies what information may be given on a lawyer's letterhead. While the names of a lawyer's "associates" may be stated, "associates" are construed to mean "associate lawyers", and not to include non-lawyer employees. In N.Y. State 261 (1972), it was stated:

> "This committee sees no benefit to the public to be advised who is office manager, investigator or legal assistant in a law firm except in case of direct communication from such person, in which case such person may sign the letter and designate himself as such, and therefore there is no valid purpose to be served by permitting the inclusion of the name of a non-lawyer on a lawyer's letterhead. Such action would be improper."

See also, N.Y. City 884 (1974); N.Y. County 641 (1975).

As indicated in the Opinions cited above, a lawyer may permit his legal assistant to sign a letter on his employer's letterhead provided his non-lawyer status is clearly disclosed by an appropriate term, such as "legal assistant", "paralegal", "law clerk."

The business card of a legal assistant, which clearly identifies him as a legal assistant, may refer to the name, address and telephone number of his lawyer or law firm employer. The distinction between business cards and letterheads was drawn in ABA 909 (1966), summarized in N.Y. State 261 (1972) as follows:

> "In ABA Inf. 909 (1966) and 1000 (1967), that committee pointed out the distinction between the business card and the letterhead in that the card is the employee's card, basically designed to identify him and to state by whom he is employed, exactly as he would do in an oral statement. It is not the professional card of the lawyer or law firm. That committee, therefore, held that the reasoning with respect to a business card need not and should not be extended to the professional letterhead, and adhered to the earlier opinions that such listing on a lawyer's letterhead was improper."

176

It should be noted in connection with the above that it was held, in N.Y. City 454 (1938), that it would not be proper for an announcement to be circulated listing a non-lawyer as associated with a law firm because "associate" implies that the legal assistant is a lawyer admitted to practice in New York.

GUIDELINE VII

A LAWYER SHALL REQUIRE THAT HIS LEGAL ASSISTANT, WHEN DEALING WITH HIS CLIENT, DISCLOSE AT THE OUTSET THAT HE IS NOT A LAWYER. HE SHALL ALSO REQUIRE SUCH DISCLOSURE AT THE OUTSET WHEN HIS LEGAL ASSISTANT IS DEALING WITH A COURT, AN ADMINISTRATIVE AGENCY, ATTORNEYS OR THE PUBLIC IF THERE IS ANY REASON FOR THEIR BELIEVING THAT HE IS A LAWYER OR ASSOCIATED WITH A LAWYER.

Commentary

A lawyer should instruct his legal assistant to disclose at the beginning of any dealings with his client that he is not an attorney. Whenever any person dealing with a legal assistant has reason to believe that the legal assistant is a lawyer or associated with a lawyer, the legal assistant shall make clear that he is not a lawyer. Even if a legal assistant appears before an administrative agency or court in which a layman is entitled to represent a party, the legal assistant should nevertheless disclose his capacity to the tribunal if his employer is named as attorney of record. Routine early disclosure of non-lawyer status when a legal assistant is dealing with persons outside the law firm in connection with legal matters is necessary to assure that there will be no misapprehension as to the responsibilities and role of the legal assistant. Disclosure may be made in any way that avoids confusion. With respect to oral communications relating to legal matters, whether face to face or by telephone, the non-lawyer status of the legal assistant should be made clear. Common sense suggests a routine disclosure at the outset of conversation. N.Y. City 884 (1974).

If a legal assistant is designated as the individual in the office of a lawyer or firm who should be contacted, disclosure of his non-lawyer status should be made at the time of such designation.

A lawyer shall require that his legal assistant not communicate or cause another to communicate on the subject of the representation with a party known to be represented by a lawyer on that matter unless he has the prior consent of the lawyer representing such other party or is authorized by law to do so. See DR7-104 (A)(1).

GUIDELINE VIII

EXCEPT AS OTHERWISE PROVIDED BY STATUTE, COURT RULE OR DECISION, RULE OR REGULATION OF ADMINISTRATIVE AGENCY, THE PROPRIETY OF THE UTILIZATION BY LAWYERS OF THE SERVICES OF LEGAL ASSISTANTS SHALL BE GOVERNED BY OPINIONS OF THE COMMITTEES ON PROFESSIONAL ETHICS, AND UNLAWFUL PRACTICE OF THE LAW HAVING JURISDICTION.

Commentary

There is set forth in the Appendix attached hereto examples of what presently may and may not be done in the rendition of services by a legal assistant. The opinions cited apply only to the particular facts considered therein, and represent but a few of the many situations which may arise.

ADVICE ON QUESTIONS

Attorneys who desire further ethical guidance concerning their personal professional conduct in the operation of their law office as it relates to paralegal employees, may write to the Association's Committee on Professional Ethics, One Elk Street, Albany 12207, requesting the Committee to issue an ethics opinion. The letter should specifically state the issue involved and any additional facts which the inquiring attorney wishes the Committee to consider in its deliberations.

As a service to paralegals in the State of New York, the Association's Committee on Unlawful Practice of Law, when requested, will issue advisory opinions as to whether proposed activity of a paralegal in the course of employment by an attorney is or is not the practice of law. Such requests should be submitted in writing to the Association's Committee on Unlawful Practice of Law, One Elk Street, Albany 12207, and set forth the specific question and related facts which they wish the Committee to consider.

SUPPLEMENT

(This Appendix is intended to refer to particular factual situations and does not purport to be exhaustive.)

ADMINISTRATIVE AGENCIES
See Court Rules, Statutes

ADVICE TO CLIENTS

A legal assistant should not independently advise a client concerning his legal rights or duties. N.Y. State 44 (1967); N.Y. City 78 (1927-28), 884, (1974); ABA 316 (1967).

AFFIDAVITS
See Litigation

ANNOUNCEMENTS

It is improper for a law firm to send an announcement listing a legal assistant as "associated" with the firm. N.Y. City 454 (1938); N.Y. County 641 (1974).

BRIEFS
See Litigation

It is permissible to give a legal assistant credit for work performed on brief. N.Y. State 299 (1973); N.Y. City 884 (1974).

CALENDAR CALLS
See Litigation

CARD

A legal assistant's business card may refer to the name, address and telephone number of his lawyer-employer, provided his status is clearly revealed on the card. N.Y. State 261 (1972); N.Y. City 884 (1974); N.Y. County 641 (1974); ABA Inf. 909 (1966), 1000 (1967), 1185 (1971).

CONFIDENCES

A legal assistant is under a duty to preserve a client's confidences and

180

secrets. A lawyer-employer is under an obligation to exercise care in selecting and training his legal assistant to prevent improper disclosure thereof. DR 4-101(D); EC 4-2; see CPLR Section 4503; N.Y. County 641 (1974); N.Y. City 884 (1974).

COURT APPEARANCE
See Litigation

COURT RULES
See Administrative Agencies, Statutes

Eligible law students and others may appear in certain Courts subject to Court approval, general supervision by attorney, and consent of client. For example, see General Rules of United States District Courts, Southern and Eastern Districts of New York, Rule 4.1 for Eastern District of New York. See also Rules Supplementing Federal Rules of Appellate Procedure, United States Court of Appeals, Second Circuit, Part II Sec. 46(e). See also Rules of Practice before the Tax Court of the United States, Rule 2.

DEEDS

A legal assistant may prepare a deed, provided his lawyer-employer assumes responsibility for it. Cf. ABA 316 (1967).

DEPOSITIONS
See Litigation

DESIRABILITY OF EMPLOYMENT OF LEGAL ASSISTANTS

The delegation of tasks to legal assistants in proper circumstances "enables a lawyer to render services more economically and efficiently." EC 3-6.

DISCLOSURE

A legal assistant's status should be disclosed at the outset of his contact with his employer's client, any attorney, or member of the public. N.Y. City 884, (1974).

EMPLOYEE BENEFIT PLANS	It is not proper for a legal assistant to provide advice or services of a legal nature in connection with the design, drafting or adoption of employee benefit plans. UPLC Advisory Opinion No. 28 (1975).
INTERVIEWING WITNESSES See Litigation	
LAW STUDENTS See Court Rules	Certain law students and law school graduates may, under supervision, engage in law-related activities in the work of a legal aid organization, in certain Family Court proceedings, and in assisting District Attorneys, Judiciary Law, Section 478, 484.
LEGAL FEES See Retirement and Pension Plans	A lawyer or law firm may not share legal fees with a non-lawyer, subject to certain exceptions. DR 3-102 (A).
LETTERHEADS	A legal assistant's name may not be listed on a lawyer's letterhead. N.Y. State 261 (1972); N.Y. City 884 (1974); N.Y. County 641 (1972); ABA Inf. 845 (1965); See DR 2-102(A)(4).
LETTERS	A legal assistant may sign letters on the lawyer's letterhead, when he is clearly designated as a non-lawyer. N.Y. State 255 (1972); N.Y. City 884 (1974). See N.Y. City 837 (1958) and N.Y. County 420 (1953).
LITIGATION See Administrative Agencies, Briefs, Court Rules, Statutes	A legal assistant may answer calendar calls where no argument is necessary, investigate questions of law, assist in the preparation of briefs, affidavits, subpoenas, pleadings, interview prospective witnesses, assist in preparation for trial, serve and file notes of issue, notices of trial. N.Y. State 44 (1967), 299 (1973); N.Y. City 78 (1927-28), 884 (1974); N.Y. County 641 (1974);

ABA 316 (1967).

In connection with court proceedings, a legal assistant may not argue motions, conduct depositions of a witness; conduct examinations before trial, or examinations in supplementary proceedings, unless permitted to do so by statute or rule of court. N.Y. State 44 (1967), 304 (1973); N.Y. City 884 (1974); N.Y. County 641 (1974); ABA 316 (1967).

MORTGAGE CLOSINGS

A legal assistant may attend mortgage closings, with limited responsibilities. N.Y. State 44 (1967).

MOTIONS
See Litigation

NOTICES ON TRIAL
See Litigation

"NO FAULT"
INSURANCE CLAIMS

It is unlawful for a legal assistant to determine which insurance forms should be selected, or to decide whether a "No Fault" claim should be filed. UPLC Advisory Opinion No. 20 (1974).

PARTNERSHIP

A lawyer may not form a partnership with a legal assistant if any of the activities of the partnership consist of the practice of law. DR 3-103; EC 3-8.

PLEADINGS
See Litigation

PREPARATION FOR
TRIAL
See Litigation

PRETRIAL CONFERENCES

It is unlawful for a legal assistant to participate in discussions concerning liability, damage or other questions of law at pretrial conferences, unless permitted to do so by statute, rule of court, or rule or regulation of an administrative

183

agency. UPCL Advisory Opinion No. 19 (1974).

PROFESSIONAL
JUDGMENTS

A legal assistant may not engage in conduct involving the exercise of a lawyer's professional judgment. EC 3-5; N.Y. State 44 (1967); N.Y. City 78 (1927-28), 884 (1974); N.Y. County 641 (1974).

RETIREMENT AND
PENSION PLANS

A legal assistant may be included in the retirement plan of a lawyer or law firm, even though the plan is based in whole or in part on a profit-sharing arrangement. DR 3-102(A)(3); EC 3-8; N.Y. State 282 (1973); N.Y. County 884 (1974); ABA 325 (1970).

STATUTES
See Administrative Agencies, Court Rules

See Judiciary Law Sections 478, 484.

SUPERVISION

A legal assistant's work must be under the supervision of a lawyer. N.Y. County 641 (1975) and 420 (1953).

SUPPLEMENTARY
PROCEEDINGS
See Litigation

TELEPHONE LISTING

It is unlawful for a legal assistant to be listed in a classified telephone directory under the heading of "Lawyers" or "Attorneys". UPL Advisory Opinion No. 22 (1974).

WILLS

A legal assistant may not supervise the execution of a will. N.Y. State 343 (1974).

WORKMEN'S
COMPENSATION

It has been held that a statute authorizing a licensed lay representative to appear on behalf of claimants before a Workmen's Compensation Board "does not speak of nor does it authorize the representation by a licensed lay representative of an attorney at law representing such claimant," and that such latter activity would constitute the unlawful practice of law. U.P.L. Advisory Opinion No. 16 (1973). (This opinion is under reconsideration by the Committee on Unlawful Practice of Law.)

ZONING APPEALS

A legal assistant may not handle cases before a zoning board of appeals where legal principles are involved. UPL Advisory Opinion No. 10 (1968).

RE: Informal Opinion 1278   November 19, 1973
      Professional Secretary Signing
      Correspondence on Firm Letterhead
      as Jane Doe, P.L.S. Legal Assistant

This is in response to your inquiry relating to your secretary who has been certified as a member of the Legal Assistant Section of the National Association of Legal Secretaries (International). Your inquiry is whether there is any ethical objection to your permitting to sign correspondence with her name followed by "PLS Legal Assistant."

We have concluded that although no violation of any disciplinary rule is involved, and the matter is up to you to decide as you think right, it would seem to us preferable for you not to permit your secretary to use the phrase "Legal Assistant." "PLS," which stands for Professional Legal Secretary, seems to us entirely proper.

Ethical Consideration 2-13 says that: "In order to avoid the possibility of misleading persons with whom he deals, a lawyer should be scrupulous in the representation of his professional status." (He should also be scrupulous in the representation of his professional status.") He should also be scrupulous in the representation of the status of his employees; for whose conduct pertaining to his professional conduct he is responsible (see Preliminary Statement to the Code of Professional Responsibility), and in the judgment of this Committee the use of the phrase "Legal Assistant" connotes a training and a status that is different from that of a legal secretary, even if she has been certified as aforesaid. However, as you may know, standards are at this very time in process of development regarding the educational standards for paraprofessionals who may be described as "Legal Assistants." See also Informal Opinion 1185. In view of this uncertainty as to who are properly to be termed "Legal Assistants," we think you would be well advised at least to defer permission to your secretary to sign as your "Legal Assistant."

Informal Opinion 1185   May 31, 1971
'Legal Assistant' on Business Card

You have inquired whether it is ethically proper to designate a paralegal employee, whose duties consist of interviewing witnesses, obtaining copies of hospital records, court records and other contacts outside the office, as a "Legal Assistant" on a business card. It is the opinion of the Committee that this would be proper, assuming that the duties which are performed by the individual are those which can properly be performed by a layman under the direction of a lawyer.

The term "Legal Assistant" appears to be coming into general use as connoting a lay assistant to a lawyer, as evidenced by its use in the title of the American Bar Association's Special Committee on Legal Assistants. EC3-6 states that:

> "a lawyer often delegates tasks to clerks, secretaries and other lay persons. Such delegation is proper if the lawyer maintains a direct relationship with his client, supervises the delegated work and has complete professional responsibility for the work product. This delegation enables a lawyer to render legal service more economically and efficiently."

Formal Opinion 316 is to the same effect.

Informal Opinion 909 permits the designation on a business card of an employee of a law firm who does investigation work for that firm as an "Investigator". By the same reasoning, it would appear to be proper to designate a legal assistant as such on a business card, provided that the designation is accurate, and the duties involved are properly performed under the direction of the lawyer. In this connection, all of the strictures set forth at some length in Informal Opinion 909 in regard to Investigators would be equally applicable to Legal Assistants.

Informal Opinion 408   January 24, 1961
Showing Name of Office Manager
On Firm Card

You have inquired of this Committee whether or not it would be proper for a layman, employed by your office as investigator and office manager, to use a regular professional card of your firm with his own name and title of office manager in the lower left hand corner.

We assume, first of all, that the use of the particular professional card you have described would be limited to its use by the lay office manager, and that such a card would not be used by any of the attorneys or associates of your office. A lawyer's letterhead, of course, may not carry the name of any layman, and a lawyer's professional card may with propriety contain only his name and those of his lawyer associates, the profession, address, and telephone number.

This Committee has not previously specifically considered the exact question which you have presented. In Formal Opinion 54 of this Committee, however, dealing with the sending out of an announcement of the association of a layman with a law office who would thereafter have charge of all collection matters, some language of the Committee is appropriate. The Committee stated,

> "In the first place, the language of the announcement would reasonably be construed as misrepresenting the lay associate to be a member of the bar. . . . Further, the use of the name of a layman on the stationery of a lawyer, representing the former as conducting or managing a department of a lawyer's professional activities, is improper, because it too readily lends itself to the solicitation of employment or the use of it for advertising purposes by the layman so employed."

Your specific question has been determined on two occasions by the New York County Lawyer's Association, each instance involving a clerk, employed by the attorney or firm of attorneys. In both instances the New York County opinion held that the use of a card in one instance showing the clerk's name as "manager, commercial department," and in the other case simply as "associated with" the law firm, was improper. In one instance the Committee stated that it was not advised of any valid reason why the clerk, not being admitted to the bar, should use a card referring to the attorney. In the other instance the Committee felt that cards should not represent a layman as conducting or managing a department of the lawyer's professional business because of the fact that it lent itself too readily to the solicitation of employment or the using of it for advertising purposes by the layman so employed. The Committee therefore believes that the use of a professional card, [which shows the firm name, address and telephone number of the attorney or firm], by a layman employee, would be improper, even though the layman's title is also shown. To permit any lay employee to use an attorney's professional card too readily lends itself to abuse. If a lay office manager were permitted the use of such a card, there would be no distinction also from any other lay employee using a similar card, such as a clerk, an accountant, or a secretary.

You have made two inquiries: first, whether "the content and operation of the proposal" to train "senior advocates" violates the Code of Professional Responsibility; and second, whether "the Community Education Program now operated by the Legal Services office constitutes unprofessional conduct so long as it is dignified in tone, does not promote or advertise individual attorneys and does not in and of itself stir up or promote litigation either in individual cases or to promote a cause."

Your report of the proposal to train and use senior advocates and your description of the operation of the present community education program were quite comprehensive: but we assume that the essential aspects of the proposal and of the program are these:

(1) In view of the problems of older Americans (such as chronic illness, isolation, lack of access to social welfare groups, lack of knowledge as to where help can be obtained, transportation problems, etc.), and in view of the fact they often are "new poor" with little experience in dealing with problems of poverty, you contemplate an expansion of your existing legal services program for the elderly poor. Your present program recognizes that the number of elderly who are eligible for legal services exceeds 7,000, yet in 1972 you served only 114. You state that you have reached only "between 1 percent and 1½ percent of the elderly population of (   ) who are eligible for the services of the program."

(2) In order to make your program more available to the eligible elderly, your present activities include: having an attorney meet with various elderly groups and clubs; encouraging referrals from existing social service agencies; and location of the areas of the county with a high concentration of elderly poor, so that the legal services program may work with other programs in working with the elderly poor in the particular area. You have found that the elderly poor particularly need legal assistance in fields such as housing and property taxes, health and nutrition, pensions and public assistance, institutionalization in nursing homes and mental health hospitals, transportation, probate and estate planning, consumer problems, and guardianship problems.

(3) Your project or proposal is designed to make the legal services program more accessible to and better known by

the elderly poor citizens of the community. Primarily you intend to accomplish this by training four or more "senior advocates," who will be elderly poor persons employed by the project and supervised by a project attorney. The project attorney, who will work under your supervision will be assisted by a law student (or, legal intern). Those senior advocates will be trained for eight weeks in regard to the needs of the elderly, the existence of community services, the nature of the problems (such as transportation, probate matters, commitment procedures) that are legal in nature and that affect the elderly, and in regard to working techniques, such as in negotiating, advocating, etc. Those senior advocates will begin their "outreach activities" after completing four weeks of training and prior to completion of all of their training. They will develop initial contacts in the residential areas of concentration of the elderly, seeking particularly to "locate senior citizens of low visibility such as those who are physically handicapped." The senior advocates will make references to other agencies as well as, when indicated, to the legal services program. Legal interns as well as senior advocates will undertake interviews at nearby sites that are convenient to the elderly, where routine advice will be given and legal problems will be referred as needed to the project attorney. In addition, each senior advocate will work with senior citizen groups and clubs if the groups or clubs have large numbers of eligible poor.

(4) Your program has been, and will continue, to operate lay advocacy workshops which are open to the elderly and which make the elderly persons aware of legal pitfalls that may warrant legal advice or consultation, such as in connection with insurance, sales contracts, mortgages, etc.

The Code of Professional Responsibility recognizes that "important functions of the legal profession are to educate laymen to recognize their problems, to facilitate the process of intelligent selection of lawyers, and to assist in making legal services fully available." (EC 2-1). Since Legal problems may not be timely noticed by laymen, "lawyers acting under proper auspices should encourage and participate in educational and public relations programs concerning our legal system with particular reference to legal problems that frequently arise." (EC 2-2).

Since your lawyers are full-time, salaried lawyers, it is difficult to see how your program for the education of the elderly poor could be improperly motivated, so long as it does not promote or advertise individual lawyers. Accordingly, from the information furnished to us it appears that your program conforms to the ethical goals of the profession as stated in the Code of Professional Responsibility. Likewise, it does not appear that your operations are calculated to, or likely to, result in a violation of any of the disciplinary rules under Canon 2.

In your inquiry, you seem to question whether a limitation on the activities of the legal aid organization might be that the activities not "stir up" litigation. Of course, whenever the legal aid organization complies with EC 2-1 and EC 2-2 by educating a member of the elderly poor to the existence of a legal problem which can be solved only by litigation, it might be said to have stirred up litigation. We point out, however, that there is no provision in either the Ethical Considerations or the Disciplinary Rules of the Code of Professional Responsibility which prohibits the stirring up of litigation. Rather, the approach of the Code is, as we have indicated above, to approve educational approaches when the motive of the lawyer is proper and to condemn approaches to laymen when the lawyer seeks to benefit himself or his firm. For example, DR 2-103 (A) does not prohibit the giving of advice that might result in litigation, but, rather, prohibits the recommendation by a lawyer of himself as a private practitioner. Similarly, DR 2-104 (A) does not prohibit the giving of unsolicited advice to a layman to take legal action, but, rather, forbids the lawyer (unless he is furnished by an organization such as legal aid) to accept employment resulting from that advice.

Use of legal assistants such as the "senior advocates" is permissible when the lawyer delegates the tasks and remains responsible for their work. See EC 3-6. It appears that much of the work which the senior advocates will perform is more in the nature of social services work rather than legal work; but to the extent that the senior advocates and legal interns do perform work that might be classified as legal in nature, the project attorney should bear in mind the admonition of EC 3-6: "Such delegation is proper if the lawyer maintains a direct relationship with his client, supervises the delegated work, and has complete professional responsibility for the work product."

In summary, we find no violation of the Code of Professional Responsibility to be implicit in your proposal or in your present operations as outlined above.

APPENDIX II

AMERICAN PARALEGAL ASSOCIATION
NATIONAL STEERING COMMITTEE

CODE OF ETHICS FOR LEGAL ASSISTANTS

COE #1 It shall be in violation of this Code of Ethics for anyone other than a duly *qualified, specially trained person,* working *under the direct supervision* of a licensed attorney, to hold themselves out as a legal assistant.

COE #2 It shall be unethical conduct for a legal assistant to "openly" solicit or otherwise advertise for legal business on behalf of a duly licensed attorney; or for themselves as individuals while in the employ of such attorney or set up business for themselves without the supervision of duly licensed attorney.

COE #3 It shall be unethical conduct for a legal assistant to endanger, in any manner, the client-attorney fiduciary relationship of the employing attorney.

COE #4 It shall be the unauthorized practice of law, as defined by the organized bar, for a legal assistant, either by omission or commission, mislead the public as to their legal status or position, while employed under the supervision of a licensed attorney.

COE #5 It shall be the unauthorized practice of law, as defined by the organized bar, for a legal assistant to give advice if said advice is given to aid a client in reaching a legal decision regarding a legal problem.

COE #6 It shall be the unauthorized practice of law, as defined by the organized bar, for a legal assistant to accept a case into a law office or set a legal fee for services of the attorney since the same requires a legal determination and legal judgment of law applicable and an analysis of the problems involved.

COE #7 It shall be the unauthorized practice of law, as defined by the organized bar, for a legal assistant to sign any legal document or pleading, in his name on behalf of the employing attorney, unless and until it is hereafter determined and allowed by the local or state bar associations and the Supreme Court of a given state that he can so sign.

COE #8 It shall further be the unauthorized practice of law, as defined by the organized bar, for a legal assistant to sign any letters addressed to a client or adversary which contains legal determination or judgment without the prior review, approval or consent of the supervising attorney.

COE #9 It shall not be the unauthorized practice of law, as defined by the organized bar for a legal assistant to carry a business card for purposes of introduction or identification as to his position or legal status in a law office.

But it shall be unethical conduct for a legal assistant to carry a business card if such card can be misleading to the public as to his legal status or position in the office of his employing attorney.

COE #10 It shall be the unauthorized practice of law, as defined by the organized bar, for a legal assistant to appear before any local, state or federal court, unless and until it is hereafter determined and allowed by the local, or state bar association and the Supreme Court of a given state that he can so appear on certain specified matters.

It shall not be the unauthorized practice of law, as defined by the organized bar, for a legal assistant as herein defined, to appear before any local, state or federal administrative agency in the name of the employing attorney, at his direction, on behalf of the client of the employing attorney.

NATIONAL ASSOCIATION OF LEGAL ASSISTANTS, INC.

CODE OF ETHICS
AND
PROFESSIONAL RESPONSIBILITY

Preamble

It is the responsibility of every legal assistant to adhere strictly to the accepted standards of legal ethics and to live by general principles of proper conduct. The performance of the duties of the legal assistant shall be governed by specific canons as defined herein in order that justice will be served and the goals of the profession attained.

The canons of ethics set forth hereafter are adopted by the national Association of Legal Assistants, Inc. as a general guide, and the enumeration of these rules does not mean there are not others of equal importance although not specifically mentioned.

Canon 1. A legal assistant shall not perform any of the duties that lawyers only may perform nor do things that lawyers themselves may not do.

Canon 2. A legal assistant may perform any task delegated and supervised by a lawyer so long as the lawyer is responsible to the client, maintains a direct relationship with the client, and assumes full professional responsibility for the work product.

Canon 3. A legal assistant shall not engage in the practice of law by giving legal advice, appearing in court, setting fees, or accepting cases.

Canon 4. A legal assistant shall not act in matters involving professional legal judgment as the services of a lawyer are essential in the public interest whenever the exercise of such judgment is required.

Canon 5. A legal assistant must act prudently in determining the extent to which a client may be assisted without the presence of a lawyer.

Canon 6. A legal assistant shall not engage in the unauthorized practice of law and shall assist in preventing the unauthorized practice of law.

Canon 7. A legal assistant must protect the confidences of a client, and it shall be unethical for a legal assistant to violate any statute now in effect or hereafter to be enacted controlling privileged communications.

Canon 8. It is the obligation of the legal assistant to avoid conduct which would cause the lawyer to be unethical or even appear to be unethical, and loyalty to the employer is incumbent upon the legal assistant.

Canon 9. A legal assistant shall work continually to maintain integrity and a high degree of competency throughout the legal profession.

Canon 10. A legal assistant shall strive for perfection through education in order to better assist the legal profession in fulfilling its duty of making legal services available to clients and the public.

Canon 11. A legal assistant shall do all other things incidental, necessary, or expedient for the attainment of the ethics and responsibilities imposed by statute or rule of court.

Adopted May 1, 1975

APPENDIX IV

ETHICS AND THE PARALEGAL

(Excerpts from the American Bar Association's Code of Professional Responsibility and Code of Judicial Conduct)

Legal ethics is the code of moral conduct that an attorney must adhere to in practicing his or her profession. These codes are promulgated by the American Bar Association and the State and County Bar Associations in which the attorney practices law. The American Bar Association's ethical code is named "Code of Professional Responsibility and Code of Judicial Conduct." This code superseded the Canons of Professional Ethics, which was the format for the present code.

This code is subject to annual changes, and the changes result from new law and the dynamics of changing times.

It was unthinkable not too many years ago that attorneys would be permitted to advertise. The American Bar Association within the past year has decided that in some instances an attorney may advertise a specialty if one exists.

CANON 1

A Lawyer Should Assist in Maintaining the Integrity and Competence of the Legal Profession

ETHICAL CONSIDERATIONS

EC 1-1   A basic tenet of the professional responsibility of lawyers is that every person in our society should have ready access to the independent professional services of a lawyer of integrity and competence. Maintaining the integrity and improving the competence of the bar to meet the highest standards is the ethical responsibility of every lawyer.

EC 1-2   The public should be protected from those who are not qualified to be lawyers by reason of a deficiency in education or moral standards or of other relevant factors but who nevertheless seek to practice law. To assure the maintenance of high moral and educational standards of the legal profession, lawyers should affirmatively assist courts and other appropriate bodies in promulgating, enforcing, and improving requirements for admission to the bar. In like manner, the bar has a positive obligation to aid in the continued improvement of all phases of pre-admission and post-admission legal education.

EC 1-3   Before recommending an applicant for admission, a lawyer should satisfy himself that the applicant is of good moral character. Although a lawyer should not become a self-appointed investigator or judge of applicants for admission, he should report to proper officials all unfavorable information he possesses relating to the character or other qualifications of an applicant.

EC 1-4   The integrity of the profession can be maintained only if conduct of lawyers in violation of the Disciplinary Rules is brought to the attention of the proper officials. A lawyer should reveal voluntarily to those officials all privileged knowledge of conduct of lawyers which he believes clearly to be in violation of the Disciplinary Rules. A lawyer should, upon request, serve on and assist comittees and boards having responsibility for the administration of the Disciplinary Rules.

EC 1-5   A lawyer should maintain high standards of professional conduct and should encourage fellow lawyers to do likewise. He should be temperate and dignified, and he should refrain from all illegal and morally reprehensible conduct. Because of his position in society, even minor violations of law by a lawyer may tend to lessen public confidence in the legal profession. Obedience to law exemplifies respect for law. To lawyers especially, respect for the law should be more than a platitude.

EC 1-6   An applicant for admission to the bar or a lawyer may be unqualified, temporarily or permanently, for other than moral and educational reasons, such as mental or emotional instability. Lawyers should be diligent in taking steps to see that during a period of disqualification such person is not granted a license or, if licensed, is not permitted to practice. In like manner, when the disqualification has terminated, members of the bar should assist such person in being licensed, or, if licensed, in being restored to his full right to practice.

CANON 2

A Lawyer Should Assist the Legal Profession in Fulfilling Its Duty to Make Legal Counsel Available

ETHICAL CONSIDERATIONS

EC 2-1 The need of members of the public for legal services is met only if they recognize their legal problems, appreciate the importance of seeking assistance, and are able to obtain the services of acceptable legal counsel. Hence, important functions of the legal profession are to educate laymen to recognize their problems, to facilitate the process of intelligent selection of lawyers, and to assist in making legal services fully available.

Recognition of Legal Problems

EC 2-2 The legal profession should assist laymen to recognize legal problems because such problems may not be self-revealing and often are not timely noticed. Therefore, lawyers acting under proper auspices should encourage and participate in educational and public relations programs concerning our legal system with particular reference to legal problems that frequently arise. Such educational programs should be motivated by a desire to benefit the public rather than to obtain publicity or employment for particular lawyers. Examples of permissible activities include preparation of institutional advertisements and professional articles for lay publications and participation in seminars, lectures, and civic programs. But a lawyer who participates in such activities should shun personal publicity.

EC 2-3 Whether a lawyer acts properly in volunteering advice to a layman to seek legal services depends upon the circumstances. The giving of advice that one should take legal action could well be in fulfillment of the duty of the legal profession to assist laymen in recognizing legal problems. The advice is proper only if motivated by a desire to protect one who does not recognize that he may have legal problems or who is ignorant of his legal rights or obligations. Hence, the advice is improper if motivated by a desire to obtain personal benefit, secure personal publicity, or cause litigation to be brought merely to harass or injure another. Obviously, a lawyer should not contact a non-client, directly or indirectly, for the purpose of being retained to represent him for compensation.

EC 2-4 Since motivation is subjective and often difficult to judge, the motives of a lawyer who volunteers advice likely to produce legal controversy may well be suspect if he receives professional employment or other benefits as a result. A lawyer who volunteers advice that one should obtain the services of a lawyer generally should not himself accept employment, compensation, or other benefit in connection with that matter. However, it is not improper for a lawyer to volunteer such advice and render resulting services to close friends, relatives, former clients (in regard to matters germane to former employment), and regular clients.

EC 2-5 A lawyer who writes or speaks for the purpose of educating members of the public to recognize their legal problems should carefully refrain from giving or appearing to give a general solution applicable to all apparently similar individual problems, since slight changes in fact situations may require a material variance in the applicable advice: otherwise, the public may be misled and misadvised. Talks and writings by lawyers for laymen should caution them not to attempt to solve individual problems upon the basis of the information contained therein.

Selection of a Lawyer: Generally

EC 2-6 Formerly a potential client usually knew the reputations of local lawyers for competency and integrity and therefore could select a practitioner in whom he had confidence. This traditional selection process worked well because it was initiated by the client and the choice was an informed one.

EC 2-7 Changed conditions, however, have seriously restricted the effectiveness of the traditional selection process. Often the reputations of lawyers are not sufficiently known to enable laymen to make intelligent choices. The law has become increasingly complex and specialized. Few lawyers are willing and competent to deal with every kind of legal matter, and many laymen have difficulty in determining the competence of lawyers to render different types of legal services. The selection of legal counsel is particularly difficult for transients, persons moving into new areas, persons of limited education or means, and others who have little or no contact with lawyers.

EC 2-8 Selection of a lawyer by a layman often is the result of the advice and recommendation of third parties — relatives, friends, acquaintances, business associates, or other lawyers. A layman is best served if the recommendation is disinterested and informed. In order that the recommendation be disinterested, a lawyer should not seek to influence another to recommend his employment. A lawyer should not compensate another person for recommending him, for influencing a prospective client to employ him, or to encourage future recommendations.

Selection of a Lawyer: Professional Notices and Listings

EC 2-9   The traditional ban against advertising by lawyers, which is subject to certain limited exceptions, is rooted in the public interest. Competitive advertising would encourage extravagant, artful, self-laudatory brashness in seeking business and thus could mislead the layman. Furthermore, it would inevitably produce unrealistic expectations in particular cases and bring about distrust of the law and lawyers. Thus, public confidence in our legal system would be impaired by such advertisements of professional services. The attorney-client relationship is personal and unique and should not be established as the result of pressures and deceptions. History has demonstrated that public confidence in the legal system is best preserved by strict, self-imposed controls over, rather than by, unlimited advertising.

EC 2-10   Methods of advertising that are subject to the objections stated above should be and are prohibited. However, the Disciplinary Rules recognize the value of giving assistance in the selection process through forms of advertising that furnish identification of a lawyer while avoiding such objections. For example, a lawyer may be identified in the classified section of the telephone directory, in the office building directory, and on his letterhead and professional card. But at all times the permitted notices should be dignified and accurate.

EC 2-11   The name under which a lawyer conducts his practice may be a factor in the selection process. The use of a trade name or an assumed name could mislead laymen concerning the identity, responsibility, and status of those practicing thereunder. Accordingly, a lawyer in private practice should practice only under his own name, the name of a lawyer employing him, a partnership name composed of the name of one or more of the lawyers practicing in a partnership, or, if permitted by law, in the name of a professional legal corporation, which should be clearly designated as such. For many years some law firms have used a firm name retaining one or more names of deceased or retired partners and such practice is not improper if the firm is a bona fide successor of a firm in which the deceased or retired person was a member, if the use of the name is authorized by law or contract, and if the public is not misled thereby. However, the name of a partner who withdraws from a firm but continues to practice law should be omitted from the firm name in order to avoid misleading the public.

EC 2-12   A lawyer occupying a judicial, legislative, or public executive or administrative position who has the right to practice law concurrently may allow his name to remain in the name of the firm if he actively continues to practice law as a member thereof. Otherwise, his name should be removed from the firm name, and he should not be identified as a past or present member of the firm; and he should not hold himself out as being a practicing lawyer.

EC 2-13   In order to avoid the possibility of misleading persons with whom he deals, a lawyer should be scrupulous in the representation of his professional status. He should not hold himself out as being a partner or associate of a law firm if he is not one in fact, and thus, should not hold himself out as a partner or associate if he only shares offices with another lawyer.

EC 2-14   In some instances a lawyer confines his practice to a particular field of law. In the absence of state controls to insure the existence of special competence, a lawyer should not be permitted to hold himself out as a specialist or as having special training or ability, other than in the historically accepted fields of admiralty, trademark, and patent law.

EC 2-15   The legal profession has developed lawyer referral systems designed to aid individuals who are able to pay fees but need assistance in locating lawyers competent to handle their particular problems. Use of a lawyer referral system enables a layman to avoid an uninformed selection of a lawyer because such a system makes possible the employment of competent lawyers who have indicated an interest in the subject matter involved. Lawyers should support the principle of lawyer referral systems and should encourage the evolution of other ethical plans which aid in the selection of qualified counsel.

EC 2-16   The legal profession cannot remain a viable force in fulfilling its role in our society unless its members receive adequate compensation for services rendered, and reasonable fees should be charged in appropriate cases to clients able to pay them. Nevertheless, persons unable to pay all or a portion of a reasonable fee should be able to obtain necessary legal services, and lawyers should support and participate in ethical activities designed to achieve that objective.

Financial Ability to Employ Counsel:
Persons Able to Pay Reasonable Fees

EC 2-17   The determination of a proper fee requires consideration of the interests of both client and lawyer. A lawyer should not charge more than a reasonable fee, for excessive cost of legal service would deter laymen from utilizing the legal system in protection of their rights. Furthermore, an excessive charge abuses the professional relationship between lawyer and client. On the other hand, adequate compensation is necessary in order to enable the lawyer to serve his client effectively and to preserve the integrity and independence of the profession.

EC 2-18   The determination of the reasonableness of a fee requires consideration of all relevant circumstances, including those stated in the Disciplinary Rules. The fees of a lawyer will vary according to many factors, including the time required, his experience, ability, and reputation, the nature of the employment, the responsibility involved, and the results obtained. Suggested fee schedules and economic reports of state and local bar associations provide some guidance on the subject of reasonable fees. It is a commendable and long-standing tradition of the bar that special consideration is given in the fixing of any fee for services rendered a brother lawyer or a member of his immediate family.

EC 2-19   As soon as feasible after a lawyer has been employed, it is desirable that he reach a clear agreement with his client as to the basis of the fee charges to be made. Such a course will not only prevent later misunderstanding but will also work for good relations between the lawyer and the client. It is usually beneficial to reduce to writing the understanding of the parties regarding the fee, particularly when it is contingent. A lawyer should be mindful that many persons who desire to employ him may have had little or no experience with fee charges of lawyers, and for this reason he should explain fully to such persons the reasons for the particular fee arrangement he proposes.

EC 2-20   Contingent fee arrangements in civil cases have long been commonly accepted in the United States in proceedings to enforce claims. The historical bases of their acceptance are that (1) they often, and in a variety of circumstances, provide the only practical means by which one having a claim against another can economically afford, finance, and obtain the services of a competent lawyer to prosecute his claim, and (2) a successful prosecution of the claim produces a res out of which the fee can be paid. Although a lawyer generally should decline to accept employment on a contingent fee basis by one who is able to pay a reasonable fixed fee, it is not necessarily improper for a lawyer, where justified by the particular circumstances of a case, to enter into a contingent fee contract in a civil case with any client who, after being fully informed of all relevant factors, desires that arrangement. Because of the human relationships involved and the unique character of the proceedings contingent fee arrangements in domestic relation cases are rarely justified. In administrative agency proceedings contingent fee contracts should be governed by the same consideration as in other civil cases. Public policy properly condemns contingent fee arrangements in criminal cases, largely on the ground that legal services in criminal cases do not produce a res with which to pay the fee.

EC 2-21   A lawyer should not accept compensation or any thing of value incident to his employment or services from one other than his client without the knowledge and consent of his client after full disclosure.

EC 2-22   Without the consent of his client, a lawyer should not associate in a particular matter with another lawyer outside his firm. A fee may properly be divided between lawyers properly associated if the division is in proportion to the services performed and the responsibility assumed by each lawyer and if the total fee is reasonable.

EC 2-23   A lawyer should be zealous in his efforts to avoid controversies over fees with clients and should attempt to resolve amicably any differences on the subject. He should not sue a client for a fee unless necessary to prevent fraud or gross imposition by the client.

EC 2-24   A layman whose financial ability is not sufficient to permit payment of any fee cannot obtain legal services, other
than in cases where a contingent fee is appropriate, unless
the services are provided for him. Even a person of moderate means may be unable to pay a reasonable fee which
is large, because of the complexity, novelty, or difficulty
of the problem or similar factors.

EC 2-25   Historically, the need for legal services of those unable
to pay reasonable fees has been met in part by lawyers
who donated their services or accepted court appointments on behalf of such individuals. The basic responsibility for providing legal services for those unable to pay
ultimately rests upon the individual lawyer, and personal
involvement in the problems of the disadvantaged can
be one of the most rewarding experiences in the life of a
lawyer. Every lawyer, regardless of professional promi-
nence or professional workload, should find time to participate in serving the disadvantaged. The rendition of
free legal services to those unable to pay reasonable fees
continues to be an obligation of each lawyer, but the efforts of individual lawyers are often not enough to meet
the need. Thus it has been necessary for the profession to
institute additional programs to provide legal services.
Accordingly, legal aid offices, lawyer referral services,
and other related programs have been developed, and
others will be developed, by the profession. Every lawyer
should support all proper efforts to meet this need for
legal services.

Acceptance and Retention of Employment

EC 2-26   A lawyer is under no obligation to act as adviser or advocate for every person who may wish to become his client;
but in furtherance of the objective of the bar to make legal
services fully available, a lawyer should not lightly decline
proffered employment. The fulfillment of this objective
requires acceptance by a lawyer of his share of tendered
employment which may be unattractive both to him and
the bar generally.

EC 2-27   History is replete with instances of distinguished and
sacrificial services by lawyers who have represented unpopular clients and causes. Regardless of his personal
feelings, a lawyer should not decline representation be-

cause a client or a cause is unpopular or community reaction is adverse.

EC 2-28   The personal preference of a lawyer to avoid adversary alignment against judges, other lawyers, public officials, or influential members of the community does not justify his rejection of tendered employment.

EC 2-29   When a lawyer is appointed by a court or requested by a bar association to undertake representation of a person unable to obtain counsel, whether for financial or other reasons, he should not seek to be excused from undertaking the representation except for compelling reasons. Compelling reasons do not include such factors as the repugnance of the subject matter of the proceeding, the identity or position of a person involved in the case, the belief of the lawyer that the defendant in a criminal proceeding is guilty, or the belief of the lawyer regarding the merits of the civil case.

EC 2-30   Employment should not be accepted by a lawyer when he is unable to render competent service or when he knows or it is obvious that the person seeking to employ him desires to institute or maintain an action merely for the purpose of harassing or maliciously injuring another. Likewise, a lawyer should decline employment if the intensity of his personal feeling, as distinguished from a community attitude, may impair his effective representation of a prospective client. If a lawyer knows a client has previously obtained counsel, he should not accept employment in the matter unless the other counsel approves or withdraws, or the client terminates the prior employment.

EC 2-31   Full availability of legal counsel requires both that persons be able to obtain counsel and that lawyers who undertake representation complete the work involved. Trial counsel for a convicted defendant should continue to represent his client by advising whether to take an appeal and, if the appeal is prosecuted, by representing him through the appeal unless new counsel is substituted or withdrawal is permitted by the appropriate court.

EC 2-32   A decision by a lawyer to withdraw should be made only on the basis of compelling circumstances, and in a matter pending before a tribunal he must comply with the rules of the tribunal regarding withdrawal. A lawyer should not withdraw without considering carefully and endeavoring to minimize the possible adverse effect on the rights of his client and the possibility of prejudice to his client as a result of his withdrawal. Even when he justifiably withdraws, a lawyer should protect the welfare of his client by giving due notice of his withdrawal, suggesting employment of other counsel, delivering to the client all papers and property to which the client is entitled, cooperating with counsel subsequently employed, and otherwise endeavoring to minimize the possibility of harm. Further, he should refund to the client any compensation not earned during the employment.

CANON 3

*A Lawyer Should Assist in Preventing the
Unauthorized Practice of Law*

ETHICAL CONSIDERATIONS

EC 3-1   The prohibition against the practice of law by a layman is rounded in the need of the public for integrity and competence of those who undertake to render legal services. Because of the fiduciary and personal character of the lawyer-client relationship the inherently complex nature of our legal system, the public can better be assured of the requisite responsibility and competence if the practice of law is confined to those who are subject to the requirements and regulations imposed upon members of the legal profession.

EC 3-2   The sensitive variations in the considerations that bear on legal determinations often make it difficult even for a lawyer to exercise appropriate professional judgment, and it is therefore essential that the personal nature of the relationship of client and lawyer be preserved. Competent professional judgment is the product of a trained familiarity with law and legal processes, a disciplined, analytical approach to legal problems, and a firm ethical commitment.

EC 3-3   A non-lawyer who undertakes to handle legal matters is not governed as to integrity or legal competence by the same rules that govern the conduct of a lawyer. A lawyer is not only subject to that regulation but also is committed to high standards of ethical conduct. The public interest is best served in legal matters by a regulated profession committed to such standards. The Disciplinary Rules protect the public in that they prohibit a lawyer from seeking employment by improper overtures, from acting in cases of divided loyalties, and from submitting to the control of others in the exercise of his judgment. Moreover, a person who entrusts legal matters to a lawyer is protected by the attorney-client privilege and by the duty of the lawyer to hold inviolate the confidences and secrets of his client.

EC 3-4   A layman who seeks legal services often is not in a position to judge whether he will receive proper professional attention. The entrustment of a legal matter may well involve the confidences, the reputation, the property, the freedom, or even the life of the client. Proper protection of members of the public demands that no person be permitted to act in the confidential and demanding capacity of a lawyer unless he is subject to the regulations of the legal profession.

EC 3-5   It is neither necessary nor desirable to attempt the formulation of a single, specific definition of what constitutes the practice of law. Functionally, the practice of law relates to the rendition of services for others that call for the professional judgment of a lawyer. The essence of the professional judgment of the lawyer is his educated ability to relate the general body and philosophy of law to a specific legal problem of a client; and thus, the public interest will be better served if only lawyers are permitted to act in matters involving professional judgment. Where this professional judgment is not involved, non-lawyers, such as court clerks, police officers, abstracters, and many governmental employees, may engage in occupations that require a special knowledge of law in certain areas. But the services of a lawyer are essential in the public interest whenever the exercise of professional legal judgment is required.

EC 3-6   A lawyer often delegates tasks to clerks, secretaries, and other lay persons. Such delegation is proper if the lawyer maintains a direct relationship with his client, supervises the delegated work, and has complete professional responsibility for the work product. This delegation enables a lawyer to render legal service more economically and efficiently.

EC 3-7   The prohibition against a non-lawyer practicing law does not prevent a layman from representing himself, for then he is ordinarily exposing only himself to possible injury. The purpose of the legal profession is to make educated legal representation available to the public; but anyone who does not wish to avail himself of such representation is not required to do so. Even so, the legal profession should help members of the public to recognize legal problems and to understand why it may be unwise for them to act for themselves in matters having legal consequences.

EC 3-8   Since a lawyer should not aid or encourage a layman to practice law, he should not practice law in association with a layman or otherwise share legal fees with a layman. This does not mean, however, that the pecuniary value of the interest of a deceased lawyer in his firm or practice may not be paid to his estate or specified persons such as his widow or heirs. In like manner, profit-sharing retirement plans of a lawyer or law firm which include non-lawyer office employees are not improper. These limited exceptions to the rule against sharing legal fees with laymen are permissible since they do not aid or encourage laymen to practice law.

EC 3-9   Regulation of the practice of law is accomplished principally by the respective states. Authority to engage in the practice of law conferred in any jurisdiction is not per se a grant of the right to practice elsewhere, and it is improper for a lawyer to engage in practice where he is not permitted by law or by court to do so. However, the demands of business and the mobility of our society pose distinct problems in the regulation of the practice of law by the states. In furtherance of the public interest, the legal profession should discourage regulation that unreasonably imposes territorial limitations upon the right of a lawyer to handle the legal affairs of his client or upon the opportunity of a client to obtain the services of a lawyer of his choice in all matters including the presentation of a contested matter in a tribunal before which the lawyer is not permanently admitted to practice.

CANON 4

*A Lawyer Should Preserve the Confidences
and Secrets of a Client*

ETHICAL CONSIDERATIONS

EC 4-1   Both the fiduciary relationship existing between lawyer and client and the proper functioning of the legal system require the preservation by the lawyer of confidences and secrets of one who has employed or sought to employ him. A client must feel free to discuss whatever he wishes with his lawyer and a lawyer must be equally free to obtain information beyond that volunteered by his client. A lawyer should be fully informed of all the facts of the matter he is handling in order for his client to obtain the full advantage of our legal system. It is for the lawyer in the exercise of his independent professional judgment to separate the relevant and important from the irrelevant and unimportant. The observance of the ethical obligation of a lawyer to hold inviolate the confidences and secrets of his client not only facilitates the full development of facts essential to proper representation of the client but also encourages laymen to seek early legal assistance.

EC 4-2   The obligation to protect confidences and secrets obviously does not preclude a lawyer from revealing information when his client consents after full disclosure when necessary to perform his professional employment, when permitted by a Disciplinary Rule, or when required by law. Unless the client otherwise directs, a lawyer may disclose the affairs of his client to partners or associates of his firm. It is a matter of common knowledge that the normal operation of a law office exposes confidential professional information to non-lawyer employees of the office, particularly secretaries and those having access to the files; and this obligates a lawyer to exercise care in selecting and training his employees so that the sanctity of all confidences and secrets of his clients may be preserved. If the obligation extends to two or more clients as to the same information, a lawyer should obtain the permission of all before revealing the information. A lawyer must always be sensitive to the rights and wishes of his client and act scrupulously in the making of decisions which may involve the disclosure of information obtained in his professional relationship. Thus, in the absence of consent of his client after full disclosure a lawyer should not associate another lawyer in the handling of a matter; nor should he, in the absence of consent, seek counsel from another lawyer if there is a reasonable possibility that the identity of the client or his confidences or secrets would be revealed to such lawyer. Both social amenities and professional duty should cause a lawyer to shun indiscreet conversations concerning his clients.

EC 4-3   Unless the client otherwise directs, it is not improper for a lawyer to give limited information from his files to an outside agency necessary for statistical, bookkeeping, accounting, data processing, banking, printing, or other legitimate purposes, provided he exercises due care in the selection of the agency and warns the agency that the information must be kept confidential.

EC 4-4 The attorney-client privilege is more limited than the ethical obligation of a lawyer to guard the confidences and secrets of his client. This ethical precept, unlike the evidentiary privilege, exists without regard to the nature or source of information or the fact that others share the knowledge. A lawyer should endeavor to act in a manner which preserves the evidentiary privilege; for example, he should avoid professional discussion in the presence of persons to whom the privilege does not extend. A lawyer owes an obligation to advise the client of the attorney-client privilege and timely to assert the privilege unless it is waived by the client.

EC 4-5 A lawyer should not use information acquired in the course of the representation of a client to the disadvantage of the client and a lawyer should not use, except with the consent of his client after full disclosure, such information for his own purposes. Likewise, a lawyer should be diligent in his efforts to prevent the misuse of such information by his employees and associates. Care should be exercised by a lawyer to prevent the disclosure of the confidences and secrets of one client to another, and no employment should be accepted that might require such disclosure.

EC 4-6 The obligation of a lawyer to preserve the confidences and secrets of his clients continues after the termination of his employment. Thus a lawyer should not attempt to sell a law practice as a going business because, among other reasons, to do so would involve the disclosure of confidences and secrets. A lawyer should also provide for the protection of the confidences and secrets of his client following the termination of the practice of the lawyer, whether termination is due to death, disability, or retirement. For example, a lawyer might provide for the personal papers of the client to be returned to him and for the papers of the lawyer to be delivered to another lawyer or to be destroyed. In determining the method of disposition, the instructions and wishes of the client should be a dominant consideration.

CANON 5

*A Lawyer Should Exercise Independent
Professional Judgment on Behalf of a Client*

ETHICAL CONSIDERATIONS

EC 5-1   The professional judgment of a lawyer should be exercised, within the bounds of the law, solely for the benefit of his client and free of compromising influences and loyalties. Neither his personal interests, the interests of other clients, nor the desires of third persons should be permitted to dilute his loyalty to his client.

Interests of a Lawyer That May Affect His Judgment

EC 5-2   A lawyer should not accept proffered employment if his personal interests or desires will, or there is a reasonable probability that they will, affect adversely the advice to be given or services to be rendered the prospective client. After accepting employment, a lawyer carefully should refrain from acquiring a property right or assuming a position that would tend to make his judgment less protective of the interests of his client.

EC 5-3   The self-interest of a lawyer resulting from his ownership of property in which his client also has an interest or which may affect property of his client, may interfere with the exercise of free judgment on behalf of his client. If such interference would occur with respect to a prospective client, a lawyer should decline employment proffered by him. After accepting employment, a lawyer should not acquire property rights that would adversely affect his professional judgment in the representation of his client. Even if the property interests of a lawyer do not presently interfere with the exercise of his independent judgment, but the likelihood of interference can reasonably be foreseen by him, a lawyer should explain the situation to his client and should decline employment or withdraw unless the client consents to the continuance of the relationship after full disclosure. A lawyer should not seek to persuade his client to permit him to invest in an undertaking of his client nor make improper use of his professional relationship to influence his client to invest in an enterprise in which the lawyer is interested.

EC 5-4   If, in the course of his representation of a client, a lawyer is permitted to receive from his client a beneficial ownership in publication rights relating to the subject matter of the employment, he may be tempted to subordinate the interests of his client to his own anticipated pecuniary gain. For example, a lawyer in a criminal case who obtains from his client television, radio, motion picture, newspaper, magazine, book, or other publication rights with respect to the case may be influenced, consciously or unconsciously, to a course of conduct that will enhance the value of his publication rights to the prejudice of his client. To prevent these potentially differing interests, such arrangements should be scrupulously avoided prior to the termination of all aspects of the matter giving rise to the employment, even though his employment has previously ended.

EC 5-5 A lawyer should not suggest to his client that a gift be made to himself or for his benefit. If a lawyer accepts a gift from his client, he is peculiarly susceptible to the charge that he unduly influenced or over-reached the client. If a client voluntarily offers to make a gift to his lawyer, the lawyer may accept the gift, but before doing so, he should urge that his client secure disinterested advice from an independent, competent person who is cognizant of all the circumstances. Other than in exceptional circumstances, a lawyer should insist that an instrument in which his client desires to name him beneficially be prepared by another lawyer selected by the client.

EC 5-6 A lawyer should not consciously influence a client to name his as executor, trustee, or lawyer in an instrument. In those cases where a client wishes to name his lawyer as such, care should be taken by the lawyer to avoid even the appearance of impropriety.

EC 5-7 The possibility of an adverse effect upon the exercise of free judgment by a lawyer on behalf of his client during litigation generally makes it undesirable for the lawyer to acquire a propriety interest in the cause of his client or otherwise to become financially interested in the outcome of litigation. Although a contingent fee arrangement gives a lawyer a financial interest in the outcome of litigation, a reasonable contingent fee is permissible in civil cases because it may be the only means by which a layman can obtain the services of a lawyer of his choice. But a lawyer, because he is in a better position to evaluate a cause of action, should enter into a contingent fee arrangement only in those instances where the arrangement will be beneficial to the client.

EC 5-8   A financial interest in the outcome of litigation also results if monetary advances are made by the lawyer to his client. Although this assistance generally is not encouraged, there are instances when it is not improper to make loans to a client. For example, the advancing or guaranteeing of payment of the costs and expenses of litigation may be the only way a client can enforce his cause of action, but the ultimate liability for such costs and expenses must be that of the client.

EC 5-9   Occasionally a lawyer is called upon to decide in a particular case whether he will be a witness or an advocate. If a lawyer is both counsel and witness, he becomes more easily impeachable for interest and thus may be less effective as a witness. Conversely, the opposing counsel may be handicapped in challenging the credibility of the lawyer when the lawyer also appears as an advocate in the case. An advocate who becomes a witness in the unseemly and ineffective position of arguing his own credibility. The roles of an advocate and of a witness are inconsistent; the function of an advocate is to advance or argue the cause of another, while that of a witness is to state facts objectively.

EC 5-10   Problems incident to the lawyer-witness relationship arise at different stages; they relate either to whether a lawyer should accept employment or should withdraw from employment. Regardless of when the problem arises, his decision is to be governed by the same basic considerations. It is not objectionable for a lawyer who is a potential witness to be an advocate if it is unlikely that he will be called as a witness because his testimony would be merely cumulative or if his testimony will relate only to an uncontested issue. In the exceptional situation where it will be manifestly unfair to the client for the lawyer to refuse employment or to withdraw when he will likely be a witness on a contested issue, he may serve as advocate even though he may be a witness. In making such decision, he should determine the personal or financial sacrifice of the client that may result from his refusal of employment or withdrawal therefrom, the materiality of his testimony, and the effectiveness of his representation in view of his personal involvement. In weighing these factors, it should be clear that refusal or withdrawal will impose an unreasonable hardship upon the client before the lawyer accepts or continues the employment. Where the question arises, doubts should be resolved in favor of the lawyer testifying and against his becoming or continuing as an advocate.

EC 5-11   A lawyer should not permit his personal interests to influence his advice relative to a suggestion by his client that additional counsel be employed. In like manner, his personal interests should not deter him from suggesting that additional counsel be employed; on the contrary, he should be alert to the desirability of recommending additional counsel when, in his judgment, the proper representation of his client requires it. However, a lawyer should advise his client not to employ additional counsel suggested by the client if the lawyer believes that such employment would be a disservice to the client, and he should disclose the reasons for his belief.

EC 5-12   Inability of co-counsel to agree on a matter vital to the representation of their client requires that their disagreement be submitted by them jointly to their client for his resolution, and the decision of the client shall control the action to be taken.

EC 5-13   A lawyer should not maintain membership or be influenced by any organization of employees that undertakes to prescribe, direct, or suggest when or how he should fulfill his professional obligations to a person or organization that employs him as a lawyer. Although it is not necessarily improper for a lawyer employed by a corporation or similar entity to be a member of an organization of employees, he should be vigilant to safeguard his fidelity as a lawyer to his employer, free from outside influences.

Interests of Multiple Clients

EC 5-14   Maintaining the independence of professional judgment required of a lawyer precludes his acceptance or continuation of employment that will adversely affect his judgment on behalf of or dilute his loyalty to a client. This problem arises whenever a lawyer is asked to represent two or more clients who may have differing interests, whether such interests be conflicting, inconsistent, diverse, or otherwise discordant.

EC 5-15   If a lawyer is requested to undertake or to continue representation of multiple clients having potentially differing interests, he must weigh carefully the possibility that his judgment may be impaired or his loyalty divided if he accepts or continues the employment. He should resolve all doubts against the propriety of the representation. A lawyer should never represent in litigation multiple clients with differing interests; and there are few situations in which he would be justified in representing in litigation multiple clients with potentially differing interests. If a lawyer accepted such employment and the interests did become actually differing, he would have to withdraw from employment with likelihood of resulting hardship on the clients; and for this reason it is preferable that he refuse the employment initially. On the other hand, there are many instances in which a lawyer may properly serve multiple clients having potentially differing interests in matters not involving litigation. If the interests vary only slightly, it is generally likely that the lawyer will not be subjected to an adverse influence and that he can retain his independent judgment on behalf of each client; and if the interests become differing, withdrawal is less likely to have a disruptive effect upon the causes of his clients.

EC 5-16   In those instances in which a lawyer is justified in representing two or more clients having differing interests, it is nevertheless essential that each client be given the opportunity to evaluate his need for representation free of any potential conflict and to obtain other counsel if he so desires. Thus before a lawyer may represent multiple clients, he should explain fully to each client the implications of the common representation and should accept or continue employment only if the clients consent. If there are present other circumstances that might cause any of the multiple clients to question the undivided loyalty of the lawyer, he should also advise all of the clients of those circumstances.

EC 5-17   Typically recurring situations involving potentially differing interests are those in which a lawyer is asked to represent co-defendants in a criminal case, co-plaintiffs in a personal injury case, an insured and his insurer, and beneficiaries of the estate of a decedent. Whether a lawyer can fairly and adequately protect the interests of multiple clients in these and similar situations depends upon an analysis of each case. In certain circumstances, there may exist little chance of the judgment of the lawyer being adversely affected by the slight possibility that the interest will become actually differing; in other circumstances, the chance of adverse effect upon his judgment is not unlikely.

EC 5-18   A lawyer employed or retained by a corporation or similar entity owes his allegiance to the entity and not to a stockholder, director, officer, employee, representative, or other person connected with the entity. In advising the entity, a lawyer should keep paramount its interests and his professional judgment should not be influenced by the personal desires of any person or organization. Occasionally a lawyer for an entity is requested by a stockholder, director, officer, employee, representative, or other person connected with the entity to represent him in an individual capacity; in such case the lawyer may serve the individual only if the lawyer is convinced that differing interests are not present.

EC 5-19   A lawyer may represent several clients whose interests are not actually or potentially differing. Nevertheless, he should explain any circumstances that might cause a client to question his undivided loyalty. Regardless of the belief of a lawyer that he may properly represent multiple clients, he must defer to a client who holds the contrary belief and withdraw from representation of that client.

EC 5-20   A lawyer is often asked to serve as an impartial arbitrator or mediator in matters which involve present or former clients. He may serve in either capacity if he first discloses such present or former relationships. After a lawyer has undertaken to act as an impartial arbitrator or mediator, he should not thereafter represent in the dispute any of the parties involved.

Desires of Third Persons

EC 5-21   The obligation of a lawyer to exercise professional judgment solely on behalf of his client requires that he disregard the desires of others that might impair his free judgment. The desires of a third person will seldom affect a lawyer unless that person is in a position to exert strong economic, political, or social pressures upon the lawyer. These influences are often subtle, and a lawyer must be alert to their existence. A lawyer subjected to outside pressures should make full disclosure of them to his client; and if he or his client believes that the effectiveness of his representation has been or will be impaired thereby, the lawyer should take proper steps to withdraw from representation of his client.

EC 5-22   Economic, political, or social pressures by third persons are less likely to impinge upon the independent judgment of a lawyer in a matter in which he is compensated directly by his client and his professional work is exclusively with his client. On the other hand, if a lawyer is compensated from a source other than his client, he may feel a sense of responsibility to someone other than his client.

EC 5-23   A person or organization that pays or furnishes lawyers to represent others possesses a potential power to exert strong pressures against the independent judgment of those lawyers. Some employers may be interested in furthering their own economic, political, or social goals without regard to the professional responsibility of the lawyer to his individual client. Others may be far more concerned with establishment or extension of legal principles than in the immediate protection of the rights of the lawyer's individual client. On some occasions, decisions on priority of work may be made by the employer rather than the lawyer with the result that prosecution of work already undertaken for clients is postponed to their detriment. Similarly, an employer may seek, consciously or unconsciously, to further its own economic interests through the actions of the lawyers employed by it. Since a lawyer must always be free to exercise his professional judgment without regard to the interests or motives of a third person, the lawyer who is employed by one to represent another must constantly guard against erosion of his professional freedom.

EC 5-24   To assist a lawyer in preserving his professional independence, a number of courses are available to him. For example, a lawyer should not practice with or in the form of a professional legal corporation, even though the corporate form is permitted by law, if any director, officer, or stockholder of it is a non-lawyer. Although a lawyer may be employed by a business corporation with non-lawyers serving as directors or officers, and they necessarily have the right to make decisions of business policy, a lawyer must decline to accept direction of his professional judgment from any layman. Various types of legal aid offices are administered by boards of directors composed of lawyers and laymen. A lawyer should not accept employment from such an organization unless the board sets only broad policies and there is no interference in the relationship of the lawyer and the individual client he serves. Where a lawyer is employed by an organization, a written agreement that defines the relationship between him and the organization and provides for his independence is desirable since it may serve to prevent misunderstanding as to their respective roles. Although

216

other innovations in the means of supplying legal counsel may develop, the responsibility of the lawyer to maintain his professional independence remains constant, and the legal profession must insure that changing circumstances do not result in loss of the professional independence of the lawyer.

CANON 6

*A Lawyer Should Represent a
Client Competently*

ETHICAL CONSIDERATIONS

EC 6-1   Because of his vital role in the legal process, a lawyer should act with competence and proper care in representing clients. He should strive to become and remain proficient in his practice and should accept employment only in matters which he is or intends to become competent to handle.

EC 6-2   A lawyer is aided in attaining and maintaining his competence by keeping abreast of current legal literature and developments, participating in continuing legal education programs, concentrating in particular areas of the law, and by utilizing other available means. He has the additional ethical obligation to assist in improving the legal profession, and he may do so by participating in bar activities intended to advance the quality and standards of members of the profession. Of particular importance is the careful training of his younger associates and the giving of sound guidance to all lawyers who consult him. In short, a lawyer should strive at all levels to aid the legal profession in advancing the highest possible standards of integrity and competence and to meet those standards himself.

EC 6-3   While the licensing of a lawyer is evidence that he has met the standards then prevailing for admission to the bar, a lawyer generally should not accept employment in any area of the law in which he is not qualified. However, he may accept such employment if in good faith he expects to become qualified through study and investigation, as long as such preparation would not result in unreasonable delay or expense to his client. Proper preparation and representation may require the association by the lawyer of professionals in other disciplines. A lawyer offered employment in a matter in which he is not and does not expect to become so qualified should either decline the employment or, with the consent of his client, accept the employment and associate a lawyer who is competent in the matter.

EC 6-4   Having undertaken representation, a lawyer should use proper care to safeguard the interests of his client. If a lawyer has accepted employment in a matter beyond his competence but in which he expected to become competent, he should diligently undertake the work and study necessary to qualify himself. In addition to being qualified to handle a particular matter, his obligation to his client requires him to prepare adequately for and give appropriate attention to his legal work.

EC 6-5   A lawyer should have pride in his professional endeavors. His obligation to act competently calls for higher motivation than that arising from fear of civil liability or disciplinary penalty.

EC 6-6   A lawyer should not seek, by contract or other means, to limit his individual liability to his client for his malpractice. A lawyer who handles the affairs of his client properly has no need to attempt to limit his liability for his professional activities and one who does not handle the affairs of his client properly should not be permitted to do so. A lawyer who is a stockholder in or is associated with a professional legal corporation may, however, limit his liability for malpractice of his associates in the corporation, but only to the extent permitted by law.

CANON 7

A Lawyer Should Represent a Client Zealously
Within the Bounds of the Law

ETHICAL CONSIDERATIONS

EC 7-1   The duty of a lawyer, both to his client and to the legal system, is to represent his client zealously within the bounds of the law, which includes Disciplinary Rules and enforceable professional regulations. The professional responsibility of a lawyer derives from his membership in a profession which has the duty of assisting members of the public to secure and protect available legal rights and benefits. In our government of laws and not of men, each member of our society is entitled to have his conduct judged and regulated in accordance with the law, to seek any lawful objective through legally permissible means, and to present for adjudication any lawful claim, issue, or defense.

218

EC 7-2   The bounds of the law in a given case are often difficult to ascertain. The language of legislative enactments and judicial opinions may be uncertain as applied to varying factual situations. The limits and specific meaning of apparently relevant law may be made doubtful by changing or developing constitutional interpretations, inadequately expressed statutes or judicial opinions, and changing public and judicial attitudes. Certainty of law ranges from well-settled rules through areas of conflicting authority to areas without precedent.

EC 7-3   Where the bounds of law are uncertain, the action of a lawyer may depend on whether he is serving as advocate or adviser. A lawyer may serve simultaneously as both advocate and adviser, but the two roles are essentially different. In asserting a position on behalf of his client, an advocate for the most part deals with past conduct and must take the facts as he finds them. By contrast, a lawyer serving as adviser primarily assists his client in determining the course of future conduct and relationships. While serving as advocate, a lawyer should resolve in favor of his client doubts as to the bounds of the law. In serving a client as adviser, a lawyer in appropriate circumstances should give his professional opinion as to what the ultimate decisions of the courts would likely be as to the applicable law.

Duty of the Lawyer to a Client

EC 7-4   The advocate may urge any permissible construction of the law favorable to his client, without regard to his professional opinion as to the likelihood that the construction will ultimately prevail. His conduct is within the bounds of the law, and therefore permissible, if the position taken is supported by the law or is supportable by a good faith argument for an extension, modification, or reversal of the law. However, a lawyer is not justified in asserting a position in litigation that is frivolous.

EC 7-5   A lawyer as adviser furthers the interest of his client by giving his professional opinion as to what he believes would likely be the ultimate decision of the courts on the matter at hand and by informing his client of the practical effect of such decision. He may continue in the representation of his client even though his client has elected to pursue a course of conduct contrary to the advice of the lawyer so long as he does not thereby knowingly assist the client to engage in illegal conduct or to take a frivolous legal position. A lawyer should never encourage or aid his client to commit criminal acts or counsel his client on how to violate the law and avoid punishment thereafter.

EC 7-6 Whether the proposed action of a lawyer is within the bounds of the law may be a perplexing question when his client is contemplating a course of conduct having legal consequences that vary according to the client's intent, motive, or desires at the time of the action. Often a lawyer is asked to assist his client in developing evidence relevant to the state of mind of the client at a particular time. He may properly assist his client in the development and preservation of evidence of existing motive, intent, or desire; obviously, he may not do anything furthering the creation or preservation of false evidence. In many cases a lawyer may not be certain as to the state of mind of his client, and in those situations, he should resolve reasonable doubts in favor of his client.

EC 7-7 In certain areas of legal representation not affecting the merits of the cause or substantially prejudicing the rights of a client, a lawyer is entitled to make decisions on his own. But otherwise the authority to make decisions is exclusively that of the client and, if made within the framework of the law, such decisions are binding on his lawyer. As typical examples in civil cases, it is for the client to decide whether he will accept a settlement offer or whether he will waive his right to plead an affirmative defense. A defense lawyer in a criminal case has the duty to advise his client fully on whether a particular plea to a charge appears to be desirable and as to the prospects of success on appeal, but it is for the client to decide what plea should be entered and whether an appeal should be taken.

EC 7-8 A lawyer should exert his best efforts to insure that decisions of his client are made only after the client has been informed of relevent considerations. A lawyer ought to initiate this decision-making process if the client does not do so. Advice of a lawyer to his client need not be confined to purely legal considerations. A lawyer should advise his client of the possible effect of each legal alternative. A lawyer should bring to bear upon this decision-making process the fullness of his experience as well as his objective viewpoint. In assisting his client to reach a proper decision, it is often desirable for a lawyer to point out those factors which may lead to a decision that is morally just as well as legally permissible. He may emphasize the possibility of harsh consequences that might result from assertion of legally permissible positions.

In the final analysis, however, the lawyer should always remember that the decision whether to forego legally available objectives or methods because of non-legal factors is ultimately for the client and not for himself. In the event that the client in a non-adjudicatory matter insists upon a course of conduct that is contrary to the judgment and advice of the lawyer but not prohibited by Disciplinary Rules, the lawyer may withdraw from the employment.

EC 7-9   In the exercise of his professional judgment on those decision which are for his determination in the handling of a legal matter, a lawyer should always act in a manner consistent with the best interests of his client. However, when an action in the best interest of his client seems to him to be unjust, he may ask his client for permission to forego such action.

EC 7-10   The duty of a lawyer to represent his client with zeal does not militate against his concurrent obligation to treat with consideration all the persons involved in the legal process and to avoid the infliction of needless harm.

EC 7-11   The responsibilities of a lawyer may vary according to the intelligence, experience, mental condition or age of a client, the obligation of a public officer, or the nature of a particular proceeding. Examples include the representation of an illiterate or an incompetent, service as a public prosecutor or other government lawyer, and appearances before administrative and legislative bodies.

EC 7-12   Any mental or physical condition of a client that renders him incapable of making a considered judgment on his own behalf casts additional responsibilities upon his lawyer. Where an incompetent is acting through a guardian or other legal representative, a lawyer must look to such representative for those decisions which are normally the perogative of the client to make. If a client under disability has no legal representative, his lawyer may be compelled in court proceedings to make decisions on behalf of the client. If the client is capable of understanding the matter in question or of contributing to the advancement of his interests, regardless of whether he is legally disqualified from performing certain acts, the lawyer should obtain from him all possible aid. If the disability of a client and the lack of a legal representative compel the lawyer to make decisions for his client, the lawyer should consider all circumstances then prevailing and act with care to safeguard and advance the interests of his client. But obviously a lawyer cannot perform any act or make any decision which the law requires his client to perform or make, either acting for himself, if competent, or by a duly constituted representative if legally incompetent.

EC 7-13   The responsibility of a public prosecutor differs from that of the usual advocate; his duty is to seek justice, not merely to convict. This special duty exists because: (1) the prosecutor represents the sovereign and therefore should use restraint in the discretionary exercise of governmental powers, such as in the selection of cases to prosecute; (2) during trial the prosecutor is not only an advocate but he also may make decisions normally made by an individual client, and those affecting the public interest should be fair to all, and (3) in our system of criminal justice the accused is to be given the benefit of all reasonable doubts. With respect to evidence and witnesses, the prosecutor has responsibilities different from those of a lawyer in private practice: the prosecutor should make timely disclosure to the defense of available evidence, known to him, that tends to negate the guilt of the accused, mitigate the degree of the offense, or reduce the punishment. Further, a prosecutor should not intentionally avoid pursuit of evidence merely because he believes it will damage the prosecutor's case or aid the accused.

EC 7-14   A government lawyer who has discretionary power relative to litigation should refrain from instituting or continuing litigation that is obviously unfair. A government lawyer in a civil action or administrative proceeding has the responsibility to seek justice and to develop a full and fair record, and he should not use his position or the economic power of the government to harass parties or to bring about unjust settlements or results.

EC 7-15   The nature and purpose of proceedings before administrative agencies vary widely. The proceedings may be legislative or quasi-judicial, or a combination of both. They may be ex parte in character, in which event they may originate either at the instance of the agency or upon motion of an interested party. The scope of an inquiry may be purely investigative or it may be truly adversary looking toward the adjudication of specific rights of a party or of classes of parties. The foregoing are but examples of some of the types of proceedings conducted by administrative agencies. A lawyer appearing before an administrative agency, regardless of the nature of the proceeding it is conducting, has the continuing duty to advance the cause of his client within the bounds of the law. Where the applicable rules of the agency impose specific obligations upon a lawyer, it is his duty to comply therewith, unless the lawyer has a legitimate basis for challenging the validity thereof. In all appearances before administrative agencies, a lawyer should identify himself, his client if identity of his client is not privileged, and the representative nature of his appearance. It is not improper, however, for a lawyer to seek from an agency information available to the public without identifying his client.

EC 7-16   The primary business of a legislative body is to enact laws rather than to adjudicate controversies, although on occasion the activities of a legislative body may take on the characteristics of an adversary proceeding, particularly in investigative and impeachment matters. The role of a lawyer supporting or opposing proposed legislation normally is quite different from his role in representing a person under investigation or on trial by a legislative body. When a lawyer appears in connection with proposed legislation, he seeks to affect the lawmaking process, but when he appears on behalf of a client in investigatory or impeachment proceedings, he is concerned with the protection of the rights of his client. In either event, he should identify himself and his client, if identity of his client is not privileged, and should comply with applicable laws and legislative rules.

EC 7-17   The obligation of loyalty to his client applies only to a lawyer in the discharge of his professional duties and implies no obligation to adopt a personal viewpoint favorable to the interests or desires of his client. While a lawyer must act always with circumspection in order that his conduct will not adversely affect the rights of a client in a matter he is then handling, he may take positions on public issues and espouse legal reforms he favors without regard to the individual views of any client.

EC 7-18   The legal system in its broadest sense functions best when persons in need of legal advice or assistance are represented by their own counsel. For this reason a lawyer should not communicate on the subject matter of the representation of his client with a person he knows to be represented in the matter by a lawyer, unless pursuant to the law or rule of court or unless he has the consent of the lawyer for that person. If one is not represented by counsel, a lawyer representing another may have to deal directly with the unrepresented person; in such an instance, a lawyer should not undertake to give advice to the person who is attempting to represent himself, except that he may advise him to obtain a lawyer.

Duty of the Lawyer to the Adversary System of Justice

EC 7-19   Our legal system provides for the adjudication of disputes governed by the rules of substantive, evidentiary, and procedural law. An adversary presentation counters the natural human tendency to judge too swiftly in terms of the familiar that which is not yet fully known, the advocate, by his zealous preparation and presentation of facts and law, enables the tribunal to come to the hearing with an open and neutral mind and to render impartial judgments. The duty of a lawyer to his client and his duty to the legal system are the same: to represent his client zealously within the bounds of the law.

EC 7-20   In order to function properly, our adjudicative process requires an informed, impartial tribunal capable of administering justice promptly and efficiently according to procedures that command public confidence and respect. Not only must there be competent, adverse presentation of evidence and issues, but a tribunal must be aided by rules appropriate to an effective and dignified process. The procedures under which tribunals operate in our adversary system have been prescribed largely by legislative enactments, court rules and decisions, and administrative rules. Through the years certain concepts of proper professional conduct have become rules of law applicable to the adversary adjudicative process. Many of these concepts are the bases for standards of professional conduct set forth in the Disciplinary Rules.

EC 7-21   The civil adjudicative process is primarily designed for the settlement of disputes between parties, while the criminal process is designed for the protection of society as a whole. Threatening to use, or using, the criminal process to coerce adjustment of private civil claims or controversies is a subversion of that process; further, the person against whom the criminal process is so misused may be deterred from asserting his legal rights and thus the usefulness of the civil process in settling private disputs is impaired. As in all cases of abuse of judicial process, the improper use of criminal process tends to diminish public confidence in our legal system.

EC 7-22 Respect for judicial rulings is essential to the proper administration of justice; however, a litigant or his lawyer may, in good faith and within the framework of the law, take steps to test the correctness of a ruling of a tribunal.

EC 7-23 The complexity of law often makes it difficult for a tribunal to be fully informed unless the pertinent law is presented by the lawyers in the cause. A tribunal that is fully informed on the applicable law is better able to make a fair and accurate determination of the matter before it. The adversary system contemplates that each lawyer will present and argue the existing law in the light most favorable to his client. Where a lawyer knows of legal authority in the controlling jurisdiction directly adverse to the position of his client, he should inform the tribunal of its existence unless his adversary has done so; but, having made such disclosure, he may challenge its soundness in whole or in part.

EC 7-24 In order to bring about just and informed decisions, evidentiary and procedural rules have been established by tribunals to permit the inclusion of relevant evidence and argument and the exclusion of all other considerations. The expression by a lawyer of his personal opinion as to the justness of a cause, as to the credibility of a witness, as to the culpability of a civil litigant, or as to the guilt or innocence of an accused is not a proper subject for argument to the trier of fact. It is improper as to factual matters because admissible evidence possessed by a lawyer should be presented only as sworn testimony. It is improper as to all other matters because, were the rule otherwise, the silence of a lawyer on a given occasion could be construed unfavorably to his client. However, a lawyer may argue, on his analysis of the evidence, for any position or conclusion with respect to any of the foregoing matters.

EC 7-25 Rules of evidence and procedure are designed to lead to just decisions and are part of the framework of the law. Thus, while a lawyer may take steps in good faith and within the framework of the law to test the validity of rules, he is not justified in consciously violating such rules and he should be diligent in his efforts to safeguard them. As examples, a lawyer should subscribe to or verify only those pleadings that he believes are in compliance with applicable law and rules; a lawyer should not make any prefatory statement before a tribunal in regard to the purported facts of the case on trial unless he believes that his statement will be supported by admissible evidence; a lawyer should not ask a witness a question solely for the purpose of harassing or embarrassing him; and a lawyer should not by subterfuge put before a jury matters which it cannot properly consider.

EC 7-26   The law and Disciplinary Rules prohibit the use of fraudulent, false, or perjured testimony or evidence. A lawyer should, however, present any admissible evidence his client desires to have presented unless he knows, or from facts within his knowledge should know, that such testimony or evidence is false, fraudulent, or perjured.

EC 7-27   Because it interferes with the proper administration of justice, a lawyer should not suppress evidence that he or his client has a legal obligation to reveal or produce. In like manner, a lawyer should not advise or cause a person to secrete himself or to leave the jurisdiction of a tribunal for the purpose of making him unavailable as a witness therein.

EC 7-28   Witnesses should always testify truthfully and should be free from any financial inducements that might tempt them to do otherwise. A lawyer should not pay or agree to pay a non-expert witness an amount in excess of reimbursement for expenses and financial loss incident to his being a witness; however, a lawyer may pay or agree to pay an expert witness a reasonable fee for his services as an expert. But in no event should a lawyer pay or agree to pay a contingent fee to any witness. A lawyer should exercise reasonable diligence to see that his client and lay associates conform to these standards.

EC 7-29   To safeguard the impartiality that is essential to the judicial process, veniremen and jurors should be protected against extraneous influences. When impartiality is present, public confidence in the judicial system is enhanced. There should be no extrajudicial communication with veniremen prior to trial or with jurors during trial by or on behalf of a lawyer connected with the case. Furthermore, a lawyer who is not connected with the case should not communicate with or cause another to communicate with a venireman or a juror about the case. After the trial, communication by a lawyer with jurors is permitted so long as he refrains from asking questions or making comments that tend to harass or embarrass the juror or to influence actions of the juror in future cases. Were a lawyer to be prohibited from communicating after trial with a juror, he could not ascertain if the verdict might be subject to legal challenge, in which event the invalidity of a verdict might go undetected. When an extrajudicial communication by a lawyer with a juror is permitted by law, it should be made considerately and with deference to the personal feelings of the juror.

EC 7-30   Vexatious or harassing investigations of veniremen or jurors seriously impair the effectiveness of our jury system. For this reason, a lawyer or anyone on his behalf who conducts an investigation of veniremen or jurors should act with circumspection and restraint.

EC 7-31   Communications with or investigations of members of families of veniremen or jurors by a lawyer or by anyone on his behalf are subject to the restrictions imposed upon the lawyer with respect to his communications with or investigations of veniremen and jurors.

EC 7-32   Because of his duty to aid in preserving the integrity of the jury system, a lawyer who learns of improper conduct by or towards a venireman, a juror, or a member of the family of either should make a prompt report to the court regarding such conduct.

EC 7-33   A goal of our legal system is that each party shall have his case, criminal or civil, adjudicated by an impartial tribunal. The attainment of this goal may be defeated by dissemination of news or comments which tend to influence judge or jury. Such news or comments may prevent prospective jurors from being impartial at the outset of the trial and may also interfere with the obligation of jurors to base their verdict solely upon the evidence admitted in the trial. The release by a lawyer of out-of-court statements regarding an anticipated or pending trial may improperly affect the impartiality of the tribunal. For these reasons, standards for permissible and prohibited conduct of a lawyer with respect to trial publicity have been established.

EC 7-34   The impartiality of a public servant in our legal system may be impaired by the receipt of gifts or loans. A lawyer, therefore, is never justified in making a gift or a loan to a judge, a hearing officer, or an official or employee of a tribunal.

EC 7-35   All litigants and lawyers should have access to tribunals on an equal basis. Generally, in adversary proceedings a lawyer should not communicate with a judge relative to a matter pending before, or which is to be brought before, a tribunal over which he presides in circumstances which might have the effect or give the appearance of granting undue advantage to one party. For example, a lawyer should not communicate with a tribunal by a writing unless a copy thereof is promptly delivered to opposing counsel or to the adverse party if he is not represented by a lawyer. Ordinarily an oral communication by a lawyer with a judge or hearing officer should be made only upon adequate notice to opposing counsel, or, if there is none, to the opposing party. A lawyer should not condone or lend himself to private importunities by another with a judge or hearing officer on behalf of himself or his client.

EC 7-36   Judicial hearings ought to be conducted through dignified and orderly procedures designed to protect the rights of all parties. Although a lawyer has the duty to represent his client zealously, he should not engage in any conduct that offends the dignity and decorum of proceedings. While maintaining his independence, a lawyer should be respectful, courteous, and above-board in his relations with a judge or hearing officer before whom he appears. He should avoid undue solicitude for the comfort or convenience of judge or jury and should avoid any other conduct calculated to gain special consideration.

EC 7-37   In adversary proceedings, clients are litigants and though ill feeling may exist between clients, such ill feeling should not influence a lawyer in his conduct, attitude, and demeanor towards opposing lawyers. A lawyer should not make unfair or derogatory personal reference to opposing counsel. Haranguing and offensive tactics by lawyers interfere with the orderly administration of justice and have no proper place in our legal system.

EC 7-38   A lawyer should be courteous to opposing counsel and should accede to reasonable requests regarding court proceedings, settings, continuances, waiver of personal formalities, and similar matters which do not prejudice the rights of his client. He should follow local customs of courtesy or practice, unless he gives timely notice to opposing counsel of his intention not to do so. A lawyer should be punctual in fulfilling all professional commitments.

EC 7-39   In the final analysis, proper functioning of the adversary system depend upon cooperation between lawyers and tribunals in utilizing procedures which will preserve the impartiality of tribunals and make their decisional processes prompt and just, without impinging upon the obligation of lawyers to represent their clients zealously within the framework of the law.

CANON 8

A Lawyer Should Assist in
Improving the Legal System

ETHICAL CONSIDERATIONS

EC 8-1   Changes in human affairs and imperfections in human institutions make necessary constant efforts to maintain and improve our legal system. This system should function in a manner that commands public respect and fosters the use of legal remedies to achieve redress of grievances. By reason of education and experience, lawyers are especially qualified to recognize deficiencies in the legal system and to initiate corrective measures therein. Thus they should participate in proposing and supporting legislation and programs to improve the system, without regard to the general interests or desires of clients or former clients.

EC 8-2   Rules of law are deficient if they are not just, understandable, and responsive to the needs of society. If a lawyer believes that the existence or absence of a rule of law, substantive or procedural, causes or contributes to an unjust result, he should endeavor by lawful means to obtain appropriate changes in the law. He should encourage the simplification of laws and the repeal or amendment of laws that are outmoded. Likewise, legal procedures should be improved whenever experience indicates a change is needed.

EC 8-3   The fair administration of justice requires the availability of competent lawyers. Members of the public should be educated to recognize the existence of legal problems and the resultant need for legal services, and should be provided methods for intelligent selection of counsel. Those persons unable to pay for legal services should be provided needed services. Clients and lawyers should not be penalized by undue geographical restraints upon representation in legal matters, and the bar should address itself to improvements in licensing, reciprocity, and admission procedures consistent with the needs of modern commerce.

EC 8-4   Whenever a lawyer seeks legislative or administrative changes, he should identify the capacity in which he appears, whether on behalf of himself, a client, or the public. A lawyer may advocate such changes on behalf of a client even though he does not agree with them. But when a lawyer purports to act on behalf of the public, he should espouse only those changes which he conscientiously believes to be in the public interest.

EC 8-5   Fraudulent, deceptive, or otherwise illegal conduct by a participant in a proceeding before a tribunal or legislative body is inconsistent with fair administration of justice, and it should never be participated in or condoned by lawyers. Unless constrained by his obligation to preserve the confidences and secrets of his client, a lawyer should reveal to appropriate authorities any knowledge he may have of such improper conduct.

EC 8-6   Judges and administrative officials having adjudicatory powers ought to be persons of integrity, competence, and suitable temperament. Generally, lawyers are qualified, by personal observation or investigation, to evaluate the qualifications of persons seeking or being considered for such public offices, and for this reason they have a special responsibility to aid in the selection of only those who are qualified. It is the duty of lawyers to endeavor to prevent political considerations from outweighing judicial fitness in the selection of judges. Lawyers should protest earnestly against the appointment or election of those who are unsuited for the bench and should strive to have elected or appointed thereto only those who are willing to forego pursuits, whether of a business, political, or other nature, that may interfere with the free and fair consideration of questions presented for adjudication. Adjudicatory officials, not being wholly free to defend themselves, are entitled to receive the support of the bar against unjust criticism. While a lawyer as a citizen has a right to criticize such officials publicly, he should be certain of the merit of his complaint, use appropriate language, and avoid petty criticisms, for unrestrained and intemperate statements tend to lessen public confidence in our legal system. Criticisms motivated by reasons other than a desire to improve the legal system are not justified.

EC 8-7   Since lawyers are a vital part of the legal system, they should be persons of integrity, of professional skill, and of dedication to the improvement of the system. Thus a lawyer should aid in establishing, as well as enforcing, standards of conduct adequate to protect the public by insuring that those who practice law are qualified to do so.

EC 8-8   Lawyers often serve as legislators or as holders of other public offices. This is highly desirable, as lawyers are uniquely qualified to make significant contributions to the improvement of the legal system. A lawyer who is a public officer, whether full or part-time, should not engage in activities in which his personal or professional interests are or foreseeably may be in conflict with his official duties.

EC 8-9   The advancement of our legal system is of vital importance in maintaining the rule of law and in facilitating orderly changes; therefore, lawyers should encourage, and should aid in making, needed changes and improvements.

CANON 9

A Lawyer Should Avoid Even the
Appearance of Professional Impropriety

ETHICAL CONSIDERATIONS

EC 9-1   Continuation of the American concept, that we are to be governed by rules of law requires that the people have faith that justice can be obtained through our legal system. A lawyer should promote public confidence in our system and in the legal profession.

EC 9-2   Public confidence in law and lawyers may be eroded by irresponsible or improper conduct of a lawyer. On occasion, ethical conduct of a lawyer may appear to laymen to be unethical. In order to avoid misunderstandings, and hence to maintain confidence, a lawyer should fully and promptly inform his client of material developments in the matters being handled for the client. While a lawyer should guard against otherwise proper conduct that has a tendency to diminish public confidence in the legal system or in the legal profession, his duty to clients or to the public should never be subordinate merely because the full discharge of his obligation may be misunderstood or may tend to subject him or the legal profession to criticism. When explicit ethical guidance does not exist, a lawyer should determine his conduct by acting in a manner that promotes public confidence in the integrity and efficiency of the legal system and the legal profession.

EC 9-3   After a lawyer leaves judicial office or other public employment, he should not accept employment in connection with any matter in which he had substantial responsibility prior to his leaving, since to accept employment would give the appearance of impropriety even if none exists.

EC 9-4   Because the very essence of the legal system is to provide procedures by which matters can be presented in an impartial manner so that they may be decided solely upon the merits, any statement or suggestion by a lawyer that he can or would attempt to circumvent those procedures is detrimental to the legal system and tends to undermine public confidence in it.

EC 9-5   Separation of the funds of a client from those of his lawyer not only serves to protect the client but also avoids even the appearance of impropriety, and therefore commingling of such funds should be avoided.

EC 9-6   Every lawyer owes a solemn duty to uphold the integrity and honor of his profession; to encourage respect for the law and for the courts and the judges thereof; to observe the Code of Professional Responsibility; to act as a member of a learned profession, one dedicated to public service; to cooperate with his brother lawyers in supporting the organized bar through the devoting of his time, efforts, and financial support as his professional standing and ability reasonably permit; to conduct himself so as to reflect credit on the legal profession and to inspire the confidence, respect, and trust of his clients and of the public; and to strive to avoid not only professional impropriety but also the appearance of impropriety.

The American Bar Association has not promulgated any codes for the paralegal. However, the National Association of Legal Assistants and the American Paralegal Association have both suggested a Code of Ethics. The following is the NALA Code of Ethics (see attached Code) and the American Paralegal Association Code of Ethics (see attached Code).

Black's Law Dictionary defines legal ethics as the usage and custom among members of the legal profession, involving their duties toward one another, toward clients, toward courts; that branch of moral science which relates the duties which a member of the legal profession owes to the public, to the court, to his professional brothers, and to his client. This definition was taken from the case of *Kraushaar v. LaVin,* 42 N.Y.S. 2d, 857, 859, 181 Misc. 518.

APPENDIX V

SELECTED BIBLIOGRAPHY OF THE LITERATURE OF WHAT LAWYERS "DO"

Allsop, P. *The Legal Profession* (1960)

A.B.A. Canons of Professional Ethics

Association of American Law Schools. *Selected Readings on the Legal Profession*

Bloom, M. *The Trouble with Lawyers* (1968)

Caplovitz, D. *The Poor Pay More* (1967)

Cheatham, E. *A Lawyer When Needed* (1963)

Chroust, A. *The Rise of the Legal Profession in America* (1965)

Countryman, V. & Finman, T. *The Lawyer in Modern Society* (1966)

Cozzens, J.G. *The Just and the Unjust* (1965) Recommended by the Harvard reading list for law students as the finest modern legal novel.

Greenbaum, E. *The Lawyer's Job* (1967)

Handler, J. *The Lawyer and His Community: The Practicing Bar in a Middle-Sized City* (1967)

Hopson, D. Johnstone Q. *Lawyers and Their Work: An Analysis of the Legal Profession* (1967)

Mayer, M. *The Lawyers* (1967)